£50.00

74285

FOREIGN & COMMONWEALTH OFFICE LIBRARY
ROOM 213
DOWNING STREET EAST
LONDON SW1A 2AL

12/2

This book is due for return on or before
the latest date stamped below

13 Mar 2002

1·4·02

18 JUN 2002

19/2/04

This book should not be passed on to
another reader. It should be returned to
the Library when no longer required.
To extend the loan period, please telephone
270–3025

Developing Countries in the WTO

Also by Constantine Michalopoulos

TRADE IN THE NEW INDEPENDENT STATES (*with David G. Tarr*)

AID AND DEVELOPMENT (*with Anne O. Krueger and Vernon W. Ruttan*)

FINANCING NEEDS OF DEVELOPING COUNTRIES: Proposals for International Action

Developing Countries in the WTO

Constantine Michalopoulos

palgrave

First published 2001 by
PALGRAVE
Houndmills, Basingstoke, Hampshire RG21 6XS and
175 Fifth Avenue, New York, N. Y. 10010
Companies and representatives throughout the world

PALGRAVE is the new global academic imprint of
St. Martin's Press LLC Scholarly and Reference Division and
Palgrave Publishers Ltd (formerly Macmillan Press Ltd).

ISBN 0–333–97016–0

This book is printed on paper suitable for recycling and
made from fully managed and sustained forest sources.

A catalogue record for this book is available
from the British Library.

Library of Congress Cataloging-in-Publication Data
Michalopoulos, Constantine
    Developing countries in the WTO / Constantine Michalopoulos.
        p. cm.
    Includes bibliographical references and index.
    ISBN 0–333–97016–0 (cloth)
    1. Developing countries—Commercial policy. 2. Free trade–
–Developing countries. 3. World Trade Organization–
–Developing countries. 4. Foreign trade regulation—Developing
countries. 5. Developing countries—Foreign economic relations.
6. International trade. I. Title.

HF1413 .M513 2001
382'.92'091724—dc21
                                                      2001035819

10   9   8   7   6   5   4   3   2   1
10   09   08   07   06   05   04   03   02   01

Printed and bound in Great Britain by
Antony Rowe Ltd, Chippenham, Wiltshire

To Eveline, a champion of free trade in the fight against poverty

Contents

List of Tables

Preface

This volume was written in the summer and autumn of 2000 when I was Senior Economic Advisor at the Brussels office of the World Bank. It is partly based on research I started in 1998–99 when I was Special Economic Advisor to the WTO in Geneva, and partly on personal experiences when working on trade and development at the two institutions. The views expressed are solely my own and should not be attributed to either the World Bank or the WTO. Many staff members of these institutions, however, contributed to the completion of this project. I am especially grateful to David Tarr of the World Bank and Peter Tulloch of the WTO for their comments on earlier drafts of several chapters. I would also like to thank Amar Breckenridge of the WTO, who contributed material on the early treatment of the developing countries in GATT, and Cato Adrian, also of the WTO, for helpful suggestions on issues of WTO accession.

I have benefited greatly from the contributions of several people whose work involves addressing the constraints that developing countries face in the WTO and more generally in world trade. In this connection I want to thank Esperenza Duran (Director of AITIC) for providing me with valuable insights into the problems that delegations from less-advantaged countries face when participating in the WTO, and for permission to use material from an article we coauthored on TRIPs; Otto Genee (Deputy Permanent Representative of the Netherlands to the WTO and driving force at the Advisory Center on WTO law) for helping me to understand the workings of developed-country delegations in Geneva, as well as the difficulties developing countries face in the WTO dispute settlement process; and Eveline Herfkens for relating her experiences on the obstacles that must be overcome in order to inject even a small degree of coherence into the policies of the international community on aid and trade towards the developing countries.

I reserve my greatest thanks for Rachael Taylor of the World Bank's office in Brussels. She provided immense help, first with research assistance and data development, especially for Chapter 2, and later in preparing this volume for publication. Neither she nor any of the others who helped with the volume are responsible for any errors or inaccuracies that may remain.

Finally, I wish to thank the Werner Publishing Company for permission to use material from an article I coauthored with E. Duran on 'Intellectual

Property Rights and Developing Countries in the WTO Millennium Round', which appeared in the *Journal of World Intellectual Property*, vol. 2, no. 6 (November 1999); and Blackwell Publishers Ltd for permission to use material from my article on 'The Developing Countries in the WTO', published in *World Economy*, vol. 22, no. 1 (January 1999).

CONSTANTINE MICHALOPOULOS

List of Abbreviations

ACP	Asia, Caribbean and Pacific Countries
AITIC	Agency for International Trade Information and Co-operation
AMS	Aggregate Measure of Support
ASEAN	Association of Southeast Asia Nations
ATC	Agreement on Textiles and Clothing
CBD	(UN) Convention on Biological Diversity
CEFTA	Central Europe Free Trade Area
CFC	Common Fund for Commodities
CFF	Compensatory Financing Facility
DSB	Dispute Settlement Body
DSM	Dispute Settlement Mechanism
EC	European Communities
EFTA	European Free Trade Area
EPZ	Export Processing Zone
EU	European Union
FAO	Food and Agriculture Organization
FOGS	Functions of the GATT System
FSU	Former Soviet Union
GATS	General Agreement on Trade in Services
GATT	General Agreement on Tariffs and Trade
GSP	Generalized System of Preferences
HS	Harmonized System
HIPC	Heavily Indebted Poor Countries
IMF	International Monetary Fund
IPRs	Intellectual Property Rights
ISO	International Standards Organization
ITC	International Trade Center
ITO	International Trade Organization
LDCs	Least Developed Countries
MAI	Multilateral Agreement on Investment
MERCOSUR	Mercado Commun de Sur
MFA	Multi-fiber Arrangement
MFN	Most Favoured Nation
NAFTA	North America Free Trade Area
NFIDC	Net food importing developing country

NTM	Non-tariff measures
OECD	Organization for Economic Co-operation and Development
OPEC	Organization of Petroleum Exporting Countries
PRSP	Poverty Reduction Strategy Paper
PTAs	Preferential Trade Agreements
Quad	Canada, the EU, Japan and the USA
R&D	Research and Development
SADC	Southern Africa Development Community
SAL	Structural Adjustment Loan
SPS	Sanitary and Phyto-Sanitary
TBT	Technical Barriers to Trade
TNC	Transnational corporation
TPR	Trade Policy Review
TPRM	Trade Policy Review Mechanism
TRIMs	Trade Related Investment Measures
TRIPs	Trade Related Intellectual Property Rights
UN	United Nations
UNCTAD	United Nations Conference on Trade and Development
UNDP	United Nations Development Programme
UPOV	Union for Protection of New Varieties of Plants
USAID	United States Agency for International Development
VAT	Value Added Tax
WIPO	World Intellectual Property Organization
WTO	World Trade Organization

1
Introduction: Developing Countries in World Trade

For more than half a century developing countries have made enormous progress in integrating their economies into the international trading system. Growth in their international trade has exceeded growth in output, the product composition of their exports has shifted dramatically in favour of manufactures and away from primary commodities, and since the early 1990s trade in some developing countries has grown exceptionally quickly and far more than trade in developed countries.

Yet for other developing countries and groups – most prominently the LDCs, very limited progress has been evident. The output and trade of these countries[1] are growing less rapidly than those of other developing countries, and they continue to rely overwhelmingly on exports of a few primary commodities with unstable prices and subject to long-term deteriorating terms of trade. These 49 countries are in many ways already marginal in the world economy – their share of world trade fell from about 0.7 per cent in the 1980s to 0.4 per cent in the 1990s.

Integration into the world trading system depends on whether countries and their trading partners establish policies and institutions that are conducive to the mutually beneficial exchange of goods and services, based on specialization and comparative advantage. The effective integration of the developing countries involves not only their own trade policies and institutions but also those of the developed countries, their main trading partners. Integration also requires them to abide by the rules of conduct that govern the multilateral trading system. These rules were established and are being implemented in the context of the agreements administered by the World Trade Organization (WTO). Therefore membership of and effective participation in the WTO is an essential element of, and perhaps even a necessary condition for, full integration into the world trading system.[2]

The draft charter of the International Trade Organization (ITO), which together with the International Monetary Fund (IMF) and the World Bank was intended to be one of the three pillars of international economic cooperation after World War II but never came into being, contained specific exceptions to general trade rules when applied in the context of development. The General Agreement on Tariffs and Trade (GATT), which was signed as an interim agreement after the failure to launch the ITO but lasted almost 50 years, had no explicit provisions on development.

Almost half of the original GATT membership consisted of developing countries. Over time these countries succeeded in incorporating a variety of development-related provisions into the agreement. Nevertheless, for a variety of reasons (discussed in detail in Chapter 3) the developing countries did not feel that GATT as an institution was responsive to their special needs in trade. As a consequence, in the 1960s they lobbied for and succeeded in establishing a new global institution, UNCTAD (the United Nations Conference on Trade and Development). Throughout the 1960s and 1970s developing countries viewed UNCTAD rather than GATT as the main institution through which to promote their trade interests. Their representation in GATT reflected this priority: many were not Contracting Parties, and the participation of those that were was rather passive. They did not engage in a significant way in the mutual exchange of trade liberalization concessions on a reciprocal basis in the GATT negotiations, but focused on securing special and more favourable treatment both for their exports and in the rules governing protection against foreign imports.

Beginning with the GATT Uruguay Round of multilateral trade negotiations in the mid 1980s, the developing countries' attitude towards their participation in GATT, and subsequently in the WTO, changed significantly: many played a very active role in the Uruguay Round negotiations, and a large number decided to become members of GATT and later the WTO during or at the end of the round. This change of attitude reflected a number of complex and interrelated developments.

The trade policies of many developing countries had been liberalized, favouring an outward orientation and lower protection. Several countries in East Asia had become major trading powers, especially as exporters of manufactures. And there was a growing appreciation of the importance of observing international rules in the conduct of trade, as well as the need to safeguard trading interests through effective participation in the activities of the new organization and in the making of general rules that govern international trade – as opposed to focusing on special rules and exceptional treatment for developing countries.

The establishment of the WTO has resulted in further changes that have placed additional demands on developing countries in respect of effective participation. First, the WTO covers a variety of new areas – such as services, standards and intellectual property rights – in which new rules governing the conduct of international trade have been agreed and whose implementation requires additional institutional capacity on the part of member governments. Second, the WTO negotiations on the liberalization of various sectors require continuous participation by the members. Third, the new WTO Dispute Settlement Mechanism (DSM) enables developing countries to address their grievances, but it also poses tremendous challenges because of their very limited institutional capacity to initiate action against developed countries.

The participation of developing countries in the WTO has increased in comparison with their earlier participation in GATT. This is especially true of a number of middle- and higher-income developing countries. The large majority, however, feel that they are still unable to pursue their trade interests effectively in the new organization. Developing-country frustration with the WTO peaked in late 1999 at the third WTO ministerial meeting in Seattle, where it was intended that agreement would be reached on the launching of a new round of multilateral trade negotiations. The trade interests of developing countries are quite diverse and their positions on different issues vary, but in Seattle many of them were united in their disagreement with both the scope and the content of the negotiations proposed by the developed countries, and the vast majority of the smaller, low-income countries were dissatisfied with the processes employed to reach agreement on an agenda for a new Round. Failure to address the concerns of these countries was one of the reasons for the failure of the Seattle meeting.

Developing countries' policies and attitudes towards further integration into the international trading system are clouded with uncertainty. There is a general unease that globalization will benefit only a few countries, and that it is progressing at a faster pace than the institutions in most others can cope with. At the same time there is awareness that exogenous forces involving technological change are pushing globalization and growth inexorably forward, and hence there is a fear of being left behind – of becoming further marginalized. In many countries the rapid expansion of international trade during the 1990s created a solid domestic base in support of a liberal trade regime and further integration into the world economy. In others, especially the LDCs and many in Africa, which are still only marginally integrated into the multilateral trading system, the Asian financial crisis heightened governments' concern about the impact of globalization on fragile economies with pervasive poverty; and about whether further commitment to trade liberalization could be supported by their weak domestic institutions.

Many developing countries are also concerned that aspects of the Uruguay Round agreements of interest to them are not being implemented as expected. In particular, they have questioned whether developed countries have lived up to their commitments on market access, involving the liberalization of products and services of interest to developing countries and strengthened restriction of developed countries' use of trade remedies such as antidumping. They also regard as inadequate the technical and other assistance they have received to strengthen their institutional capacity and to cushion the adjustment costs resulting from a more rational and liberal international economic system. These concerns have been manifested in a reluctance to make commitments in new areas of international trade cooperation.

In this global environment, developing countries are participating in a series of important trade negotiations. The WTO negotiations on agriculture and services, which involve all developing-country members of the WTO, are already under way. An important issue is whether a wider set of trade negotiations will be launched by the WTO in the near future, and if so, what its focus will be. At the same time there are several regional negotiations involving groups of developing countries, such as those between the ACP countries and their EU partners since the Cotonou Agreement, and regional arrangements among developing countries, such as MERCOSUR, the Andean Pact and the Southern Africa Development Community (SADC).

In the currently unsettled international environment, it seems useful to take stock of where developing countries stand in terms of their policies and institutions, their integration into the international trading system, the challenges they face at the beginning of the twenty-first century and what they and the international community can do to address them. This volume attempts such a stock-taking after several years of implementation of the Uruguay Round Agreements. It then considers what needs to be done to strengthen the institutional capacity of the developing countries so that they can participate effectively in both the WTO and the international trading system. It analyses the issues of importance to developing countries that need to be addressed before and as part of a new Round of multilateral negotiations under WTO's auspices. It examines the relationship between regional and multilateral approaches to trade integration, and considers how trade policy reform can be linked to economic assistance by developed countries and international organizations such as the World Bank so that a more coherent international policy for development can emerge.

The emphasis is on integrating developing countries into the trading system as it has emerged and as it is reflected in the WTO agreements, as well as on how the system can be modified in order better to reflect the interests of developing countries. The focus is on trade in goods and to a lesser extent on trade in services, but special attention is devoted to the implications for developing countries of WTO rules on trade-related intellectual property rights (TRIPS).

The volume is organized as follows. Chapter 2 presents a summary of developing countries' trade performance in goods and services between 1980 and 1999. This includes a review of indicators of integration into the trading system (for example the ratio of trade to GDP) and export structure (for example the share of manufactures in total exports), as well as an analysis of the differing performance of various developing-country groupings (by region and income group). Chapter 3 reviews the evolution of thinking on trade policies suitable for development, and how this is reflected in GATT/WTO rules and in the concept of 'special and differential' treatment for developing countries.

Chapters 4–7 are devoted to an analysis of some of the key trade policies and institutions at the beginning of the millennium. Chapters 4 and 5 discuss developing-country trade policies and institutions respectively. Chapter 6 analyzes issues of developed-country policies that affect developing-country market access in goods and services, plus a number of issues that are pertinent to the implementation of the URA. Chapter 7 explores the special challenges the TRIPS agreement poses for development.

The next two chapters address institutional aspects of developing countries' participation in the WTO, including their participation in the DSM (Chapter 8) and the problems posed by the WTO accession process for new members, which tend to be either developing countries or economies in transition (Chapter 9).

Chapter 10 discusses the prospects of and the issues that might be discussed in a new Round of multilateral trade negotiations from a developing-country perspective. Chapter 11 deals with coherence – the links between international trade policies for development and other national and international development policies, including the links between the WTO, the IMF and the World Bank. The final chapter summarizes the main conclusions and recommendations of the analysis, and looks at the main challenges developing countries will face in the world trading system in the coming decades.

Notes

1. These are the 49 developing countries formally designated as 'least developed' by the UN. This designation is based on a number of criteria, including per capita income, structure of production and so on.

2. WTO members can be countries or customs territories, such as Hong Kong (now part of China), which joined the WTO when it was a British colony. Similarly the European Union is a member, but there are separate delegations from each of the 15 constituent states. For purposes of simplicity, in this volume the term 'country' is used irrespective of the legal status of the member.

2
Trends in Developing-Country Trade, 1980–99

General trends

The period covered in this study, 1980–1999, witnessed a rapid expansion of world trade and a slightly more rapid expansion of developing-country trade. The share of developing-country trade in total world merchandise trade (exports plus imports) was somewhat higher at the end of the period than at the beginning – 28.8 per cent as opposed to 27.4 per cent (Tables 2.1 and 2.2). A similar picture emerged in trade in services. While the data on services are much less complete than for merchandise trade, there is little doubt about the overall trends: trade in services grew even faster than merchandise trade; and there was a rise in the share of developing-country exports.

At the same time, on average, GDP growth was much less than the growth in trade for developed and developing countries alike. Using the ratio of total trade to GDP as an indicator of integration into world trade, on average developing countries were more integrated at the end of the century than they had been 20 years earlier. This was the result of a long-term trend and an important dimension of the globalization process.

These overall trends, however, disguise very different patterns during some of the subperiods and among different developing countries and groups. Broadly speaking, the data show that the 1980s were pretty much a 'lost' decade for many different developing countries and groups, but during the 1990s the trade of practically all major developing-country groupings grew faster than that of the developed countries, and in many cases it was very rapid indeed. The major exceptions were the LDCs and some low-income countries whose growth in the 1990s was less than world trade as a whole. As a consequence these countries, whose trade was already marginal in terms of the world totals, were marginalized even further.

Table 2.1 World merchandise exports 1980–99 (billion $ and per cent)

	1980		1985		1990		1995		1999	
	Value	%	Value	%	Value	%	Value	%	Value	%
By income level										
Developed economies	1273	62.7	1288	66.2	2466	71.9	3464	68.3	3725	66.4
Developing and transition economies*	757	37.3	657	33.8	964	28.1	1608	31.7	1881	33.6
Least developed countries	14	0.7	12	0.6	16	0.5	20	0.4	24	0.4
Low income	92	4.5	85	4.4	143	4.2	268	5.3	333	5.9
Low income excl. China	74	3.6	58	3.0	81	2.4	119	2.4	138	2.5
Lower middle income	225	11.1	206	10.6	209	6.1	281	5.5	344	6.1
Upper middle income	295	14.5	222	11.4	336	9.8	557	11.0	677	12.1
High income	131	6.4	132	6.8	261	7.6	482	9.5	504	9.0
Total	2030		1944		3431		5072		5607	
By region										
Developed economies	1273	62.7	1288	66.2	2466	71.9	3464	68.3	3725	66.4
Developing economies	612	30.2	509	26.2	850	24.8	1435	28.3	1657	29.5
Sub-Saharan Africa	77	3.8	50	2.6	67	1.9	74	1.5	76	1.4
Asia	165	8.1	210	10.8	454	13.2	933	18.4	1054	18.8
Latin America & Caribbean	109	5.4	108	5.5	145	4.2	225	4.4	293	5.2
Middle East and Mediterranean	261	12.8	141	7.3	184	5.4	203	4.0	235	4.2
Transition economies	145	7.1	148	7.6	115	3.3	173	3.4	225	4.0
Developing economies excl. OPEC	313	15.4	354	18.2	662	19.3	1233	24.3	1433	25.6
42 developing economies	275	13.5	285	14.7	515	15.0	955	18.8	1086	19.4
Total	2030		1944		3431		5072		5607	

* For the definition of country groupings see Appendix 1.
Sources: WTO; World Bank.

Table 2.2 World merchandise imports, 1980–99 (billion $ and per cent)

	1980		1985		1990		1995		1999	
	Value	%	Value	%	Value	%	Value	%	Value	%
By income level										
Developed economies	1409	68.3	1380	69.0	2584	73.3	3423	66.8	3913	68.0
Developing and transition economies*	655	31.7	619	31.0	939	26.7	1698	33.2	1841	32.0
Least developed countries	23	1.1	20	1.0	23	0.6	31	0.6	38	0.7
Low income	87	4.2	101	5.0	134	3.8	256	5.0	293	5.1
Low income excl. China	67	3.2	58	2.9	80	2.3	124	2.4	127	2.2
Lower middle income	211	10.2	204	10.2	233	6.6	324	6.3	337	5.8
Upper middle income	220	10.7	181	9.0	295	8.4	577	11.3	671	11.7
High income	114	5.5	114	5.7	254	7.2	511	10.0	503	8.7
Total	2064		1999		3523		5121		5755	
By region										
Developed economies	1409	68.3	1380	69.0	2584	73.3	3423	66.8	3913	68.0
Developing economies	510	24.7	476	23.8	813	23.1	1526	29.8	1613	28.0
Sub-Saharan Africa	66	3.2	43	2.1	56	1.6	78	1.5	81	1.4
Asia	181	8.8	224	11.2	473	13.4	988	19.3	958	16.6
Latin America and Caribbean	121	5.9	82	4.1	124	3.5	246	4.8	329	5.7
Middle East and Mediterranean	142	6.9	127	6.4	160	4.5	213	4.2	245	4.3
Transition economies	145	7.0	143	7.2	126	3.6	173	3.4	229	4.0
Developing economies excl. OPEC	380	18.4	376	18.8	699	19.8	1376	26.9	1458	25.3
42 developing economies	294	14.3	266	13.3	538	15.3	1076	21.0	1074	18.7
Total	2064		1999		3523		5121		5755	

* For the definition of country groupings see Appendix 1.
Sources: WTO; World Bank.

Trends in merchandise trade

Developing-country merchandise exports grew at an annual rate of 5.4 per cent in the period 1980–99 compared with 5.8 per cent for developed countries (Table 2.3). But the performance was very different in the 1980s compared with the 1990s. In the 1980s developing-country exports grew only at 3.3 per cent while the exports of developed countries rose by nearly 7 per cent per annum. In the 1990s the situation was reversed, with developing-country exports rising by 7.7 per cent per annum compared with 4.7 per cent for the developed countries. The performance of transition economies was poor for the period as a whole, with exports falling in absolute terms in the 1980s but growing at about the same pace as those of developing countries in the 1990s (Table 2.3). But for these countries the data are so unreliable as to require great caution when making anything other than the broadest of judgements about their overall trade performance.

The trends in merchandise imports parallel those in exports for developed and developing countries alike. But in both periods, the developing countries' imports grew faster than their exports (Table 2.3).

One very interesting feature of the 20 years in question was the performance of the 11 developing-country members of OPEC.[1] Because oil prices peaked in 1980, the performance of these countries and other oil-exporting countries (which have not diversified their economies since that time) was very weak. Table 2.3 shows that if we were to exclude these OPEC members the trade performance of the remaining developing countries would look far better and the growth of their merchandise exports and imports over the period would far exceed that of the developed countries. Of course if data were available for 2000, when the price of oil increased significantly, the trade picture for OPEC and other oil exporting countries would be significantly better, while that of oil importing countries would be worse.[2]

Table 2.3 shows the performance of developing countries by region. In practically all cases and periods, Asia enjoyed the highest growth and Sub-Saharan Africa the lowest, with Latin America and the Middle East and Mediterranean in between. In the 1980s, however, the latter group, which includes many oil exporting countries, did worse than the other regions as a consequence of the large decline in oil prices from the high reached in 1980.

Also shown in Table 2.3 is the performance of 42 developing-country members of the WTO, whose trade policies are subjected to a more systematic analysis in Chapters 4 and 5. The total trade of these

Table 2.3 World merchandise exports and imports, growth rates by region (per cent per annum)

	1980–1990		1990–1999		1980–1999	
	Exports	*Imports*	*Exports*	*Imports*	*Exports*	*Imports*
Developed economies	6.84	6.25	4.69	4.72	5.82	5.52
Developing economies	3.33	4.78	7.70	7.91	5.38	6.25
Sub-Saharan Africa	−1.44	−1.62	1.42	4.23	−0.10	1.11
Asia	10.65	10.07	9.80	8.16	10.25	9.16
Latin America and Caribbean	2.86	0.24	8.13	11.42	5.32	5.39
Middle East and Mediterranean	−3.44	1.24	2.75	4.84	−0.56	2.93
Transition economies	−2.31	−1.38	7.77	6.84	2.34	2.43
Developing economies excl. OPEC	7.77	6.28	8.95	8.52	8.33	7.33
42 developing economies	6.48	6.21	8.65	7.99	7.50	7.05
World Total	5.39	5.49	5.61	5.60	5.49	5.55

Source: WTO.

42 countries in 1999 accounted for 93 per cent of the trade of developing WTO countries. The remaining countries – mostly LDCs and other small economies – accounted for only 7 per cent. The sample includes few OPEC members (many of which are not members of the WTO) and no transition economies.[3] Thus with the exception of the LDCs, the performance of this group can be seen as reflecting the performance of developing-country WTO members in general. The trade for these 42 countries increased at about the same rate as for developing countries as a whole (excluding OPEC) in both the 1980s and the 1990s, and there was a similar trend in the two subperiods and for merchandise exports and imports.

The trends for various geographic groups disguise some very important differences between the performance of developing countries and transition economies during the period that are associated with the level of per capita income. No conclusions can be drawn at this point about the direction of the causal link between level of development (as reflected in per capita income) and growth in trade, but the data in Table 2.4 are striking. The table shows that if China (which enjoyed phenomenal growth in trade) is excluded from the group of low-income countries, growth in trade tended to be higher the higher the level of per capita income.[4]

The performance of the high-income developing countries was substantially better than that of the developed countries for the period as a whole and for each subperiod for both merchandise exports and imports. Their growth in exports for the period 1980–99 averaged 7.4 per cent per annum compared with 5.8 per cent for the developed countries. At the other extreme, the LDCs experienced very slow trade growth during the 1980s and it picked up less than the trade of the other developing countries in 1990s. The performance of the middle-income countries was somewhere in between.

On the face of it the trade performance of the low-income category – a group of countries with very similar income levels as the LDCs but which do not qualify as LDCs as they do not meet all the defining criteria – was far superior to that of the LDCs. Exports for this group grew at 4.5 per cent in the 1980s and over 7 per cent in the 1990s. But the group's performance was dominated by that of China. If China is excluded, their growth in trade was little higher than that of the LDCs and both experienced a reduction in their share of total world trade (Tables 2.1 and 2.2).

The other group of countries to experience a large reduction in their share of world trade – and negative growth in the 1980s – were the lower-middle-income countries, with per capita incomes of US$750–3000 in 1999. While the trade of a number of these countries, such as Colombia,

Table 2.4 World merchandise exports and imports, growth rates by income level (per cent per annum)*

	1980–1990		1990–1999		1980–1999	
	Exports	*Imports*	*Exports*	*Imports*	*Exports*	*Imports*
Developed economies	6.84	6.25	4.69	4.72	5.82	5.52
Developing and transition economies	2.45	3.67	7.71	7.77	4.91	5.59
Least developed countries	1.12	-0.08	4.53	5.91	2.72	2.71
Low income	4.50	4.43	9.83	9.10	7.00	6.62
Low income excl. China	0.93	1.88	6.09	5.23	3.34	3.45
Lower middle income	-0.75	1.02	5.69	4.15	2.25	2.49
Upper middle income	1.29	2.99	8.11	9.54	4.47	6.04
High income	7.17	8.31	7.59	7.92	7.37	8.12
World Total	5.39	5.49	5.61	5.60	5.49	5.55

*Based on World Bank definitions and estimates for 1998: low per capita income = $760 or less; lower middle = $761–3030; upper middle = $3031–9360; high = $9361 or more; see also Appendix A. Most of the LDCs would have been in the low-income category as defined by the World Bank. However they are shown separately and are not included in the other per capita income groups in the table.
Source: WTO.

Table 2.5 Developing country trade: manufactures and non-manufactures, 1989–97 (annual growth rates, per cent)

	Manufactures	Non-manufactures
42 developing countries	14.2	5.5
Latin America and the Caribbean	15.3	6.7
Asia	12.6	6.0
Sub-Saharan Africa	15.2	1.7
Middle-East and Mediterranean	11.1	6.9

Source: Michalopoulos (1999b).

Costa Rica, Morocco and the Philippines, increased substantially during the period, the group's performance was dominated by the decline in trade experienced by the transition economies and the OPEC members.

These findings highlight the similarity between the poor performance of the LDCs and that of other low-income developing countries (except China) during this period. This begs the question of whether the attention of the international community should be so heavily focused on the problems faced by the LDCs to the detriment of other low-income countries.

The findings also highlight the fact that the strong overall growth in total developing-country trade over the period, and particularly during the 1990s, derived to a significant extent from the very rapid growth enjoyed by a relatively small number of these countries, most of which (again with the exception of China) are middle- and higher-income economies. This explains the concern expressed by many of the poorer developing countries that they are being left behind.

As noted in many studies, the trade performance of the various groups of developing countries depends very much on the composition of their exports, that is whether their exports consist mainly of manufactures, primary commodities or foodstuffs. Overall, developing countries have more than doubled their share of world exports of manufactures since the 1980s (World Bank, 2000a). Table 2.5 looks at the trade performance of 42 developing countries by regional group in manufactures and non-manufactures over the period 1989–97. There was strong growth in manufactured exports from Latin America and, somewhat surprisingly, the Sub-Saharan African countries, although the latter group started from a low base. The table also shows that there was very slow growth in non-manufactured exports from the Sub-Saharan countries, explained in good part by the weak price of their main raw material exports. Other studies (for example Hertel and Martin, 1999) have shown that a significant proportion of the growth in manufactured exports in Latin America and Asia was the result of increased trade among the developing countries themselves.

The improved export performance of developing countries during the 1990s was due mainly to increased world trade in the commodities they exported, and to a much lesser extent to diversification or increases in the market share of their traditional exports. While this was true for the developing countries as a whole, different regions had different experiences: both Asia and Latin America improved their competitive position, but Sub-Saharan Africa experienced slow growth in its export basket, reflecting the continued decline in primary commodity prices and the slow growth in demand for these commodities. The same was true for the LDCs (World Bank, 2000d).

The weak export performance of the LDCs was largely due to their dependence upon a small range of primary commodities (usually two or three) for the bulk of their export earnings. On average the top three export commodities of the LDCs accounted for over 70 per cent of each country's exports, and with the exception of Bangladesh, few countries had any significant exports of manufactures. On average manufactures, mainly textiles and clothing, constituted about 20 per cent of total LDC exports (WTO, 1997b). Although these exports grew substantially over the period, this did not compensate for the weak performance of primary commodities, which accounted for the bulk of LDC merchandise exports.

Trade in services

Data on trade in services are far less easy to obtain than data on merchandise trade. Indeed many countries do not report data on certain service categories (Whichard, 1999), and no data are available for a number of countries for certain periods.[5] Nonetheless it appears that the growth of world trade in services in the 1980s and 1990s was faster than that of goods. Developing-country service exports grew faster than those of developed countries for the period as a whole (8.2 per cent compared with 6.9 per cent), although export growth was slightly slower in the 1980s (Table 2.7). Service imports by developing countries, on the other hand, grew slightly less than those by developed countries, and growth was poorer in the 1980s than in the 1990s.

The regional growth patterns in services were similar to those in goods. The Asian developing countries' trade grew the fastest and Sub-Saharan Africa's the slowest, with Latin America and the Middle East and the

Table 2.6 World commercial services exports 1980–1999 (billion $ and per cent)

	1980 Value	1980 %	1985 Value	1985 %	1990 Value	1990 %	1995 Value	1995 %	1999 Value	1999 %
By income level										
Developed economies	275	78.1	287	77.5	605	79.2	852	73.7	973	75.0
Developing and transition economies*	77	21.9	83	22.5	159	20.8	304	26.3	325	25.0
Least developed countries	2	0.4	2	0.4	2	0.3	4	0.3	4	0.3
Low income	9	2.6	9	2.5	17	2.2	35	3.0	49	3.8
Low income excl. China	7	1.9	6	1.7	11	1.5	16	1.4	22	1.7
Lower middle income	18	5.1	18	5.0	33	4.3	60	5.2	61	4.7
Upper middle income	30	8.6	33	8.8	58	7.6	110	9.5	119	9.2
High income	18	5.2	21	5.8	49	6.4	96	8.3	92	7.1
Total	352		371		764		1156		1297	
By region										
Developed economies	275	78.1	287	77.5	605	79.2	852	73.7	973	75.0
Developing economies	66	18.6	73	19.8	142	18.6	273	23.6	292	22.5
Sub-Saharan Africa	7	1.9	5	1.2	8	1.1	10	0.9	11	0.8
Asia	26	7.5	33	9.0	77	10.1	175	15.2	182	14.1
Latin America and Caribbean	16	4.5	17	4.5	27	3.5	40	3.4	46	3.6
Middle East and Mediterranean	17	4.7	19	5.1	30	4.0	48	4.1	53	4.1
Transition economies	11	3.3	10	2.7	16	2.1	32	2.7	32	2.5
42 developing countries	44	12.6	52	14.0	109	14.3	207	17.9	202	15.6
Total	352		371		764		1156		1297	

* For definition of the country groupings see Appendix 1. The total for the transition economies excludes the former Soviet Union.
Sources: WTO; World Bank.

Mediterranean in between (Table 2.7). Growth over the period as a whole was again associated with the per capita income level of the various groups when China is excluded from the low-income group (Table 2.8). Growth was highest for the high-income countries and lowest for the LDCs, with the exports of the other groups remaining stable throughout the period. Interestingly, however, the low-income countries (excluding China) and LDCs performed very strongly during the 1990s. This was due to the rapid expansion of service exports from India and Bangladesh during this period.

The overall picture that emerges from these findings on service exports is again a differential performance by the various groups, although the differences are less marked than was the case with merchandise trade. Much of the slow export growth in the low-income countries and LDCs is accounted for by the very low figures for the Sub-Saharan African countries.

Integration into world trade

A key indicator of a country's integration into world trade is the ratio of its total trade in goods and services (exports plus imports) to GDP. Essentially this shows how much of a country's economy is directly affected by international trade. This indicator is especially useful in determining the links between a country's economy and international trade over time, but it has to be used with caution when making comparisons between countries. This is because large countries tend to have smaller ratios of trade to GDP than small economies. Also, the existence of large enclave-type export sectors in some developing countries may give the false impression that the economy is well integrated into the world trading system, when in practice the bulk of economic activity may be subsistence domestic production.

Table 2.9 shows the evolution of this indicator in developing countries for the period 1980–98. The trade to GDP ratio was highest for the high- and upper-middle-income countries at both the beginning (1980) and the end of the period (1998). It was lowest for the LDCs and in between for the low- and lower-middle-income countries. If China is excluded from the low-income group, the group's share in 1980 was higher than that of the LDCs, despite the fact that some of the low-income countries have very large populations – such as India, Nigeria and Pakistan – and low trade to GDP ratios.

During this period the developing countries as a whole became more integrated into the international trading system but the degree of

Table 2.7 World commercial services exports and imports, growth rates by region (per cent per annum)

	1980–1990		1990–1999		1980–1999	
	Exports	*Imports*	*Exports*	*Imports*	*Exports*	*Imports*
Developed economies	8.20	8.62	5.41	5.14	6.87	6.96
Developing economies	8.05	4.50	8.33	8.04	8.18	6.16
Sub-Saharan Africa	2.00	-1.32	3.46	3.67	2.69	1.01
Asia	11.33	10.08	10.02	10.77	10.71	10.41
Latin America and Caribbean	5.30	1.95	6.23	6.29	5.74	3.98
Middle East and Mediterranean	6.16	1.42	6.40	3.69	6.27	2.49
Transition economies	3.60	2.65	7.86	7.38	5.60	4.86
42 developing economies	9.41	5.73	7.13	7.28	8.33	6.46
World total	8.04	7.49	6.06	5.83	7.10	6.70

Source: WTO.

Table 2.8 World commercial services exports and imports, growth rates by income level (per cent per annum)

	1980–1990		1990–1999		1980–1999	
	Exports	*Imports*	*Exports*	*Imports*	*Exports*	*Imports*
Developed economies	8.20	8.62	5.41	5.14	6.87	6.96
Developing and transition economies*	7.48	4.33	8.28	7.99	7.86	6.05
Least developed countries	2.78	2.05	8.53	5.78	5.47	3.80
Low income	6.32	2.25	12.54	13.23	9.23	7.31
Low income excl. China	5.14	1.42	8.03	8.07	6.50	4.52
Lower middle income	6.16	3.02	7.09	7.14	6.60	4.95
Upper middle income	6.80	2.87	8.24	6.57	7.48	4.61
High income	10.32	11.59	7.31	7.61	8.88	9.69
World total	8.04	7.49	6.06	5.83	7.10	6.70

* These data exclude the former Soviet Union countries.
Sources: WTO; World Bank.

Table 2.9   Ratio of total trade to GDP by income level (per cent)

	1980	*1998*
Least developed countries	0.33	0.35
Low income	0.33	0.40
Low income excl. China	0.40	0.41
Lower middle income	0.53	0.59
High and upper middle income	0.58	0.83
Total developing countries	0.50	0.65

Sources: WTO; World Bank.

integration varied between income groups. The trade to GDP ratio for the LDCs and the low-income countries (excluding China) on average increased very little, it was greatest for the upper-middle and high-income group and the other groups fell in between. Hence we see a repeat of the same pattern: it appears that the developing countries as a group are becoming better integrated into the world economy; but the individual performances differ considerably, with many poor countries being left behind and the gap between them and the rest of the world increasing.

Frankel and Romer (1999) estimate that the ratio of trade to GDP is strongly and positively related to growth in incomes: an increase in the ratio by 1 per cent can raise the level of income by anywhere between 0.5 per cent and 2 per cent. Dollar and Kraay (2001) identify a group of 'recent globalizers' – developing countries that experienced a rapid increase in the ratio of trade to GDP during the 1980s and 1990s and at the same time substantially reduced their applied tariff rates. These countries fall into different income groups, with Argentina and Brazil at the top of the income scale and Bangladesh and Ghana at the bottom.[6] Most are WTO members and the remaining are at various stages of the accession process. Dollar and Kraay show that the growth performance of these countries in the 1990s was far superior to that of the other developing countries. Their per capita GDP grew on average by 5.1 per cent compared with around zero or negative growth for the other developing countries and transition economies. Dollar and Kraay also show that overall income growth in these countries is strongly associated with higher incomes for the poor.

Policy implications

The above findings, taken together with our analysis, have striking and disquieting implications: the fact that integration into the world economy (as measured by the trade to GDP ratio) is proceeding much more slowly for the lower-income countries and the LDCs than for the other developing countries, together with the links between integration and GDP growth and hence poverty alleviation, suggests a polarizing trend in the world economy. Some developing countries, primarily those in the middle- and higher-income groups, are integrating more quickly, growing faster and reducing their poverty levels; but many others, especially the poorest, are neither integrating (or very little) nor growing and hence are making slow progress in reducing poverty.

The fact that integration and growth has generally been slowest among the LDCs and low-income countries is especially worrisome in that it suggests a further polarization of economic wellbeing in the world as a whole. On the other hand the successful performance of the 'recent globalizers', several of which are low-income countries, suggests that marginalization, stagnation and poverty are not inevitable. Countries can integrate into the world economy, grow and alleviate poverty. The key factors are the policies and institutions employed in the countries themselves and in the international environment to support this objective; and in this context a vital consideration is the role played by international trade and the WTO.

Notes

1. For definitions, see Appendix 1.
2. It is estimated that with an average oil price of $28 a barrel in 2000, developing-country oil exporters will improve their current account balance by $135 billion. Developing-country oil importers, however, can expect their current account balance to deteriorate by $45 billion (World Bank, 2000b).
3. It also excludes China (a star performer during the period), which was not a GATT/WTO member.
4. The classification of countries is based on the World Bank's definitions of income categories and groups as of 1998 (see Appendix 1).
5. For example no data are available on countries of the former Soviet Union for the period before 1995.

3
Trade and Development in GATT and the WTO

Introduction

The increasing integration of many developing countries into the world economy since the start of the 1980s has occurred in the context of a changing international and institutional environment in respect of the rules affecting developing-country participation in international trade. In particular the establishment of the WTO in 1995 introduced profound changes to the institutional and legal setting for the conduct of trade. The rules affecting developing-country participation in the multilateral trade system have reflected, sometimes with a considerable lag, the evolution in thinking about the role of trade in development.

This chapter reviews how development concerns have been addressed within GATT and subsequently the WTO. It traces the evolution of developing-country participation in these organizations and links this to changes in the types of international trade policy that are deemed conducive to development. Particular attention is paid to the concept of differential and more favourable treatment for developing countries in respect of their rights and obligations in GATT/WTO and to its changing content and emphasis over time.

The next section reviews the main principles and practices of developing-country participation in GATT from the time of its establishment through to the mid 1980s, and links them to the concerns about the relationship between trade and development that prevailed during this period. The subsequent section discusses developing-country participation in the Uruguay Round as well as the Round's significance for the treatment of development issues within the WTO. The last sections focus on the special treatment issues awarded to developing countries in general and the LDCs in particular, the manner in which they have been addressed by the WTO and questions about future implementation.

Principles and practices of developing countries in GATT, 1947–86

Trade and development in the early days of GATT[1]

The draft charter of the International Trade Organization (ITO), which was never ratified, provided for exceptions to be made to the general trade rules when dealing with issues of development. For example one provision allowed Contracting Parties to use protective measures during the establishment, development or reconstruction of particular industries or branches of agriculture, provided they obtained the permission of the other Contracting Parties.[2] When GATT was established in 1947, 11 of the original 23 Contracting Parties would have been considered developing countries.[3] At the time, however, there was no formal recognition of developing countries as a group, nor were there any special provisions or exceptions in the agreement in respect of their rights or obligations. The preamble to the agreement stressed the importance of substantially reducing discriminatory treatment and emphasized reciprocal and mutually advantageous arrangements (GATT, 1948). The fundamental principle was that all rights and obligations should apply equally to all contracting parties.

Today developing countries make up more than two thirds of the 140-strong WTO membership, and the WTO agreements contain a very extensive set of provisions on the rights and obligations of developing countries and LDCs. Despite this, there is still no official definition of what constitutes a 'developing country'. Rather, countries use the designation on the basis of self-selection. As a consequence Singapore, with a per capita income of $30170 in 1998, and Ghana, with a per capita income of $390 (World Bank, 2000a), are both supposed to benefit from the same provisions. On the other hand there is an official UN list of 49 LDCs, 30 of which are currently members of the WTO.

The original GATT contained no explicit provisions for developing countries, but developing countries soon started to voice their concern about the special challenges they faced in international trade. Their starting point was that sustainable increases in income and output could only be brought about by increased industrialization. In most countries there was a consensus that liberal trade policies would not promote industrialization and development because of the prevailing patterns of international specialization. Developing countries tended to specialize in raw materials and primary commodity exports, which were characterized by low price, low income elasticity of demand and considerable price volatility. Furthermore they were dependent on imports for manufactures, especially the capital goods and intermediate inputs needed for investment and industrialization. It was felt that liberal trade policies would stymie the development of infant industries, while their continued dependence on primary commodity and raw material exports would result in volatile export earnings and deteriorating terms of trade (Prebisch, 1950; Singer, 1950). Moreover it was thought that the development process was inherently associated with balance of payments difficulties, which could be addressed in the short term through trade controls. The trade strategy that emerged from this thinking and was practiced by most developing countries at the time had three main strands: (1) the promotion of industrialization through import substitution with protective tariff and non-tariff barriers; (2) the promotion of manufactured exports in order to diversify the export structure, in part through export subsidies, which were perceived as necessary to offset the advantages enjoyed by established developed-country producers; and (3) the use of trade controls in response to actual or potential balance of payments difficulties.

The trade strategies pursued by developing countries during this early period gave rise to requests for changes to be made to the multilateral trading system in four main areas: improved market access for developing-country exports of manufactures to developed markets (through the provision of trade preferences) in order to overcome the disadvantages developing countries faced when attempting to break into these markets; non-reciprocity – or less than full reciprocity – in trade relations between developing countries and developed countries in order to permit developing countries to maintain protective measures that were deemed necessary to promote development; for the same reason, flexibility in the application by developing-country members of the GATT and later WTO disciplines; and stabilization of the world commodity markets.

GATT and the developing countries, 1954–86

The manner in which the international community sought to accommodate the specific concerns of developing countries between the early 1950s and the 1980s was heavily influenced by the consensus prevailing at the time on the type of trade strategy that was best suited to meeting development objectives. Throughout this period developing countries sought to emphasize the uniqueness of their development problems and challenges and their need to be treated differently and more favourably in

GATT, in part by being permitted not to liberalize their own trade and in part by being awarded preferential access to developed-country markets.

In the 1954–55 GATT review session, for the first time provisions were adopted to address the needs of developing countries as a group within GATT. Three main provisions were agreed, two of which related to Article XVIII of the agreement. Reflecting the argument that developing-country members were likely to face balance-of-payments difficulties for an extended period of time, Article XVIII (B) was revised to include a specific provision to allow countries at 'an early stage of their development' to adopt quantitative restrictions on imports whenever their monetary reserves were deemed inadequate in terms of their long-term development strategy.[4] Article XVIII (C) was revised to allow for the imposition of trade restrictions (both tariffs and quantitative restrictions) to support infant industries with a view to improving living standards. And a provision granting the right of veto to certain affected contracting parties was deleted, thus facilitating the imposition of quantitative restrictions (GATT, 1954).

Commodity issues were first addressed in GATT as early as 1956, when the Contracting Parties (CP) adopted a joint resolution on the particular difficulties connected with trade in primary commodities. Characteristically for these early attempts to cope with what would turn out to be a very thorny problem, the resolution called for an annual review of trends and developments in commodity trade, and the convening of an intergovernmental meeting if it was felt that international joint action would usefully contribute to the solution of the problem. In 1958 the Haberler report – by an expert panel appointed at the 1957 GATT ministerial meeting – concluded, in quaint and guarded language, that 'there is some substance in the feeling of disquiet among primary producing countries that the present rules and conventions about commercial policies are relatively unfavorable to them'. The report went on to recommend (1) stabilization programmes to address commodity price fluctuations through buffer stocks, and (2) a reduction in developed countries' internal taxes on primary products such as coffee, tea and tobacco as these taxes served to constrain consumption and import demand (GATT, 1958).

In 1961 GATT adopted a declaration on the promotion of trade of less developed countries, which *inter alia* called for preferential market access for developing countries not covered by the preferential tariff systems (such as the Commonwealth preferences) or by preferences in customs unions or free trade areas, which were subsequently established. This was the first mention of what would later become the generalized system of preferences (GSP) for developing countries.

In 1964 GATT adopted a specific legal framework within which the concerns of developing countries could be addressed. Part IV dealt specifically with trade and development and contained three new articles XXXVI to XXXVIII. Article XXXVI stated that Contracting Parties should provide, 'in the largest possible measure', more favourable and acceptable market access conditions for products of export interest to developing countries, notably primary products and processed or manufactured products. Paragraph 8 of the article addressed the principle of less than full reciprocity by specifying that developing-country members 'should not be expected' to make contributions that would be inconsistent with their level of development in the process of trade negotiations.[5] Article XXXVII called for the highest priority to be given to the elimination of restrictions that served to 'differentiate unreasonably' between primary and processed products, and required Contracting Parties to take full account of the impact that trade policy instruments permitted by the agreement would have on developing-country members. Article XXXVIII called for joint action by the Contracting Parties through international arrangements to improve market access for products of export interest to developing countries. The Committee on Trade and Development was established and mandated to review the application of Part IV provisions, carry out or arrange any consultations required for the application of these provisions, and consider any extensions, and modifications to Part IV suggested by CP with a view to furthering the objectives of trade and development.

A decided pattern appears to have evolved during these early years: the Contracting Parties accommodated the developing countries desire not to liberalize their import regimes, partly on infant industry grounds and partly for balance of payments reasons, but on the question of improved access to developed-country markets and commodity price stabilization no action was taken or legally binding commitments made. For example none of the provisions of Part IV legally bound developed countries to undertake specific actions in favour of developing-country Contracting Parties. The Committee on Trade and Development was then, and still is, primarily a forum to discuss developing-country issues but not to negotiate legal commitments in their favour. During this period many developing countries were not party to GATT, and those that were participated minimally in its deliberations.

Partly because developing countries felt that their trade concerns were not being effectively addressed in GATT, they successfully lobbied for the establishment of a separate organization to deal explicitly with problems of trade and development. This organization, UNCTAD, came into being in 1964 and was the main institution through which developing countries pursued their international trade agenda during this period. The establishment of a system of preferences for developing-country manufactured exports in developed-country markets and the stabilization of commodity trade were important topics on the agenda of the new institution during the 1960s and 1970s.

In 1968 the developing countries succeeded in establishing a GSP under the auspices of UNCTAD. The system was established on a voluntary basis by the developed countries, meaning they were not legally bound under GATT to maintain it; but a GATT waiver from MFN obligations was granted in 1971, initially for a period of ten years (GATT, 1972), along with another waiver allowing developing-country CP to grant preferences amongst themselves.

While pursuing the GSP, developing countries were at the same time benefiting from significant gains in market access that were the product of tariff reductions implemented on an MFN basis for all the parties to GATT, leading in effect to the creation of two-track market access. The stability and predictability of market access resulting from the practice of binding tariffs in GATT was a further gain: in general, developed countries' tariff bindings throughout the history of GATT and the WTO have corresponded to the rates actually applied.

Both the Kennedy Round of GATT negotiations, which ended in 1967, and the Tokyo Round, which ended in 1979, resulted in cuts on tariffs on industrial goods on the basis of an agreed formula.[6] However the average reduction in tariffs following each Round was less favourable to developing countries than to developed ones: 26 per cent compared with an average of 36 per cent on goods of export interest to developed countries after the Kennedy Round (UNCTAD, 1968) and 26 per cent compared with 33 per cent after the Tokyo Round (GATT, 1979). This was because many such goods were either exempt from formula cuts or subject to lower than formula cuts. On the other hand a number of developed countries extended to developing countries non-reciprocal reductions in the duty on tropical products.

The relatively less favourable outcome of the two GATT Rounds for the developing countries was partly attributable to their limited participation in the process of negotiating concessions (Kemper, 1980; Hudec, 1987). The basic formula having being agreed, it was the developed countries that negotiated exceptions to the cuts specified in the formula. Final concessions were then extended to all CP by virtue of the MFN provisions of GATT. While developed countries did consider developing countries' demands in respect of products of export interest, these demands tended to be met or rejected without substantial further negotiation.

In the Kennedy and Tokyo Rounds, developing countries placed at least as much emphasis on discussing the extent to which and the manner in which they should undertake the rights and obligations of the multilateral trading system, as on negotiating specific concessions and commitments. The principal result of these 'framework discussions' of the Tokyo Round was the Enabling Clause of 1979. The clause established the principle of differential and more favourable treatment for developing countries, reciprocity and fuller participation by developing countries (GATT, 1980). It provided for: (1) preferential market access by developing countries to developed-country markets on a non-reciprocal, non-discriminatory basis; (2) more favourable treatment for developing countries in respect of other GATT rules on non-tariff barriers; (3) the introduction of preferential trade regimes between developing countries; and (4) special treatment of LDCs in the context of specific measures for developing countries.

The introduction of the Enabling Clause thus established a stronger legal basis for the special and differential treatment of developing countries within the rules of the multilateral trading system. While the clause formally embodied the concept of special and differential treatment, it did so in discretionary and permissive rather than legally binding terms.

In terms of concrete measures in favour of developing countries, the Enabling Clause transformed the 10-year waivers for the GSP and for trade preferences among developing countries into permanent waivers. In this regard the clause did not create any new legally binding obligations for developed country members, rather it made possible the introduction of preferential and non-reciprocal market access schemes, with the extent of preferences and the level of reciprocity being left to the discretion of each country that extended them. In bringing together the key elements of preferential market access, non-reciprocity and flexibility in the implementation of rules and commitments, the Enabling Clause was a summation, rather than an extension, of the efforts made since 1954 to address the concerns of developing countries within the multilateral trading system.

The permissiveness of special and differential treatment was also reflected in the non-participation of developing countries in a number of agreements negotiated during the Tokyo Round on such matters as export subsidies, countervailing duties, technical barriers to trade and government procurement. Although these agreements contained specific special measures for developing countries, most of them chose not to join, arguing that they had not been invited to do so until late in the negotiations, which had been conducted without their full participation – a complaint that would be repeated frequently in subsequent years.

As a counterweight to the provisions in the Enabling Clause for special and differential treatment and relaxation of Article XVIII disciplines,[7] the Contracting Parties agreed to the principle of 'graduation'. Behind the idea of graduation was the expectation that the capacity of developing countries to undertake negotiated conditions and to make contributions – within the framework of rights and obligations of the multilateral trading system – would increase with the improvement over time of their economic status and trade situation. This provided the formal basis for developed countries to phase out non-reciprocal preferential market access measures to Contracting Parties that over time, were deemed to have attained a sufficient level of progress (GATT, 1980, p. 205). Because the preferences permitted by the Enabling Clause were permissive and non-binding, and because of the 'fuller participation' clause, developing countries had no legal recourse within GATT against such action.

Finally, following a series of negotiations in UNCTAD the Common Fund for Commodities (CFC) was established in 1980 and went into effect in 1989. The CFC comprised two accounts: the first was intended to finance international buffer stocks and internationally coordinated national stocks, and the second to finance measures for commodity development, and promote coordination and consultation on commodity issues.

Rethinking trade and development in the 1980s

It could be argued that by the beginning of the 1980s developing countries had achieved their objectives of establishing international trade rules that were responsive to their perceived needs for development:

- They had ample flexibility under the existing GATT rules to provide protection on infant industry or balance of payments grounds.
- They did not have to liberalize their trade on a reciprocal basis in the context of multilateral trade negotiations.
- They could support their exports through subsidies, although they remained open to the risk of countervailing duties.
- They had preferential access to developed-country markets under the GSP.
- They had a new fund to support their commodity stabilization schemes.

Yet all was not well with the international rules governing developing-country trade. There were two main problems. First, access to developed-country markets was far more difficult than one might suspect given the existence of the GSP and the extensive reductions on tariffs on manufactures negotiated in previous GATT rounds. Second, just as the developing countries appeared to have successfully secured a set of trading rules that would be beneficial to their development, the intellectual underpinnings of these rules started to be extensively questioned.

There were many serious problems with market access. First, while the tariffs on manufactured imports had been reduced considerably, non-tariff barriers had tended to increase, especially on products of interest to developing countries. This was especially true in the case of textiles and clothing (under the MFA), and in respect of the so-called 'voluntary' export restraints imposed by developed countries on emerging develop-ing-country suppliers in such products as shoes, iron and steel, and non-ferrous metals. Second, despite the tariff reductions, tariff escalation was substantial, restraining developing-country entry into the processed goods markets and thereby inhibiting their industrialization efforts. Third, the agricultural sector remained essentially outside GATT, permit-ting developed-country exporters to constrain imports and subsidize exports at will, including on a number of products of export interest to developing countries.

The GSP turned out to be less than it has been touted to be at its inception. It was important for some products, for some countries, for some of the time. But it was not serving to strengthen the integration of developing countries into the world trading system. Because it was a voluntary scheme, developing-country suppliers were less certain about market conditions than under the contractual arrangements involving bound tariffs in GATT. At the same time the benefits of preferences seemed to be accruing to the more advanced developing countries that needed them least. According to Karsenty and Laird (1987) four beneficiaries – Brazil, Hong Kong, Korea and Taiwan – enjoyed more than 50 per cent of all GSP benefits. But perhaps most importantly, a number of products of great export interest to developing countries, such as textiles, were either excluded from preferential treatment or severely limited. In addition the margin of preference was eroded as a consequence of the MFN tariff reductions agreed in successive multilateral trade negotiations.[8]

Recourse by developed countries to 'graduating' higher-income or more competitive developing counties from the GSP (along with occasional recourse to political or non-trade-related graduation criteria) increased the relative importance of reciprocal liberalization with 'bound' concessions. Over time other preferential systems emerged and were applied to different developing-country groupings in various developed-country markets, such as the so-called Lomé preferences extended to Asian, Caribbean and Pacific countries (ACP) in the EU markets. This preferential treatment was deeper and more secure than that offered by the GSP. Indeed it appeared that developed countries saw measures such as the GSP as a substitute for thoroughgoing action to liberalize trade (Leutwiler *et al.*, 1985).

At the same time a serious rethinking of trade policies appropriate for development was taking place in many developing countries. In the early 1970s many had begun seriously to question the effectiveness of infant industry protection – supported by trade controls and foreign exchange restrictions – as a vehicle for industrialization and long-term sustainable development. Various potential perils in persisting with import substitution strategies had been identified. Trade barriers designed to protect infant industries created a disincentive to export, since high rates of effective protection distorted relative prices in favour of import-substitution production. As a result many infant industries remained inefficient and failed to achieve export competitiveness.[9]

In cases where selective incentives were provided, the overall trade regime often proved too complex to administer. The use of quantitative restrictions and exchange controls increased the scope for rent-seeking activities (Krueger, 1974). The inefficiency and waste implicit in some import-substitution policies led to increased vulnerability to external shocks, even in countries that had achieved rapid rates of growth in real income in the earlier stages of import substitution. At the same time, import substitution based industrialization policies typically discriminated against the agricultural sector, contributing to increased rural poverty (Krueger *et al.*, 1988). Moreover the use of fiscal and monetary instruments was far superior to trade and exchange control measures to address external imbalances as the former did not entail the resource misallocation costs typically associated with latter. Consequently there seemed to be little justification for the use of trade restrictions to address balance-of-payments difficulties (Bhagwati, 1978).

The experiences at the 1960s and 1970s also seemed to suggest that countries that pursued more open trade policies – for example those which broadly balanced incentives for import-substitution production with incentives for export manufacturing – enjoyed strong growth in both exports and per capita income. On the other hand countries that had persisted with import substitution behind high trade barriers had broadly experienced slow growth or a decline in per capita income.

While the direction of causality between trade and income growth is controversial, there is no doubt that a large number of developing countries opted for more open trade regimes in the 1980s and many countries undertook autonomous trade liberalization involving fewer trade restrictions in the belief that such regimes were more conducive to the attainment of their development objectives. Many developing countries introduced stabilization and adjustment programmes during this period (supported by the World Bank and/or the IMF), which frequently involved the conversion of quantitative restrictions into tariffs, tariff reductions, the phasing out of selective export subsidies and the liberalization of foreign exchange markets.[10]

All this was done outside GATT and involved no changes to the formal commitments of developing countries in that context. Indeed it was argued that the emphasis within GATT on the provisions for special and differential treatment – as embodied, *inter alia*, in the Enabling Clause – created scope within the multilateral trading system for the implementation, and in some cases entrenchment, of development strategies with deleterious consequences. In addition, by allowing a great deal of flexibility in the implementation of GATT rules and commitments, the provisions for special and differential treatment may have introduced a bias in favour of protection and against exports in the formulation of commercial policy.[11]

At the same time as developing countries were starting to take steps to liberalize their trade policies in the 1980s, there was growing recognition of the value of participating actively in multilateral negotiations with a view to securing market access in areas of export interest through the agreement of reciprocal commitments and concessions. This was in turn connected to the recognition that, partly as a consequence of the emphasis on non-reciprocity, the MFN tariff concessions agreed in the Kennedy and Tokyo Rounds were on the whole less favourable for products of export interest to developing countries than were concessions relating to products of interest to developed countries.

Finally, the usefulness of buffer stocks and commodity agreements as instruments for commodity market stabilization started to be questioned. Many developing countries continued to depend heavily on a few primary commodity exports and the terms of trade for primary commodity exporters continued to deteriorate (Sapsford and Balasubramanyam, 1999). But efforts to use such agreements to reverse or slow the deterioration of the terms of trade through supply management failed. By the early 1990s new market-based approaches to guard against price fluctuations started to be explored, and by 1996 the economic provisions in all the major commodity agreements had either lapsed or failed (ITF, 1999). While the Common Fund provided technical assistance to increase the productivity and supply response of countries producing primary products, no funds from its first account were ever used to support buffer-stock management of commodity agreements.

As a consequence of the waning interest in the GSP and commodity stabilization, and of the emerging consensus that the liberalization of policies was more conducive to development, as well as the growing importance of reciprocal liberalization as a means of attaining greater market access, GATT's importance as an institution within which developing countries could pursue their trade objectives started to rise. This was manifested in the decision by a number of developing countries, especially in Latin America (for example Mexico), to join GATT. It was against this background that the Uruguay Round was launched – symbolically enough, in a developing country – in 1986. The Round, which did not conclude until eight years later, brought about a fundamental restructuring of the rules guiding the international trading system as well as a significant change in the role played by developing countries within the system.

The Uruguay Round and the development dimension of the WTO

The Uruguay Round resulted in the multilateral trading system being greatly strengthened and deepened in ways that offered to developing countries the possibility of greater integration. This was achieved through the extension of trade rules to cover services, trade-related intellectual property rights and investment measures, as well as through the establishment of a strengthened dispute settlement mechanism. One of the issues that emerged in the late 1990s, however, was precisely whether this potential was being realized.

Two aspects of the Uruguay Round agreements were of great potential importance to developing countries. First, several of the agreements offered significantly improved market access in areas of interest to developing countries. Specifically the market access negotiations in the Uruguay Round covered areas of interest not previously subject to GATT disciplines, such as agriculture, and textiles and clothing. Moreover the agreement on safeguards benefited developing members' market access though the elimination of voluntary export restraints, which had acted as significant barriers in the case of goods such as footwear and leather products. And of course the negotiations on tariffs resulted in further reductions in tariffs on industrial imports, with the average trade-weighted tariff rate on such imports from developing countries falling by 34 per cent. Second, the strengthening of the dispute settlement mechanism by introducing greater certainty about the adoption of quasijudicial decisions by dispute settlement panels was of great potential benefit to developing countries: it offered judicial protection against the larger and more powerful developed countries and a better chance of prevailing in a bilateral trade dispute with them than would be the case outside the WTO.

At the end of the Uruguay Round a number of studies attempted to estimate, through quantitative model simulations, some of the net benefits that might accrue to developing countries. Invariably these studies concluded that large gains might be made by developing countries in the aggregate, although the distribution of benefits was expected to favour countries in Latin America and East Asia, while countries in Africa would benefit little, if at all. This was partly due to the fact that the African countries had engaged in less trade liberalization, and partly because they could be expected to suffer from the likely increase in the prices of food imports following the reduction of agricultural export subsidies in developed countries. Moreover the expected dynamic benefits resulting from increased trade and incomes world-wide dwarfed the estimated static effects of trade liberalization (Harrison *et al.*, 1996).

At the same time, by participating in the Uruguay Round agreements on services, trade-related intellectual property rights (TRIPS) and trade-related investment measures (TRIMS), developing countries would have to conform to rules and policy disciplines in areas where they had previously enjoyed complete latitude. The same was true of the new agreements on subsidies, technical barriers to trade, customs valuation, and sanitary and phytosanitary measures, all of which converted previous plurilateral agreements, in which few developing countries had participated, into general developing-country commitments to abide with the multilaterally agreed rules, albeit within a framework of certain special provisions (see below). Tighter discipline was also introduced on actions taken under Article XVIIIb that ran counter to trade liberalization. The agreed 'Understanding about the Article' encouraged the use of price-based measures, extended the documentation and notification requirements, and provided procedures for the phasing out of restrictions. These modifications were at least partly informed by the developments in economic policy described earlier, most notably in respect of the greater effectiveness of fiscal and monetary instruments in meeting balance-of-payments shocks.

The Uruguay Round also saw an evolution in the developing countries' attitude towards the special and differential treatment provisions. The Round continued to be guided by the general principles agreed in previous Rounds, and these were even extended in a number of ways. But without formally relinquishing the principle of non-reciprocity, developing countries eschewed past practices and agreed to participate more actively in the reciprocal liberalization of goods and services. In particular, as part of the agreement on agriculture they agreed to bind all their tariffs in that sector, and they also increased their share of bound industrial tariffs from 14 per cent to 59 per cent. But the level of the vast majority of these bindings was much higher than the applied levels, leaving developing countries considerable scope to increase their tariffs should they so decide (see Chapter 4).

In other areas the special treatment provisions on market access through the GSP were maintained. Flexibility was maintained, for example, by permitting developing countries to engage in certain agricultural support practices that were not allowed to other countries, and similarly regarding export subsidies. Moreover the Uruguay Round agreements introduced new elements of special treatment by providing transitional time frames and technical assistance in the implementation of the various agreements reached in the WTO. The basic reason for the extension of special treatment through these two new elements was simply that developing countries did not have the institutional capacity to implement the commitments demanded of them in some of the new areas covered by the WTO. They would not have signed the Uruguay Round agreements had they not been promised additional time and technical assistance to develop the necessary capacity.[12]

The conceptual justification for special and differential treatment

The legal texts of the agreements embodied in the WTO contain a very large number of provisions on the differential and more favourable treatment of developing countries and LDCs. There are additional provisions for the LDCs, for example a longer transition period for the implementation of certain agreements, such as TRIPS. Thus while a lot has been made of the fact that the developing countries participated in the Uruguay Round agreements on the same basis as other members, the agreements are replete with special provisions for them (GATT, 1995). Some provisions are in the nature of exhortations, the implementation of which is difficult to evaluate; others, although also of a general nature, underpin programmes such as the GSP; still others are very specific and relate to a particular aspect of developed- or developing-country policy.

There are several conceptual premises underlying the provision of special treatment over time and as reflected in the WTO agreements. The fundamental one is that developing countries are intrinsically disadvantaged when participating in international trade, and therefore any multilateral agreement involving them and developed countries must take this weakness into account when specifying their rights and responsibilities. A related premise is that trade policies aimed at maximizing sustainable development in developing countries necessarily differ from those of developed economies, and hence policy disciplines applying to the latter should not apply to the former. The final premise is that it is in the interest of developed countries to assist developing countries to integrate fully into the international trading system.

Based on these premises, the new provisions in the WTO agreements fall into two broad categories: (1) positive actions by developed-country Members or international institutions; and (2) exceptions to the overall rules for developing countries, and some additional exceptions for the LDCs (Michalopoulos, 2000a).

Positive steps to be taken by developed countries

The developed countries have agreed to take three kinds of actions to support developing countries' participation in international trade: (1) to provide preferential access to their markets; (2) to provide technical and other assistance to permit them to meet their WTO obligations and enhance the benefits that developing countries can derive from international trade; and (3) to implement the overall agreements in ways that are beneficial or least damaging to the interests of developing countries and LDCs.

Preferential market access

As noted earlier, in recognition of the importance of developing countries diversifying their exports into manufacturing and the difficulties that they may face in breaking into international markets for such products, developed countries have provided tariff preferences for manufactured exports from developing countries under the GSP, and within that context, for special treatment of the LDCs. As already discussed, the key issue with these programmes is whether in practice they will significantly enhance the market access prospects of developing countries.

Technical and other assistance

The WTO agreements contain numerous references to the provision by developed-country Members and international institutions of technical assistance to developing countries and LDCs. The main purpose of such assistance is to strengthen the institutional capacity of the latter countries in a way that will enable them to meet their obligations under the agreements. The main areas in which technical assistance is envisaged include technical barriers to trade, sanitary and phytosanitary measures, customs valuation, preshipment inspection, dispute settlement, trade policy reviews and TRIPS.[13] Most cases of the relevant articles call for such assistance to be provided upon request by the developing country or LDC on terms and conditions appropriate to the countries concerned.

The conceptual underpinning of these provisions relates to the emerging analytical consensus that institutional constraints significantly inhibit the effective integration of poorer countries and LDCs into the multilateral trading system. While it may be relatively easy to promulgate policies to liberalize trade, it is far more difficult to develop the capacity to take advantage of the opportunities that international trade provides. Weaknesses in the human and physical infrastructure and the institutions that deal with international trade have been identified as key impediments to developing countries' ability to benefit from international trade, and technical support by developed countries and international institutions (as well as longer transition periods, see below) has been recommended to address these problems.[14] Concern has also been expressed about the high cost of implementing the Uruguay Round agreements (Finger and Schuler, 2000), and whether technical assistance alone will be sufficient to ensure the physical and human capital needed to build capacity in areas where the developing countries have assumed WTO commitments (see the discussion in Chapter 5).

Pursuant to the mandate provided by the relevant articles and decisions such as the 'Decision on Measures in Favour of LDCs', a range of technical assistance and programmes are being provided to developing countries and LDCs by international organizations, in particular the WTO, UNCTAD, the International Trade Centre (ITC) and the World Bank. The main question that arises in this respect concerns the overall adequacy and effectiveness of the WTO's efforts and those of the WTO members and the international community in general.

Implementation of the WTO provisions in a manner favourable to developing-country members

The WTO agreements contain many references, in the preambles and in the substantive provisions of the various texts, to Members implementing the agreements in ways that take into account the interests of developing countries and LDCs. Some of these references are general in nature and are expressed in broad 'best efforts' terms, but in a few cases there are more explicit provisions on how developing countries should be treated more favourably or in ways that will least damage their interests. Examples of the general preambular statements include 'the need for positive efforts designed to ensure that developing countries and especially the least developed secure a share in the growth in international trade commensurate with the needs of their economic development' (Preamble of the Agreement for establishing the WTO); 'Members shall give particular attention to the provisions of this agreement (the TBT) concerning developing country Members' rights and obligations' (Article 12.2); and 'special regard must be given by developed country Members to the special situation of developing country Members when considering the application of antidumping measures' (Article 15).

While a strong case can be made that these provisions are not legally enforceable (Kessie, 2000) developing countries have questioned whether the developed countries have lived up to the spirit of their commitments, an issue that will be discussed in Chapter 6.

Differential commitments and obligations by developing countries

There are two fundamental ways in which developing countries and LDCs have differential obligations under the WTO agreements: (1) they enjoy the freedom to undertake policies that limit access to their markets or provide support to domestic producers or exporters in ways that are not allowed to other members, which can be viewed as exemptions from WTO disciplines to take into account particular developing-country circumstances; and (2) they are provided with more time to meet their obligations or commitments under the agreements. In some cases more favourable treatment involves a combination of (1) and (2).

Exemption from disciplines

The most general and fundamental way in which developing countries continue to be exempted from WTO disciplines in respect of market access policies is through the principle of non-reciprocity in trade negotiations, whereby developed countries reduce or remove tariffs and other barriers to trade. This principle is recognized in GATT Article XXXVI and in the Enabling Clause. Consistent with these provisions, many developing countries have not bound the tariffs on their industrial products to the same extent as developed countries, or have agreed to bind at levels that are substantially higher than the applied levels. Similar provisions for non-reciprocity are included in Article XIX(2) of GATS, which states that 'There shall be appropriate flexibility for individual developing country Members for opening fewer sectors, liberalizing fewer types of transactions, [and] progressively extending market access in line with their development situation'.

Protection of domestic industry

A second way in which developing countries have greater flexibility in protecting domestic industry is through the provisions laid down in Article XVIII of GATT, which enables developing countries to (1) implement the tariff protection required to establish a particular industry and (2) apply quantitative restrictions for balance of payments purposes. Since the establishment of the WTO there have been very few instances of these provisions being invoked.

The Agreement on Agriculture contains a variety of measures that exempt developing countries and, to an even greater extent, LDCs from disciplines and obligations that apply generally, and it extends longer timetables or more modest reductions in government support and subsidies than are required from other members. For example investment subsidies or input subsidies to low-income producers are exempt from the calculation of aggregate measures of support; reductions in export subsidies are either set lower or may take place over a longer period of time; and there are specific provisions for the operation of government stockholding programmes aimed at enhancing food security, as well as less demanding minimum-access provisions for primary agricultural products that are the predominant staple in the traditional diet of the developing country in question. A number of developing countries have notified the WTO that they are implementing programmes that take into account the specific exemptions contained in these provisions.

There are similar exemptions in the Agreement on Subsidies and Countervailing Measures. This agreement permits LDCs and countries with a per capita income of less than $1000 to retain certain kinds of export subsidy that are otherwise prohibited, and for other developing countries the period over which subsidies can be provided is longer. Again, a number of developing countries have invoked these provisions by notifying the WTO that they are maintaining their export subsidy programmes.

Finally, the agreements contain a number of other provisions that allow developing countries greater flexibility in meeting certain requirements. For example the Enabling Clause allows greater flexibility in respect of adherence to the GATT provisions on the formation of free trade areas and customs unions among developing countries; the agreement on TRIMS permits temporary deviations for developing countries in the case of balance of payments measures; and the dispute settlement agreement provides for special procedures for LDCs.

Flexibility has thus emerged as the most widespread instrument of special and differential treatment. It could be argued that flexibility, as applied in the WTO, is not the negation of reciprocity. Commitments were agreed on a reciprocal basis, and flexibility applies to the differential application of such commitments. However the Uruguay Round agreements, by placing flexibility in the context of reciprocity, marked a significant shift away from the concept of non-reciprocity in the handling of development issues within the multilateral trading system.

With regard to the flexibility afforded to developing countries when pursuing different policies, a fundamental question is whether the latitude permitted, for example in respect of tariff bindings, results in policies that are more suited to development. A more narrow issue is that developing countries' right to differential treatment in certain instances, for example in the case of subsidies and countervailing duties as well as in the Agreement on Agriculture, are conditional on their notifying the existence of certain subsidies at a particular time. While a number of developing countries have indeed availed themselves of these provisions and provided such notification, it is thought that many countries have not fully notified measures they have been implementing, and therefore at some point in the future they may face challenges to their policies.

Time extensions

The final way in which special and differential treatment is conferred on developing countries and LDCs in the WTO is extension of the time in which certain obligations under the agreements must be implemented. Such flexibility is included in practically all the WTO agreements, with the exception of the Agreements on Antidumping Procedures and Preshipment Inspection. Time extensions are allowed for a variety of obligations, especially those under the TBT, SPS and TRIPS agreements. Flexibility in transition times has also allowed the conclusion of a number of agreements on a multilateral basis, such as those on Customs Valuation, Import Licensing, Subsidies and Safeguards, which had been dealt with only on a plurilateral basis prior to the Uruguay Round. In addition there are provisions in the Subsidies and Countervailing Duties Agreement and the Agreement on Agriculture that permit developing countries to continue to subsidize exports for a certain period and in a variety of ways that are prohibited to other members. In the majority of cases, flexibility takes the form of slower implementation of the agreed commitments. For instance the agreement on subsidies and countervailing duties permits a transition period of eight years, while the TRIPS agreement permits a transition period of five years. In the case of the Agreement on Textiles and Clothing, flexibility takes the form of accelerated phasing out of MFA quotas for developing countries.

Transition-time flexibility, like the other types of flexibility discussed in the previous section, is thus a mechanism for providing special and differential treatment the context of reciprocal multilateral commitments.[15] And a strong case can be made that the special provisions extended to developing countries – unlike the provisions calling for developed-country actions – are legally enforceable (Kessie, 2000).

The main justification for granting additional time for the implementation of agreed measures is the weak institutional capacity of developing countries and LDCs. It is assumed that, given extra time and technical assistance (which is often also provided in these areas), developing countries and LDCs will be able to strengthen their institutions sufficiently to implement the agreements. In the case of subsidies, the presumption is that additional time will enable countries to introduce alternative means of support (for agriculture or exports in general) that are acceptable under the agreement.

The main issues that arise in connection with this aspect of special and differential treatment are the adequacy of the time extensions and the cost of building the institutional capacity needed for full implementation of the obligations laid down in the agreements. The negotiators do not appear to have systematically consulted anybody involved in institution building in developing countries about the transition periods agreed upon. In many cases the extensions have already expired and there is little evidence that countries have made sufficient progress with institution building to allow them to meet their obligations fully. Consequently a systematic WTO review of all the relevant cost and time factors is urgently required.

Special measures for LDCs

The Enabling Clause of 1979 provided the basis for special treatment at LDCs 'in the context of any general or specific measures in favour of developing countries'. The Uruguay Round agreements contain 17 provisions that apply specifically to LDC members, in addition to those applicable to all developing-country members. These include a longer transition period than that granted to developing countries under the TRIPS, TRIMS and SPS Agreements. In addition the agreements on agriculture and subsidies exempt LDCs from all reduction commitments, with the subsidies agreement allowing for an extended phasing out of subsidies once export competitiveness is established.

A number of other initiatives have been adopted for LDC members since the establishment of the WTO. For example the Decision on Measures in Favour of Least Developed Countries (1994) allows LDC members to limit their commitments and concessions to an extent that is compatible with their individual development, financial and trade needs, and which is consistent with their administrative and institutional capabilities.

The high-level WTO meeting on LDCs in October 1997 formalized the twin-track approach in respect of special treatment of these countries, with one track emphasizing the latter's limited commitment to liberalization and the other increased commitment by the developed countries in respect of market access and technical assistance. In this context a number of WTO members have announced measures aimed at improved and preferential market access for LDCs. With regard to technical assistance, an 'Integrated Framework for Trade Related Technical Assistance to Support Least Developed Countries in their Trade Related Activities' has been developed, involving the IMF, ITC, UNCTAD the United Nations Development Program (UNDP), the World Bank and the WTO. This integrated framework seeks to address shortcomings in technical and institutional capacity, particularly in the areas of trade policy, human resources, export supply capability and regulatory regimes (see Chapter 5).

The key issues to be addressed in connection with the special provisions for the LDCs are much the same as with developing countries as a whole. Are the commitments for preferential market access and treatment offered by developed countries meaningful in light of the constraints these countries face in integrating into the world trading system? Is the international technical assistance provided to these countries adequate and effective? And will the flexibility offered to these countries in terms of meeting their WTO commitments assist their long-term trade and development objectives?

Issues for a new Round of multilateral negotiations

The above review of GATT and WTO provisions shows that since the 1950s developing countries have succeeded in establishing the principle that the trade rules applying to them and the LDCs will differ in many ways from those which apply to other WTO Members. While increasing their commitment to various aspects of participation in the international trading system, they have ensured that this participation is guided by the principle of special and differential treatment, which itself has been amplified in a number of ways, especially with regard to the provision of technical assistance and securing extra time for the implementation of their WTO commitments. These additional aspects of special and differential treatment reflect the increasing recognition that the integration of developing countries into the international trading system is constrained by their institutional weakness, which will require additional time and technical assistance to overcome. In light of the even poorer capacities of the LDCs, they have been given even more time for and greater flexibility in the implementation of their commitments.

One of the key questions raised by the developing countries in the discussions on a possible new Round of multilateral trade negotiations has been whether the developed countries have lived up to their Uruguay Round commitments in general, and specifically with regard to the provision of special and differential treatment. Another question, of equal importance, is whether the additional flexibility granted to developing countries is conducive to their development. The final question concerns the nature of the special treatment to be extended to developing countries in the context of the ongoing negotiations on agriculture and services as well in a new Round, if one is agreed upon. The next four chapters provide some answers to these questions, starting with how developing countries' policies and institutions have evolved in the aftermath of the Uruguay Round.

Notes

1. This section draws in part on material from the WTO (1999a).
2. This provision was introduced as an amendment to the GATT in 1948.
3. These were Brazil, Burma, Ceylon, Chile, China, Cuba, India, Lebanon, Pakistan, Rhodesia and Syria.
4. The *Report of the Review Working Party on Quantitative Restrictions* (GATT, 1955) argued that the safeguard provisions in Article XII, paras 1 and 2, which allowed for quantitative restrictions on imports in response to an imminent decline in monetary reserves, were not adequate in the case of developing-country members, for whom insufficient reserves was deemed to be a more chronic problem.
5. The Decision on Tropical Products approved the objective of duty free access by tropical products to developed-country markets (GATT, 1964). Article XXXVI stopped short of extending the total non-reciprocity affirmed in this decision to other aspects of trade between developed- and developing-country members.
6. The formula for the Kennedy Round required a cut of 50 per cent on tariffs on industrial goods. The so-called 'Swiss' formula for the Tokyo Round reduced tariffs to a level z, where $z = 14x/(x + 14)$, where x is the pre-round tariff. It thereby generated greater reductions in higher tariffs than in lower ones.

7. The requirement for advance warning was removed (GATT, 1980, p. 209).
8. The trade-weighted preferential margin on imports (agricultural and industrial) into the EC, the US and Japan fell by 27.3 per cent after the Tokyo Round (UNCTAD, 1980).
9. Several intensive studies of developing-country trade regimes during this period reached these conclusions. The two most important were a five-volume effort sponsored by the OECD, whose findings are summarized in Little *et al.* (1970), and a 12-volume study under the auspices of the National Bureau of Economic Research, whose findings are summarized in Bhagwati (1978) and Krueger (1978).
10. 'In the broad swing of the pendulum, developing countries have been shifting from severe and destructive protection to free trade fever' (Dornbush, 1992); 'The 1980s have seen the beginnings of a change of heart among developing country policy makers with regard to trade policy. The import substitution consensus of the previous decades, with its preference for high levels of tariff and non-tariff barriers, has all but evaporated' (Rodrik, 1992).
11. See Michalopoulos (1985).
12. Participants in the final negotiations on the establishment of the WTO have indicated that there was a tacit understanding that transition periods in the implementation of some of these agreements were linked to transition periods in the implementation of the agreement on textiles and clothing.
13. See *inter alia* SPS Agreement, Article 9.1; TBT Agreement, Articles 11, 12.7; Implementation of GATT Articles VII – 20.3; The Agreement on Preshipment Inspection, Article 1.2; TRIPS, Article 67; DSB, Article 27.2 and TPRM.
14. See UNCTAD/WTO (1996) for a discussion of the specific structural weaknesses in developing country trade that would justify differential treatment and policies.
15. However, developing countries seeking to accede to the WTO do not benefit automatically from transitional provisions (Drabek and Laird, 1998).

4
Developing-Country Policies

Introduction

During the 1990s the developing countries' trade policies underwent consolidation and further liberalization. Consolidation was important in developing countries such as Chile and Morocco, which had liberalized significantly during the 1980s and needed to ensure continued domestic support for their existing trade regimes. Other developing countries, for example Brazil, the Dominican Republic and Zambia, only began to initiate and implement liberalizing reforms in the 1990s. All developing-country members of the WTO had to make a considerable effort to internalize their commitments under the Uruguay Round agreements. Many developing countries were also especially active in forging closer regional trade links, through preferential trade arrangements with both developing and developed countries.

The GATT/WTO published findings of the Trade Policy Reviews, (TPRs) conducted on a regular basis since the beginning of the 1990s, are an important source of primary information on the evolution of developing-country policies, which has yet to be systematically analyzed. The main objective of the review mechanism is to 'contribute to improved adherence by all WTO members to rules, disciplines and commitments under the Multilateral Trade Agreements by achieving greater transparency and understanding of the trade policies and practices of members' (WTO, 1995, p. 434). The reviews provide detailed information on policies and institutions that affect imports and exports on a consistent basis over time. All this information has been reviewed and discussed by the countries in question and the WTO Members (and previously the GATT Contracting Parties) and can therefore be considered accurate and authoritative. While various aspects of the reviews could be strengthened (Keesing, 1998), there is little dispute about the accuracy of the information they provide.

The analysis of trade policies in this chapter and of trade-related institutions in Chapter 5 is based in considerable part on information on the 42 developing countries for which a TPR had been conducted, from the very first in 1989 through to mid 1999. The group includes 13 economies in Latin America and the Caribbean, 13 in Asia, 11 in Sub-Saharan Africa and 5 in the Middle-East and the Mediterranean.[1] Together they account for over 90 per cent of the total trade of the developing members of the WTO (see Chapter 2). Their policies and problems can be taken as representative of the developing countries as a whole, with the exception of the LDCs, only four of which have been reviewed at the time of writing (Bangladesh, Benin, Uganda and Zambia). In their case the analysis has been augmented by incorporating the conclusions of the 'needs assessments' prepared in 1998–99 for most of the 49 LDCs under the Integrated Framework referred to in Chapter 3.[2]

The analysis that follows documents the great progress made by many developing-country WTO Members in liberalizing their trade regimes since the early 1990s (see also Drabek and Laird, 1998; Finger and Schuknecht, 1999). The liberalization has had several dimensions: (1) applied tariffs have been lowered; (2) the overall use of non-tariff barriers to trade has decreased in practically all countries; (3) services have been liberalized in many sectors; and (4) in general the incidence of government intervention in trade has declined. The analysis also throws light on a number of outstanding issues in the reform agenda and some new challenges that have emerged. For example a lot of the tariff bindings are at much higher levels than the applied tariffs, creating a degree of uncertainty among exporters wishing to access these countries' markets as well as an opportunity for resurgent protectionism. Also, while the overall use of non-tariff measures has declined, the use of certain trade remedies, such as antidumping, is on the increase. The next two sections of this chapter are devoted to a review of developing-country trade policies that directly affect imports and exports.

No effort will be made to discuss other policies that affect trade performance, including exchange rate and macroeconomic policies or domestic subsidies and taxes. It is important to note in this connection, however, that all the evidence that has been collected on this issue points to a significant improvement in developing-country policies that affect exchange rate management. At the same time there is some evidence that military conflicts, both domestic and international, have played an important role in undermining trade performance in a number of developing countries, especially in Africa (World Bank, 2000d).

Trade policies that affect merchandise imports

Tariffs

The simple average applied MFN tariff level and the standard deviation in the applied tariff level for the latest year available, as well as the average level of binding, the average difference between the applied and Uruguay Round bound rates and the proportion of tariff lines unbound for the 42 developing countries in the sample are presented in Table 4.1. The table reveals the great variation in developing-country trade regimes. The average applied rates range from zero in Hong Kong and Singapore, to 10–20 per cent in many countries in Latin America, to over 30 per cent in Egypt, India, Kenya, Pakistan, Tunisia and Thailand and several African countries.[3] The simple average applied tariff rate for the countries in the sample was 19 per cent.[4]

Tariff rates also vary substantially within each country, with overall standard deviations in excess of 10 for several countries, and similarly high coefficients of variation. Interestingly, however, the variation in the applied tariff rate structure of the developing countries in the sample is not substantially different from that of many developed countries (see OECD, 1997, Tables 1.1–1.4). The main reason for this similarity is the increased variation of the agricultural tariffs in developed countries as a consequence of tariffication in agriculture.

The table also shows significant variations in the proportion of total tariff lines developing countries have bound since the Uruguay Round. On the whole, of course, the proportion of tariff lines bound by developing countries increased during the Round. But while the WTO Members have bound all their agricultural tariff lines, many developing-country Members have bound only a small proportion of the lines in the rest of their tariff schedules.

There is an apparent regional pattern. In Latin America all the countries analyzed have bound virtually all their tariff lines. But in Africa and Asia many countries have bound only a small proportion of tariffs outside agriculture. In Hong Kong and Singapore, which are committed to low applied tariff rates, 62 per cent and 34 per cent respectively of the tariff schedule is unbound. Their practice appears to be motivated primarily by a desire to use the portion of the unbound tariff as a bargaining chip in future negotiations. In other countries, for example India, Nigeria and Pakistan, where an equal or even higher proportion of the tariff schedules

Table 4.1 Developing-country tariffs (per cent)

	Year	Bound	Applied	SD	CV	Margin	% unbound
Argentina	1997	35	14	2.1	0.2	22	0
Bangladesh	1996	84	29	15.0	0.5	54	N/a
Benin*	1998	114	13	6.4	0.5	101	N/a
Bolivia	1995	40	10	0.1	0.0	30	0
Brazil	1996	32	12	2.9	0.2	20	0
Cameroon	1994	80	21	4.7	0.2	59	N/a
Chile	1996	25	11	0.2	0.0	14	0
Colombia	1996	52	13	3.4	0.3	39	0
Costa Rica	1995	44	12	5.5	0.4	32	0
Côte D'Ivoire	1994	13	21	0.3	0.0	−7	N/a
Cyprus	1996	43	15	10.4	0.7	28	16
Dominican Rep.	1994	40	20	5.0	0.2	20	0
Egypt	1993	48	32	16.2	0.5	15	N/a
El Salvador	1994	38	10	7.6	0.8	28	0
Fiji*	1997	40	12	N/a	N/a	28	48
Ghana	1993	78	17	4.0	0.2	61	N/a
Hong Kong, China	1999	0	0	0.0	0.0	0	62
India*	1997	54	35	N/a	N/a	19	67
Indonesia*	1999	38	10	N/a	N/a	29	6
Kenya	1994	93	36	7.6	0.2	57	N/a
Korea	1996	26	15	57.1	3.9	11	17
Malaysia	1996	19	9	14.4	1.7	10	21
Mauritius*	1996	70	29	N/a	N/a	41	2
Mexico	1996	49	14	N/a	N/a	35	0
Morocco	1995	42	25	13.1	0.5	17	0
Nigeria*	1999	117	24	N/a	N/a	94	80
Pakistan	1996	68	68	16.3	0.2	0	70
Paraguay	1996	35	11	3.4	0.3	24	0
Peru	1993	32	19	2.3	0.1	13	0
Philippines	1996	28	30	10.1	0.3	−2	40
Senegal**	1989	17	12	N/a	N/a	5	42
Singapore	1995	9	0	0	0	8	34
South Africa	1993	22	16	9.7	0.6	6	2
Sri Lanka	1995	50	24	8.0	0.3	26	73
Thailand	1995	29	25	8.9	0.3	4	36
Tunisia	1995	69	31	7.5	0.2	38	47
Turkey	1995	30	11	4.8	0.4	19	55
Uganda	1996	62	17	4.7	0.3	45	75
Uruguay*	1999	31	12	7.3	0.6	19	0
Venezuela	1995	39	14	2.7	0.2	25	0
Zambia	1996	101	16	4.0	0.3	85	85
Zimbabwe	1994	123	17	6.4	0.4	106	9
Average		49	19	8.0	0.5	30	
Average***		38	14	4.3	0.3	24	

Notes:

N/a = not available.

Bound = simple average bound rate at the end of implementation of URA.

Applied = simple average applied rate (latest year available).

SD = standard deviation for applied tariff lines.

CV = coefficient of variation: SD divided by the applied tariff.

% unbound = proportion of total tariff lines unbound.

Margin = difference between the average bound and applied rates.

* WTO, TPRs,

** Import weighted.

*** Average for 100 per cent bound only.

Sources: WTO, IDB; Finger *et al.* (1996).

are unbound, there may be a mixture of motivations, including a desire to retain the freedom to increase protection as needed for development or other objectives.

Table 4.1 also illustrates the large differences, on average, between the bound and applied rates in most developing countries. The bound rates reflect the Uruguay Round bindings. In a few cases, for example Pakistan and the Philippines, the average applied rates exceed the Uruguay Round bound rates as during the Round these countries committed themselves to reducing their tariff rates (usually in agriculture) over time. With these exceptions, most developing countries have bound their tariffs at substantially higher rates than those actually applied, if they have bound them at all. For example Brazil has bound all its tariff schedule, but at ceiling rates of 32 per cent. For some countries (for example Zimbabwe) the difference is in excess of 100 per cent. For countries that have bound all their tariff schedule (Latin America and a few others, for example Morocco) the average difference between the applied and bound rates is 30 percentage points. Other countries, such as India, Nigeria and Pakistan, have bound a small portion of their tariff schedule and used ceiling bindings with high average rates for that part which has been bound.

Ceiling bindings, just like unbound rates, allow flexibility in developing-country policy when governments feel the need to increase protection. In recent years a number of developing countries, notably Mexico and the Philippines, have increased their applied tariffs, largely in response to balance of payments pressure.

However ceiling bindings also carry significant risks. First, domestically they are an invitation to particular interest groups to exert pressure on governments for increased protection. Second, for foreign suppliers they reduce predictability and increase uncertainty in terms of the market access barriers they will be facing. This in turn impedes the activity of private agents, especially where investments are marked by a degree of irreversibility, and could result in reduced inflows of foreign investment. At the same time their widespread existence undermines the developing countries' argument that their development requires intrinsically higher levels of protection than those agreed in the WTO. Perhaps the greatest use to which ceiling bindings could be put would be to bargain them away in a new Round of negotiations on non-agricultural tariffs in exchange for developed-country concessions that would improve developing-country market access.

Table 4.2 provides similar information to that in Table 4.1, but distinguishes between agriculture (HS1–24) and manufactures (HS25–97). The table shows that with the exception of six countries, the average

Table 4.2   Developing-country tariff rates, by sector (per cent)

	HS2	Bound	Applied	SD	CV	Margin
Argentina	Agriculture	23	9	1.4	0.2	14
	Manufactures	31	14	2.4	0.2	18
Bangladesh	Agriculture	84	30	14.5	0.5	54
	Manufactures	84	27	14.9	0.6	56
Benin*	Agriculture	79	N/a	N/a	N/a	N/a
	Manufactures	119	N/a	N/a	N/a	N/a
Bolivia	Agriculture	40	10	0.0	0.0	30
	Manufactures	40	10	0.1	0.0	30
Brazil	Agriculture	36	11	2.4	0.2	30
	Manufactures	32	13	3.0	0.2	26
Cameroon	Agriculture	80	23	4.9	0.2	57
	Manufactures	79	20	4.6	0.2	59
Chile	Agriculture	32	11	0.0	0.0	21
	Manufactures	25	11	0.2	0.0	14
Colombia	Agriculture	85	14	3.0	0.2	71
	Manufactures	40	12	3.5	0.3	28
Costa Rica	Agriculture	44	17	9.9	0.6	27
	Manufactures	45	11	4.1	0.4	34
Côte d'Ivoire	Agriculture	15	17	0.2	0.0	-2
	Manufactures	13	22	0.3	0.0	-9
Cyprus	Agriculture	47	29	24.9	0.9	18
	Manufactures	40	10	5.6	0.5	29
Dominican Republic	Agriculture	40	21	4.8	0.2	19
	Manufactures	40	20	5.1	0.3	20
Egypt	Agriculture	92	34	24.6	0.7	58
	Manufactures	33	31	13.5	0.4	1
El Salvador	Agriculture	47	14	6.0	0.4	33
	Manufactures	37	9	4.9	0.5	27
Fiji*	Agriculture	41	12	N/a	N/a	29
	Manufactures	40	13	N/a	N/a	27
Ghana	Agriculture	87	20	3.9	0.2	67
	Manufactures	67	16	4.0	0.3	52
Hong Kong, China	Agriculture	0	0	0.0	0.0	0
	Manufactures	0	0	0.0	0.0	0
India*	Agriculture	112	N/a	N/a	N/a	N/a
	Manufactures	44	N/a	N/a	N/a	N/a
Indonesia*	Agriculture	47	9	24.3	2.8	39
	Manufactures	37	10	15.7	1.6	27
Kenya	Agriculture	98	40	7.1	0.2	59
	Manufactures	84	35	7.7	0.2	49
Korea	Agriculture	60	49	131.7	2.7	11
	Manufactures	19	8	12.9	1.7	11
Malaysia	Agriculture	17	5	8.3	1.7	12
	Manufactures	20	9	14.9	1.6	10
Mauritius*	Agriculture	119	18	N/a	N/a	101
	Manufactures	65	30	N/a	N/a	35
Mexico	Agriculture	47	22	36.9	1.7	25
	Manufactures	49	13	7.2	0.6	36

Table 4.2   Developing-country tariff rates, by sector (per cent) (*continued*)

	HS2	Bound	Applied	SD	CV	Margin
Morocco	Agriculture	44	29	13.8	0.5	16
	Manufactures	42	24	12.9	0.5	18
Nigeria*	Agriculture	150	N/a	N/a	N/a	N/a
	Manufactures	46	N/a	N/a	N/a	N/a
Pakistan	Agriculture	101	71	16.6	0.2	30
	Manufactures	51	67	16.2	0.2	−16
Paraguay	Agriculture	0	10	2.6	0.3	−10
	Manufactures	0	11	3.7	0.3	−11
Peru	Agriculture	38	18	2.5	0.1	20
	Manufactures	30	19	2.2	0.1	11
Philippines	Agriculture	35	35	12.6	0.4	0
	Manufactures	26	29	9.2	0.3	−3
Senegal**	Agriculture	30	0	0	0.0	30
	Manufactures	12	13	N/a	N/a	0
Singapore	Agriculture	10	0	0.0	0.0	10
	Manufactures	8	0	0.0	0.0	8
South Africa	Agriculture	38	14	9.1	0.7	24
	Manufactures	16	16	9.9	0.6	0
Sri Lanka	Agriculture	50	35	10.6	0.3	15
	Manufactures	50	20	7.2	0.4	30
Thailand	Agriculture	34	38	8.0	0.2	−4
	Manufactures	27	21	9.1	0.4	6
Tunisia	Agriculture	115	35	7.4	0.2	80
	Manufactures	49	30	7.5	0.3	19
Turkey	Agriculture	53	18	10.1	0.6	35
	Manufactures	21	8	3.1	0.4	12
Uganda	Agriculture	61	23	5.6	0.2	38
	Manufactures	63	15	4.4	0.3	48
Uruguay*	Agriculture	35	13	7.3	0.6	22
	Manufactures	30	12	5.4	0.4	18
Venezuela	Agriculture	50	15	2.7	0.2	35
	Manufactures	35	14	2.7	0.2	22
Zambia	Agriculture	118	18	4.0	0.2	100
	Manufactures	80	15	4.0	0.3	64
Zimbabwe	Agriculture	134	15	6.4	0.4	119
	Manufactures	106	18	6.4	0.4	88
Average	Agriculture	59	21	12.2	0.6	34
	Manufactures	42	17	6.3	0.4	23

Notes:
N/a = not available
Agriculture products: HS1-24
Manufactured products: HS25-97.
* WTO, TPRs.
** Import weighted.
Sources: WTO, IDB; Finger *et al.* (1996).

applied tariffs on agricultural products are higher than the tariffs on the rest of the product groups, which include raw materials and fuels as well as manufactures. The same is true for bound tariffs, with the exception of

Table 4.3 Tariff averages (per cent)

	Bound			Applied			Margin		
	M	A	T	M	A	T	M	A	T
By income level:									
High income (4)*	17	29	20	5	20	8	12	10	12
Middle income (23)	34	48	39	16	18	17	18	30	22
Low Income (15)	64	86	75	24	27	25	38	52	50
By region:									
Latin America and the Caribbean (13)	33	40	38	13	14	13	21	26	25
Asia (12)	34	49	37	19	26	21	14	18	16
Sub-Saharan Africa (12)	63	84	74	20	19	20	39	59	54
Middle-East and Mediterranean (5)	37	70	46	21	29	23	16	41	23
42 Developing countries	42	59	49	17	21	19	23	34	30

Notes:
* = Number of countries in parentheses.
M = Manufactures.
A = Agriculture.
T = Total.
Sources: WTO, IDB; Finger *et al.* (1996).

12 countries whose ceiling bindings are the same for both agricultural and other products.

A comparison of the tariff rates for developing countries with those for industrial countries (see Chapter 6) shows that the average applied tariff rates for agriculture are broadly similar for the two groups of countries. However the tariffs on manufactures are on average substantially higher for developing countries.

Finally, Table 4.3 shows the simple averages for applied and bound tariffs as well as the differences between the two for the various developing-country income groups and regions. The averages presented in this table should be viewed with caution for reasons discussed earlier, (see footnote 4) and because of the small size of some groupings (for example the high-income developing countries). It is nonetheless interesting to note that both the average bound and the applied tariffs tend to vary inversely with per capita income: the poorer the country, the higher the tariffs. This holds for all sectors and groups with the exception of applied tariffs in agriculture, where there is little difference between the average for the high-income and middle-income countries. Similarly the average differences in the margins between applied and bound tariffs tend to be highest in the low-income countries and lowest in the high-income ones.

There are a few points to note in the regional breakdown as well. First, the few Sub-Saharan African countries that have bound tariffs have done so at levels that on average are much higher than in the other regions. Also, the simple average bound tariffs on agricultural products in Africa and the Middle East and Mediterranean region tend to be much higher than in Asia and Latin America. In terms of applied tariffs, Latin America and the Caribbean countries have the lowest average tariffs in both manufactures and agriculture, but the differences between the other three regions are not large.

For most countries the trade policy reviews also include a systematic estimation of tariff-schedule escalation. Escalation is measured by calculating the average tariff rates applied to three groups of products – raw materials, intermediate products and final goods – which are consistently defined at the HS six-digit level. Table 4.4 summarizes this information and reflects the judgements contained in the reviews: thus a rating of 1 is given to countries where substantial escalation has been found, involving rising average applied tariffs for all three product groups in ascending order. Negative escalation, 2, is defined as declining average rates as the stage of processing increases. A mixed rating, 3, is given to countries where the average tariffs are higher for final goods but there is no significant difference between raw materials and intermediates, or, as is sometimes the case, the average for intermediates is higher than for raw materials. A rating of zero is given when escalation is low or not significant.

The table shows that while progress has been made in reducing tariff escalation in some country schedules since the Uruguay Round (for example Korea, Mexico, South Africa and Thailand), the tariff schedules of 38 per cent of the countries on which information is available have escalated considerably. In some countries (for example Pakistan) the escalation in the tariff schedules has been designed explicitly to promote industrialization. Whatever the justification and merits of the policy, the fact is that tariff escalation in a large number of developing countries is quite extensive and involves higher degree of effective protection than escalation in developed countries (see below).

Countries whose tariff schedules reveal substantial escalation (as shown in Table 4.4) as well as high average applied rates (30 per cent or more, as shown in Tables 4.1 and 4.2) and high dispersion (for example Egypt, Kenya, Pakistan, the Philippines and Tunisia) are likely to have effective rates of tariff protection of several hundred per cent in a number of products/sectors.

Table 4.4 Developing-country tariffs: escalation and exemptions

	Escalation	Exemptions		Escalation	Exemptions
Argentina (1990)*	1	0	Malaysia (1997)	1	i
Argentina (1998)	1	i	Mauritius	N/a	i,x,r
Bangladesh	3	i,r	Mexico (1993)	1	i,x
Benin	2	x	Mexico (1997)	3	i,x
Brazil (1992)	1	i,x	Morocco (1989)	N/a	i,x
Brazil (1996)	1	0	Morocco (1996)	1	i,x
Bolivia	0	i,x	Nigeria (1991)	0	i,x
Cameroon	3	0	Nigeria (1998)	0	i
Chile (1991)	0	x	Pakistan	1	x
Chile (1997)	0	x	Paraguay	3	i,x
Colombia (1990)	1	x	Peru	N/a	x
Colombia (1996)	N/a	x	Philippines	1	x
Costa Rica	0	x	Senegal	3	i
Côte d'Ivoire	1	i	Singapore (1992)	0	x
Cyprus	3	0	Singapore (1996)	0	X
D. Republic	3	0	S Africa/SACU (1993)	1	i,x,r
Egypt	1	i,r	S Africa/SAC7 (1997)	3	i,x,r
El Salvador	1	x	Sri Lanka	1	i,x
Fiji	1	x	Thailand (1991)	1	i,x,r
Ghana	1	i,x,r	Thailand (1995)	3	i,x,r
Hong Kong, China (1990)	0	0	Tunisia	1	N/a
Hong Kong, China (1998)	0	0	Turkey (1994)	3	i,x,r
India (1993)	1	i,r	Turkey (1998)	3	i,x
India (1997)	1	x	Uganda	0	i,x
Indonesia (1991)	1	i,x,r	Uruguay (1992)	1	i,x
Indonesia (1998)	1	x	Uruguay (1998)	1	i,x
Kenya	1	0	Venezuela	N/a	x
Korea (1992)	1	i,x	Zambia	3	x
Korea (1996)	0	i,x	Zimbabwe	N/a	i,x,r

Notes:

*TPR year in parentheses.

Tariff escalation: 0 = low or not significant, 1 = significant, 2 = negative, 3 = mixed, N/a = not available.

Tariff exemption: 0 = *de minimis*, i = investment, r = regional development, x = exports, N/a = not available.

Sources: GATT TPRs (1989–94); WTO TPRs (1995–99).

Something else that the data bring out quite clearly are the large differences between the applied MFN rates and the rates actually paid by importers. These differences are due to two factors. First, there are a growing number of PTAs, usually of a regional nature, resulting in an increasing proportion of imports coming in at lower preferential rates. Second, most developing countries provide tariff exemptions on a large number of products for a variety of purposes. Practically all countries do not impose duties and other taxes on a limited amount of goods imported by international and charitable organizations and diplomats. Most also exempt products used in the manufacture of exports, either directly or indirectly (see the section on export policies below). This is essential in order to eliminate the disadvantages export industries would face if they had to pay higher than world prices for their inputs. Many countries also provide duty exemptions on goods that help meet a variety of objectives, ranging from regional development, investment in general (resulting in duty-free importation of capital goods and raw materials) or investment in particular sectors or industries (see Table 4.4). For example in 1996 Mauritius collected US$26 million in duties on imports (including sales and excise taxes) but exempted others to the tune of US$150 million, less than half of which was related to exports. In the same year Benin collected less than 10 per cent of the duties that would have been due if the MFN rates had been applied.

Non-tariff measures

The analysis of Non-tariff Measures (NTM) has three main dimensions:

- The relative importance of the different policy measures employed by all developing countries in the sample, as measured by the frequency of their use.
- The main product categories whose importation is affected by non-tariff measures across the countries in the sample.
- The overall use of non-tariff measures by developing countries to control imports over the period 1989–98, as measured by the overall frequency of application of such measures.

The analysis relies on frequency ratios as indicators of the existence and scope of protective measures on different products by various countries. The advantages and limitations of frequency ratios as indicators of protection are well understood (Nogués *et al.*, 1986; OECD, 1997). These ratios are indicators of the extent to which countries resort to particular measures and of the proportion of total products in terms of tariff lines or product groups that are affected by such measures, irrespective of the value of the products actually imported. They do not necessarily capture the protective effect of the measures taken. The protective effect of a prohibition of the importation of a product into, for example, Thailand will be completely different from the application of a variable levy in Uruguay or the use of a non-automatic license by India. The frequency ratios are presented here in order to give an overall impression of the trade regimes in place in individual countries, and the various measures used by different countries for different products – not to measure the actual protection provided to each product or product group. A detailed discussion of the estimating procedures followed and their limitations is presented in Appendix 2. It is important to bear these limitations in mind and to view the estimates of the prevalence of non-tariff measures with caution. These indicators are probably more useful for tracing the evolution of trade regimes in a country over time, than for making intercountry comparisons, especially when the differences in indicator values are small.

The non-tariff measures include import licensing (and approvals), import prohibitions (partial or total), quotas, tariff quotas, variable levies and/or minimum pricing, and import monitoring. Frequency ratios were calculated for each measure as well as a total for each country.

The relative importance of different kinds of non-tariff measure

The relative importance of different kinds of non-tariff measure (NTM) employed by developing countries is shown in Table 4.5. The table shows the product coverage of each NTM employed by each developing country for 97 product categories at the HS-2 level. Thus, for example, the line for Argentina shows that non-automatic licensing affected products in 3 per cent of the 97 product categories during 1989–94. Note that this table (and several others similar to it) presents a snapshot of a country's non-tariff measures at the time its Trade Policy Review was conducted, not a period average. The averages by measure show the relative frequency for each measure used only for the 17 developing countries for which two reviews had been conducted, one in each period.

The data reveal several policy tendencies among the developing countries analyzed. First, non-automatic import licensing (including various forms of administrative approval) affects by far the greatest number of products imported into these countries, with prohibitions of various kinds ranking second. An effort was made to exclude from these calculations the large number of products that are subject to licensing to ensure public health, safety, environmental and other standards. These

Table 4.5 Non-tariff measures in developing countries, 1989–98 (frequencies in per cent of total HS 2 categories)

Country	Non-automatic licensing		Prohibitions		Quotas		Tariff quotas		Import monitoring		Variable levies min. pricing	
	1989–94	1995–98	1989–94	1995–98	1989–94	1995–98	1989–94	1995–98	1989–94	1995–98	1989–94	1995–98
Argentina	3	1	0	0	2	1	0	0	0	0	0	1
Bangladesh	34	N/a	43	N/a	0	N/a	0	N/a	0	N/a	0	N/a
Benin	N/a	0	N/a	1	N/a	0	N/a	0	N/a	0	N/a	0
Bolivia	0	N/a	0	N/a	0	N/a	0	N/a	0	N/a	0	N/a
Brazil	10	11	7	11	0	1	0	0	100	0	0	1
Cameroon	8	N/a	0	N/a	0	N/a	0	N/a	0	N/a	0	N/a
Chile	0	0	1	1	0	0	0	0	0	0	5	4
Colombia	55	6	7	1	3	0	0	0	0	0	0	6
Costa Rica	N/a	6	N/a	0	N/a	0	N/a	6	N/a	0	N/a	0
Côte d'Ivoire	N/a	31	N/a	0	N/a	5	N/a	0	N/a	0	N/a	0
Cyprus	N/a	1	N/a	0	N/a	0	N/a	21	N/a	0	N/a	0
Dominican Rep.	N/a	5	N/a	1	N/a	0	N/a	0	N/a	1	N/a	0
Egypt	14	N/a	53	N/a	0	N/a	0	N/a	0	N/a	0	N/a
El Salvador	N/a	5	N/a	1	N/a	1	N/a	0	N/a	0	N/a	0
Fiji	N/a	5	N/a	0	N/a	0	N/a	0	N/a	0	N/a	0
Ghana	0	N/a	3	N/a	0	N/a	0	N/a	0	N/a	0	N/a
Hong Kong, China	2	2	0	0	0	0	0	0	16	0	0	0
India	99	94	3	1	0	0	0	0	0	0	1	0
Indonesia	53	31	5	0	3	0	0	0	0	0	0	0
Kenya	87	N/a	0	N/a	3	N/a	0	N/a	0	N/a	0	N/a
Korea	32	0	0	0	3	0	26	25	0	0	0	0
Malaysia	55	20	4	14	2	2	0	7	0	0	0	0
Mauritius	N/a	9	N/a	7	N/a	0	N/a	0	N/a	0	N/a	0
Mexico	28	6	0	1	2	0	0	0	0	0	2	0
Morocco	51	13	14	0	0	0	0	1	0	0	24	0
Nigeria	0	2	14	9	0	0	0	0	0	0	0	0
Pakistan	0	N/a	17	N/a	1	N/a	0	N/a	0	N/a	0	N/a

Table 4.5 Non-tariff measures in developing countries, 1989–98 (frequencies in per cent of total HS 2 categories). *(continued)*

Country	Non-automatic licensing		Prohibitions		Quotas		Tariff quotas		Import monitoring		Variable levies min. pricing	
	1989–94	1995–98	1989–94	1995–98	1989–94	1995–98	1989–94	1995–98	1989–94	1995–98	1989–94	1995–98
Paraguay	N/a	0	N/a	0	N/a	0	N/a	0	N/a	0	N/a	0
Peru	0	N/a	0	N/a	0	N/a	0	N/a	0	N/a	6	N/a
Philippines	7	N/a	4	N/a	1	N/a	0	N/a	0	N/a	0	N/a
Senegal	10	N/a	0	N/a	5	N/a	0	N/a	0	N/a	0	N/a
Singapore	1	1	0	1	0	0	0	0	0	0	0	0
South Africa	36	5	0	0	0	3	0	0	0	0	0	0
Sri Lanka	N/a	23	N/a	0	N/a	0	N/a	0	N/a	0	N/a	0
Thailand	36	11	0	6	2	1	0	12	2	0	3	0
Tunisia	54	N/a	0	N/a	0	N/a	0	N/a	0	N/a	2	N/a
Turkey	5	0	0	0	0	8	0	11	0	0	0	0
Uganda	N/a	3	N/a	0	N/a	0	N/a	0	N/a	0	N/a	0
Uruguay	0	0	0	0	1	0	1	0	0	4	31	0
Venezuela	N/a	2	N/a	3	N/a	0	N/a	0	N/a	0	N/a	13
Zambia	N/a	0	N/a	1	N/a	0	N/a	0	N/a	0	N/a	0
Zimbabwe	23	N/a	0	N/a	0	N/a	0	N/a	0	N/a	0	N/a
Average	24	10	6	2	1	1	1	3	4	0	3	1

Sources: GATT, TPRs (1989–94), WTO, TPRs (1995–99).

are frequently justified by reference to GATT Article XX in the TPR. Even so, during the early period considered (1989–94) non-automatic licensing affected a large proportion of developing-country imports: non-automatic licensing was present in about one-quarter of the product categories. Several countries, such as Bangladesh, India, Nigeria and Pakistan, have indicated that the licensing and prohibition measures they used were due to balance of payments difficulties.

No effort was made in this study to determine the consistency of these licensing arrangements, or for that matter any other Member policies with GATT provisions. Only 39 WTO Members have reported quantitative restrictions, of which 22 are included in our study. Of the latter, 16 reported the use of quantitative restrictions that are mostly justified under GATT Article XX. Three Members – India, Korea and the Philippines – also justified restrictions under the balance of payments provisions of Article XVIIIb.[5] A report by the WTO Committee on Import Licensing (WTO, 1998d) showed that 19 of the 42 developing countries analyzed in this study invoked the delayed application provisions of the WTO agreement on licensing procedures, and that one quarter of the total (13) had not submitted a notification in respect of publications and/or legislation on licensing procedures.

Second, while caution is needed when interpreting the findings on the evolution of policy over time because the sample of countries is slightly different in the two subperiods examined, the data strongly suggest that the utilization of all 'core' non-tariff measures with a clearly protective effect – such as licensing, prohibitions, quotas and administered pricing – has declined over time. This is shown by the decreasing frequency ratios for the 1995–98 period for the large majority of countries for which data are available for each of the two subperiods. The only measure clearly showing an increase is the use of tariff quotas, which is permitted under the Uruguay Round agreement on agriculture. Furthermore the tables do not show the further liberalization of import regimes that has taken place since the reviews were conducted (for example, Tunisia) or the commitments that some countries have made (for example India) to liberalize non-tariff measures in the future.

The main products

The main products whose importation is controlled by NTM in these developing countries, which account for the bulk of WTO developing-country trade, are listed in Table 4.6. The table shows the percentage of countries using each measure to affect imports in each product category during the GATT period (1989–94) and the WTO period (1995–98). Thus,

Table 4.6 Non-tariff measures by product group, 1989–98 (percentage of countries using measure)

		Non-automatic licensing		Prohibitions		Quotas		Tariff quotas		Variable levies & administered pricing	
		1989–94	1995–98	1989–94	1995–98	1989–94	1995–98	1989–94	1995–98	1989–94	1995–98
I	Animal products	40	14	10	3	2	0	1	9	3	3
II	Vegetables	37	19	5	3	4	2	1	9	3	3
III	Fats and oils	45	17	14	7	0	0	0	10	3	13
IV	Prepared foodstuff	32	11	7	2	1	1	1	4	3	3
V	Minerals	34	24	3	6	0	0	1	2	0	0
VI	Chemicals	18	9	4	1	0	0	1	2	1	0
VII	Plastics	21	17	5	7	0	0	3	2	5	2
VIII	Leather	14	2	2	0	0	0	1	0	0	0
IX	Wood	14	6	2	2	0	0	2	2	1	0
X	Pulp and paper	22	4	3	1	0	0	1	2	3	0
XI	Textiles	24	7	10	1	0	2	1	2	5	0
XII	Footwear	14	3	3	0	0	0	0	1	1	0
XIII	Glass	16	6	9	1	0	0	0	1	2	0
XIV	Pearls	34	17	3	0	0	0	0	0	0	0
XV	Base metals	17	7	2	2	0	0	1	2	2	0
XVI	Machinery and electrical equipment	45	22	12	7	0	0	0	3	7	0
XVII	Vehicles	24	11	6	6	4	2	0	1	3	0
XVIII	Instruments	16	4	3	0	0	0	0	0	0	0
XIX	Arms	21	3	3	0	3	0	0	3	0	0
XX	Other manufactures	13	7	8	1	0	0	0	0	1	0
XXI	Works of art, antiques	10	3	0	0	0	0	0	0	0	0

Source: GATT, TDRs (1989–94); WTO, TDRs (1995–99).

for example, the line on HS product group VII (plastics), under non-automatic licensing for 1995–98, shows that 17 per cent of the 30 countries reviewed in that period used non-automatic licensing procedures to control some products in this group.

The data show that agricultural products (groups I–IV or HS1–HS24) were subjected most to overall controls, especially in the earlier period. The number of countries imposing these controls substantially declined in the period 1995–98, following the tariffication of agriculture under the Uruguay Round agreements. In addition to agriculture, mineral products (in particular fuels, HS27), rubber products (HS40), machinery (especially electrical machinery, HS85) and precious stones and metals continued to be subject to controls, especially through licensing, in a significant number of countries during this period (see also Michalopoulos, 1999b, Table A-3).[6]

The Uruguay Round Agreement on Agriculture has been praised for subjecting the agricultural sector to the same trade disciplines that apply to other sectors. However it has been criticized for not resulting in significant liberalization of developed-country policies. At the time the agreement was being negotiated the developing countries' main concern was market access and the benefits that some of the key agricultural exporters would obtain, as well on the possible adverse effects that reduced export subsidies in developed countries would have on net-food-importing developing countries (see Chapter 6).[7] Little attention was focused, until recently, on the level of support and the kinds of measure that were appropriate for developing countries to implement in pursuit of agricultural development, which is essential to the elimination of poverty, itself very often mainly a rural phenomenon.

The Uruguay Round Agreement on Agriculture contains provisions that permit developing countries to increase their support of agriculture (and of poor consumers) through means not available to developed countries. For example direct and indirect investment and input subsidies to poor farmers are excluded from the calculation of aggregate measures of support (AMS); reduction of the support commitments by developing countries may take 10 years to implement, while LDCs are totally exempt; and food subsidies to urban and rural poor are excluded from the calculation of AMS. However a number of critics have pointed to the unfairness of the agriculture agreement as it still permits greater support levels in developed countries (which in the past have given a great deal of assistance to their agricultural sector) than in the developing countries, which penalized agriculture in the base period (Das, 1998b). In addition there may be some problems for LDCs in respect of the limits on AMS after the expiry of the transition periods (UNCTAD, 1998). Thus, the issue is whether the limits to aggregate support and export subsidies contained in the Agreement (and their possible further tightening in the new negotiations), would impact on their capacity to increase support to the agriculture sector should they, in future, decide to do so.

Unfortunately, very little information has been systematically compiled on how the specific agricultural policies that developing countries are pursuing relate to their WTO commitments in this respect. Both the findings of the trade policy reviews and other analyses of agricultural issues in developing countries (for example Binswanger and Lutz, 2000) discuss current agricultural policies and measures, but give little indication of whether these policies are constrained by WTO provisions at present or are likely to in the future.

The overall use of non-tariff measures

The overall use of non-tariff measures by developing countries during the GATT and WTO subperiods is shown in Table 4.7. Column one shows each country's per capita GDP, averaged over the period 1991–95. Column two shows the openness index for each country, calculated as the ratio of exports plus imports divided by GDP over the period 1991–95. Column three shows the total frequency ratios (Tf_m) for core non-tariff measures (see Appendix 2 for a discussion of the meaning of total frequency ratios). Core measures are defined as those that involve quantitative restrictions or price controls on imports, such as non-automatic licensing of all kinds, prohibitions, quotas and tariff quotas as well as variable import levies and administrative/minimum pricing.[8] As a particular product category may be affected by more than one NTM, double measures have been excluded from this calculation. For example, if both a tariff quota and an import license are imposed on the same product in HS17, it is counted only once.

The first point to note in the table is that in the GATT part of the period covered (1989–94) the values of the total frequency ratios for NTM were extremely high for several countries, covering more than 50 per cent of products in such countries as Bangladesh, Colombia, Egypt, Kenya, India, Indonesia, Malaysia, Morocco and Tunisia. Without doubt NTM at that time were an important feature of many developing countries in all regions. Subsequently the data strongly suggest that the total frequency ratios were substantially reduced.[9]

Second, as with tariffs there is a tendency for the total frequency ratios of NTM to be greater in countries with lower per capita incomes and lower degrees of openness.

Table 4.7   Developing countries, total core non-tariff measures, 1989–98

	GDP/cap (US$000)	Openness	Total core non-tariff measures (%)	
	1991–95	1991–95	1989–94	1995–98
Argentina	3.73	0.25	3.1	2.1
Bangladesh	0.19	0.32	54.2	N/a
Benin	0.35	0.48	N/a	1.0
Bolivia	0.77	0.43	0.0	N/a
Brazil	1.96	0.23	16.5	21.6
Cameroon	0.77	0.50	8.2	N/a
Chile	2.29	0.76	5.2	5.2
Colombia	1.29	0.43	55.2	10.3
Costa Rica	1.83	0.89	N/a	6.2
Côte d'Ivoire	0.74	0.66	N/a	30.9
Cyprus	7.15	1.07	N/a	21.6
Dominican Rep.	0.88	0.80	N/a	6.2
Egypt	0.73	0.56	57.3	N/a
El Salvador	0.95	0.64	N/a	5.2
Fiji	2.12	0.67	N/a	5.2
Ghana	0.41	0.59	3.1	N/a
Hong Kong	11.21	4.03	2.1	2.1
India	0.39	0.17	99.0	93.8
Indonesia	0.64	0.47	53.6	31.3
Kenya	0.38	0.62	86.6	N/a
Korea	4.99	0.86	50.0	25.0
Malaysia	2.76	1.80	56.3	19.6
Mauritius	2.37	1.32	N/a	16.7
Mexico	1.84	0.53	27.8	13.4
Morocco	0.91	0.61	58.3	13.4
Nigeria	0.36	0.5	14.4	11.5
Pakistan	0.37	0.34	17.7	N/a
Paraguay	1.03	1.17	N/a	0.0
Peru	0.93	0.31	6.3	N/a
Philippines	0.61	0.76	11.5	N/a
Senegal	0.64	0.55	10.3	N/a
Singapore	11.78	3.71	1.0	2.1
South Africa	2.17	0.62	36.5	8.3
Sri Lanka	0.47	0.74	N/a	22.7
Thailand	1.60	0.89	36.5	17.5
Tunisia	1.40	0.87	54.2	N/a
Turkey	1.81	0.43	5.2	19.8
Uganda	0.51	0.23	N/a	3.1
Uruguay	2.70	0.58	32.3	0.0
Venezuela	2.73	0.49	N/a	17.7
Zambia	0.28	0.71	N/a	1.0
Zimbabwe	0.62	0.63	22.7	N/a

Notes:
GDP/cap = per capita GDP in constant 1987 US$000 (average, 1991–95).
Openness = merchandise exports plus imports divided by GDP (average, 1991–95).
Total core NTM = frequency ratio in per cent relative to total 2-digit HS categories.
Sources: GATT, TPRs (1989–94); WTO, TPRs (1995–99).

Finally, while there has been a great deal of progress in liberalizing trade, there are still a number of countries where non-tariff measures continue to be applied to a wide range of imports. But some of these countries, for example Korea and India, have already made a commitment, sometimes after the most recent TPR was conducted, further to liberalize NTM that affect their imports.

Trade remedies

Trade remedies include antidumping, countervailing duties and safeguard measures. In principle such actions are consistent with the GATT provisions.

The legal basis of and procedures for the imposition of trade remedies are as various as the remedies, which usually do not involve quantitative restrictions but changes in duties and charges to address the problem appropriately in each case. In the case of antidumping and countervailing duties, these remedies are intended to correct distortions that occur when exporters are obtaining subsidies and engaging in discriminatory pricing practices that result in injury to domestic producers. In the case of safeguards, the result is simply injury to domestic producers, even if no unfair trade practices are involved.

Evidence of the frequency with which developing countries have taken trade remedy actions is presented in Table 4.8. As it has been argued that the mere initiation of an investigation on antidumping action tends to have a restraining effect on imports – irrespective of the outcome of the case (Finger, 1993; OECD, 1997) – the main indicator used is the number of antidumping investigations that had been initiated at the time of the TPR. For safeguards and countervailing duties, actions were so infrequent that the data shown refer to the number of specific products, usually narrowly defined, on which there was either affirmative action in place or an ongoing investigation at the time of the most recent TPR, using both review data and WTO notifications. Thus while the two sets of data in Table 4.8 are not directly comparable, the frequency of safeguard and countervailing actions was likely to have been much lower than those for antidumping.

The data verify the increasing use of antidumping action, especially by higher-middle-income developing countries, and that antidumping has been the remedy most frequently used by both developed and developing countries (Miranda *et al.*, 1998; Finger and Schuknecht, 1999). The countries in our group that resorted to such action increased from 11 in 1989–94 to 18 in 1995–98. These include most of the developing-country members of the WTO that have taken antidumping action.[10] The table

Table 4.8 Trade remedies by developing countries, 1989–98 (per cent and number of products)

	Antidumping (%)*		Countervailing**		Safeguards**	
	1989–94	1995–98	1989–94	1995–98	1989–94	1995–98
Argentina	0.70	1.12	2	3	–	2
Bangladesh	–	–	–	–	–	–
Benin	–	–	–	–	–	–
Bolivia	–	–	–	–	–	–
Brazil	1.28	0.54	2	2	–	1
Cameroon	–	–	–	–	–	–
Chile	0.01	0.74	2	5	–	–
Colombia	–	0.14	–	–	–	–
Costa Rica	–	0.23	–	–	–	–
Côte d'Ivoire	–	–	–	–	–	–
Cyprus	–	–	–	–	–	–
Dominican Rep.	–	–	–	–	–	–
Egypt	–	–	–	–	–	–
El Salvador	–	–	–	1	–	1
Fiji	–	–	–	–	–	–
Ghana	–	–	–	–	–	–
Hong Kong, China	–	–	–	–	–	–
India	0.07	0.72	–	–	–	–
Indonesia	–	0.16	–	–	–	–
Kenya	–	–	–	–	–	–
Korea	0.27	0.53	–	–	–	3
Malaysia	–	0.16	–	–	–	–
Mauritius	–	–	–	–	–	–
Mexico	16.31	28.12	–	3	–	–
Morocco	–	–	–	–	–	–
Nigeria	–	–	–	–	–	–
Pakistan	–	–	–	–	–	–
Paraguay	–	–	–	–	–	–
Peru	0.05	3.50	–	–	–	–
Philippines	0.06	0.51	–	–	–	–
Senegal	–	–	–	–	–	–
Singapore	–	0.02	–	–	–	–
South Africa	–	0.76	–	–	–	–
Sri Lanka	–	–	–	–	–	–
Thailand	0.05	0.05	–	–	–	–
Tunisia	–	–	–	–	–	–
Turkey	0.45	0.22	–	–	–	–
Uganda	–	–	–	–	–	–
Uruguay	–	–	–	–	–	–
Venezuela	0.03	0.12	–	1	–	–
Zambia	–	–	–	–	–	–
Zimbabwe	–	–	–	–	–	–

* Investigations based on WTO database. Frequency ratio relative to total tariff lines.
** Number of products, based on TPRs and WTO notifications.
Sources: GATT, TPRs (1989–94); WTO, TPRs (1995–99); WTO Antidumping Measures Database; WTO (1999d).

also shows that only four developing countries out of the 42 in our sample used safeguard actions and only six countries took countervailing action, mostly after 1994, and in each instance the actions affected only a few isolated products.

The average frequency ratio of antidumping action taken by developing countries that took action in both periods increased from an average of 1.75 per cent of tariff lines to 3.29 per cent. Despite this increase a comparison between Table 4.7 and Table A2.1 in Appendix 2 (keeping in mind some of the methodological and data differences) suggests that antidumping action affects fewer product categories and tariff lines than non-tariff measures such as licensing. This conclusion is reinforced if one considers that the number of developing countries and products on which provisional and definitive measures are taken is typically significantly smaller than that for investigations.

Among developing countries, antidumping is for the most part a middle-and higher-income developing-country practice. With the exception of India, all 17 developing countries that have taken antidumping action had per capita income of more than US$785 in 1996. It is interesting to note that these countries (with one exception, Pakistan) have initiated trade complaints through the WTO dispute settlement mechanism (DSM) and can broadly be considered as more fully integrated into the WTO than other developing countries (see Chapter 8).

Mexico's antidumping actions have affected by far the largest number of product lines – 16 per cent of its total tariff lines in the early period and 28 per cent in the later one. The main reason for the percentage increase was not that Mexico took more antidumping actions in the later period, but rather that it applied antidumping measures across broad categories of products, such as all the tariff lines in several HS2 product groups, for instance textiles.[11]

Trade policies affecting merchandise exports

There are clear links between a country's trade policies that affect its exports and those that affect its imports: for example measures to control exports of raw materials that are used as inputs by domestic industries distort resource allocation in much the same way as import protection measures for that industry. Similarly the imposition of measures that restrict the quantity and increase the domestic price of imports, may adversely affect the profitability of exports and cause a country to take offsetting measures in favour of exporters.[12] Thus it is not surprising to find that over the period reviewed the developing countries liberalized their policies that affected exports in much the same way as they liberalized their policies that affected imports.

Developing countries' policies towards exports are characterized by the following broad tendency: they have tended to impose controls and taxes on their exports of primary products and foodstuffs while providing incentives and subsidies on their exports of manufactures. The control and taxation of exports of primary products have had two purposes: to capture some of the rents from the production and sale of raw materials; and to provide incentives for industrialization by taxing exports of raw materials and other inputs, thereby making them available to domestic industries at lower than world prices. For foodstuffs, the main justification is the promotion of food security. Manufactured or non-traditional exports (some of which may involve processed agricultural or agriculture-related products) are being backed by incentives because they are believed to contribute to long-term growth and development, and because it is felt that without government assistance exporters will have difficulty breaking into foreign markets due to externalities of various kinds. Also, some of the so-called incentives amount to little more than a government effort to offset the disincentives to non-traditional exports created by the import regime.

Measures that tend to tax or regulate exports

Table 4.9 shows the frequency of developing-country use of various kinds of policy measure to tax or regulate their exports. The table is constructed much like those on imports and shows snapshots of the frequency of use of different measures by various countries in two time periods. The frequencies are defined in terms of the proportion of total product groups at the HS2 level, which may contain products that are differently taxed or regulated by different measures in different countries. The measures include export taxes or similar levies, minimum export prices, non-automatic export licensing (or approval), export prohibitions (total or partial) and export quotas.

Just as with imports, non-automatic licensing procedures are the most commonly used measure, with export levies the next most important. The variation among countries, especially during the earlier period, is rather large, with some countries – such as Brazil, Indonesia, Korea, Mexico and the Philippines – controlling more than 20 per cent of export product groups through licensing or other approval procedures, while many others limit such licensing to the implementation of health and safety standards and environmental obligations.[13]

Table 4.9 Developing-country trade policies affecting exports (frequencies in per cent of total 2-digit HS categories affected by each measure)

	Export levies		Minimum export prices		Export licensing		Export prohibitions		Export quotas	
	1989–94	1995–98	1989–94	1995–98	1989–94	1995–98	1989–94	1995–98	1989–94	1995–98
Argentina	1	2	1	0	0	0	1	0	0	0
Bangladesh	3	N/a	1	N/a	20	N/a	9	N/a	1	N/a
Benin	N/a	3	N/a	0	N/a	1	N/a	2	N/a	0
Bolivia	0	N/a	0	N/a	1	N/a	0	N/a	0	N/a
Brazil	1	3	1	0	29	1	0	1	3	3
Cameroon	6	N/a	0	N/a	3	N/a	1	N/a	2	N/a
Chile	0	0	0	0	0	0	0	0	0	0
Colombia	1	3	2	3	0	2	1	1	0	1
Costa Rica	N/a	4	N/a	1	N/a	0	N/a	0	N/a	1
Côte d'Ivoire	N/a	5	N/a	9	N/a	2	N/a	0	N/a	3
Cyprus	N/a	0	N/a	0	N/a	0	N/a	0	N/a	0
Dominican Rep.	N/a	0	N/a	0	N/a	0	N/a	0	N/a	1
Egypt	1	N/a	0	N/a	1	N/a	4	N/a	3	N/a
El Salvador	N/a	0	N/a	0	N/a	0	N/a	1	N/a	1
Fiji	N/a	2	N/a	0	N/a	7	N/a	0	N/a	0
Ghana	1	N/a	24	N/a	3	N/a	1	N/a	0	N/a
Hong Kong, China	0	0	0	0	1	0	0	0	0	0
India	1	13	4	1	10	9	2	3	4	5
Indonesia	6	5	0	0	33	19	6	0	3	0
Kenya	10	N/a	0	N/a	16	N/a	0	N/a	0	N/a
Korea	0	0	0	0	42	0	0	0	0	4
Malaysia	9	10	0	0	15	35	0	0	0	0
Mauritius	N/a	1	N/a	0	N/a	4	N/a	3	N/a	0

Table 4.9 Developing-country trade policies affecting exports (frequencies in per cent of total 2-Digit HS categories affected by each measure) (continued)

	Export levies		Minimum export prices		Export licensing		Export prohibitions		Export quotas	
	1989–94	1995–98	1989–94	1995–98	1989–94	1995–98	1989–94	1995–98	1989–94	1995–98
Mexico	3	14	0	0	24	7	0	9	0	0
Morocco	2	2	0	0	5	2	0	0	0	2
Nigeria	0	1	0	1	2	2	5	5	0	1
Pakistan	21	N/a	3	N/a	20	N/a	13	N/a	0	N/a
Paraguay	N/a	0	N/a	0	N/a	6	N/a	1	N/a	1
Peru	0	N/a	0	N/a	0	N/a	1	N/a	0	N/a
Philippines	0	N/a	0	N/a	26	N/a	0	N/a	15	N/a
Senegal	1	N/a	3	N/a	4	N/a	0	N/a	0	N/a
Singapore	1	0	0	0	6	2	0	0	0	0
South Africa	1	1	0	0	9	8	2	1	0	0
Sri Lanka	N/a	6	N/a	1	N/a	7	N/a	1	N/a	0
Thailand	3	4	2	0	11	8	0	4	0	1
Tunisia	0	N/a	1	N/a	0	N/a	1	N/a	1	N/a
Turkey	4	2	1	0	0	3	1	0	1	0
Uganda	N/a	1	N/a	1	N/a	4	N/a	0	N/a	0
Uruguay	5	3	0	0	0	0	0	0	0	0
Venezuela	N/a	1	N/a	0	N/a	7	N/a	0	N/a	0
Zambia	N/a	0	N/a	0	N/a	1	N/a	0	N/a	0
Zimbabwe	0	N/a	0	N/a	9	N/a	0	N/a	0	N/a

Note:
N/a = not available
Sources: GATT, TPRs (1989–94); WTO, TPRs (1995–99).

As was also the case with imports, it appears that the use of these measures declined over time, particularly with respect to export licensing. On the other hand it appears that on average export taxation increased slightly in those countries for which information is available in both periods. For the other measures the results are ambiguous and are affected by the inclusion of different countries in the different periods.

The data permit a broad analysis of the product groups most likely to be affected by export regulation or taxation. Table 4.10 shows the proportion of all countries in each of the two subperiods that applied different types of export measure to product groups I–XXI. The purpose of the table is to reveal which product groups developing countries tend to tax or regulate most frequently. Thus, for example, the data for group VII (textiles and products) shows that on average 7 per cent of the countries subjected such products to export licensing in 1989–94 (Michalopoulos, 1999b, Appendix B, Table B-3).

The trade policy reviews (GATT, 1989–94; WTO, 1995–99) suggest that a combination of measures – sometimes a quantitative measure such as a license plus a price-linked measure such as an export levy – are usually used. Nevertheless a rather crude adding up of the number of countries and measures imposed shows that the five most frequently regulated/ taxed product groups of exports by developing countries in 1989–94, at the HS-2 level, were live animals, coffee and tea, fuels, hides and skins, and cotton. The list was more or less identical in 1995–98, except that wood and wood products replaced cotton.

Again, these findings suggest that there are two main motivations for export restrictions: to gain revenue from taxation; and to promote the development of downstream manufacturing activities using domestically produced raw materials as inputs. However the results should not be used to draw inferences about the restrictiveness of the measures or the impact of the export regulation or controls on the volume or value of developing-country exports.

Export incentives

Practically all the countries reviewed have a variety of policies and institutional support measures for non-traditional exports. In some cases explicit export subsidies have been introduced. But more frequently the measures involve policies aimed at offsetting the impact of import controls, as well as institutional support through the provision of export financing – sometimes on concessional terms – and insurance, marketing and the establishment of export processing zones (EPZs) or similar arrangements of temporary admission aimed at export promotion.

Table 4.10 Non-tariff export measures by product group, 1989–98 (percentage of countries using measure)*

		Export taxes/levies prices		Minimum export licensing		Export		Export prohibition		Export quotas	
		1989–1994	1995–1998	1989–1994	1995–1998	1989–1994	1995–1998	1989–1994	1995–1998	1989–1994	1995–1998
I	Animal products	7	5	3	1	19	9	7	4	3	3
II	Vegetables	8	7	3	2	15	9	5	2	3	3
III	Fats and oils	0	10	3	3	10	10	3	7	7	0
IV	Prepared foodstuff	2	4	2	1	11	7	0	0	2	1
V	Minerals	6	9	2	4	29	14	2	3	2	2
VI	Chemicals	1	1	0	0	4	3	0	1	1	0
VII	Plastics	3	2	2	0	7	2	2	0	0	0
VIII	Leather	8	10	2	1	10	7	6	3	2	0
IX	Wood	5	4	1	1	10	8	6	6	1	1
X	Pulp and paper	1	0	0	0	9	1	5	0	0	0
XI	Textiles	2	3	4	0	14	3	0	0	4	0
XII	Footwear	0	0	0	0	4	2	0	0	0	1
XIII	Glass	0	0	0	0	3	2	0	0	0	0
XIX	Pearls	3	10	3	0	21	17	0	7	0	0
XV	Base metals	3	1	1	0	5	2	1	0	0	0
XVI	Machinery and electrical equipment	0	2	0	0	16	2	0	0	0	2
XVII	Vehicles	0	0	0	0	10	3	0	0	0	0
XVIII	Instruments	0	0	0	0	1	1	0	0	0	0
XIX	Arms	0	0	0	0	3	3	0	0	0	0
XX	Other manufactures	0	0	0	0	6	0	0	0	0	0
XXI	Works of art, antiques	0	3	0	0	7	0	7	3	0	0

* Total number of countries: 1989–94 = 29; 1995–98 = 30.
Sources: GATT, TPRs (1989–94); WTO, TPRs (1995–99).

In most cases the measures are not product specific but apply to broad categories of products – usually defined as non-traditional or manufacturing exports. Sometimes the incentives are available only to certain groups of producing/exporting units, such as small and medium-sized enterprises. For these reasons it is not possible to undertake an analysis at the tariff-line or product-group level, as has been done for other policies that affect imports or exports; rather it is only possible to note the presence or absence of a particular kind of programme and its main characteristics. Nor is it possible to evaluate the effectiveness of any of the programmes or institutions reported. While some TPRs have identified problems or constraints affecting the effectiveness of programmes, this has not been the general rule. Hence the results reported here should not be taken to mean that the programmes mentioned accomplished their intended objectives in support of export.

Table 4.11 shows the main programmes and institutional arrangements to support exports. It shows that 41 per cent of the countries for which TPRs are available for the period reported the use of export subsidies (column three), and that several others (India, Korea, Malaysia and Venezuela) used more generalized production support that did not differentiate between support for sales in the domestic market and exports. Some of the countries, such as Costa Rica, that reported the existence of export subsidy programmes indicated their intention to terminate them at some specific date in the future. Most of the countries reported the establishment of incentives regimes aimed at attracting foreign direct investment geared to the production of exportables.

The experience of a number of countries with export subsidies suggests that they are frequently needed to offset the incentive to sell to the domestic market that is created by protection. But when protection is relatively low and the exchange rate is not overvalued, subsidies tend to be an expensive way of promoting exports whose main impact is the provision of additional profits to established exporters.

On the other hand practically all the countries have introduced some type of duty drawback system (column two).[14] In many of the countries the system is intended to cover both duties and other border taxes as well as domestic taxes such as VAT. In an increasing number of cases it also covers taxes on domestically produced inputs. Frequently, in order to facilitate administration the actual tax rebate mechanism involves reimbursement or credit for a certain percentage of a firm's overall tax liability, rather than a rebate for specific duties or taxes. As a consequence some of these programmes may contain an element of implicit export subsidy. On the other hand this is one area where several of the TPRs

Table 4.11 Developing-countries measures to support or promote exports

	Duty drawback	Export subsidy	Export finance	Export marketing	Export insurance	Export processing zones
Argentina (1992)	2	1	1	N/a	1	1
Argentina (1998)	3	1	1	1	1	1
Bangladesh	2	1	2	1	1	2
Benin	0	0	0	0	0	0
Brazil (1992)	3	1	1	1	1	2
Brazil (1996)	3	1	2	1	0	2
Bolivia	2	0	2	1	N/a	1
Cameroon	0	1	0	0	0	1
Chile (1991)	3	1	1	1	1	1
Chile (1997)	3	N/a	1	1	1	1
Colombia (1990)	3	1	1	1	1	2
Colombia (1996)	2	1	1	1	1	2
Costa Rica	3	1	1	1	1	2
Côte d'Ivoire	0	0	0	0	0	1
Cyprus	1	0	N/a	1	1	1
Dominican Rep.	0	0	1	1	0	3
Egypt	1	1	2	1	0	2
El Salvador	1	0	1	1	0	3
Fiji	2	0	2	0	0	2
Ghana	3	0	1	1	0	0
Hong Kong, China (1990)	0	0	N/a	N/a	1	0
Hong Kong, China (1998)	0	0	N/a	1	1	0
India (1993)	2	1	2	N/a	1	2
India (1997)	3	2	2	N/a	1	3
Indonesia (1991)	2	1	2	1	1	1

Table 4.11 Developing-countries measures to support or promote exports (continued)

	Duty drawback	Export subsidy	Export finance	Export marketing	Export insurance	Export processing zones
Indonesia (1998)	3	1	1	1	1	1
Kenya	2	0	1	1	0	1
Korea (1992)	3	1	2	1	1	2
Korea (1996)	3	2	1	1	1	0
Malaysia (1993)	3	2	1	1	1	3
Malaysia (1997)	3	2	1	1	1	3
Mauritius	1	1	1	1	N/a	3
Mexico (1993)	3	1	2	1	1	3
Mexico (1997)	2	1	N/a	1	1	3
Morocco (1989)	3	1	N/a	1	1	N/a
Morocco (1996)	3	1	N/a	1	1	N/a
Nigeria (1992)	3	0	1	1	N/a	2
Nigeria (1998)	1	1	1	N/a	0	1
Pakistan	2	1	2	N/a	1	0
Paraguay	3	0	1	0	N/a	0
Peru	3	0	1	1	1	2
Philippines	2	0	1	N/a	1	2
Senegal	2	3	2	1	1	2
Singapore (1992)	3	0	1	1	1	0
Singapore (1996)	0	0	1	1	1	0
S Africa/SACU (1993)	3	1	1	1	1	0
S Africa/SACU (1997)	3	3	2	1	1	0
Sri Lanka	2	0	1	1	1	2
Thailand (1991)	3	1	2	1	0	2
Thailand (1995)	3	0	1	1	0	0

Table 4.11 Developing-countries measures to support or promote exports (*continued*)

	Duty drawback	Export subsidy	Export finance	Export marketing	Export insurance	Export processing zones
Tunisia	N/a	N/a	N/a	1	1	3
Turkey (1994)	3	1	2	1	1	2
Turkey (1998)	2	1	1	1	1	2
Uganda	2	3	2	1	0	0
Uruguay (1992)	2	0	1	1	1	2
Uruguay (1998)	3	0	2	1	1	2
Venezuela	3	2	2	1	1	2
Zambia	3	3	2	0	N/a	2
Zimbabwe	2	N/a	2	1	1	0

Notes: For all measures: 0 = no program; N/a = no information ; 1 = programme in place.
Duty drawback: 1 = duty drawback only; 2 = duties plus domestic taxes; 3 = duties, domestic taxes plus indirect taxes.
Export subsidies: 1 = export subsidy; 2 = production subsidies; 3 = *de minimis.*
Export finance: 1 = market terms; 2 = concessional terms.
Export processing zones: 1 = *De minimis*; 2 = less than 20 per cent of exports affected; 3 = more than 20 per cent of exports affected.
Sources: GATT, TPRs, (1989–94); WTO, TPRs, (1995–99).

reported problems and difficulties with delays in payment and rebates, *de facto* penalizing exporters relative to their overseas competitors (World Bank, 2000d).

Over three quarters of the countries reported the existence of one or more export processing zones or temporary admission schemes, but only a small number of these countries, including the Dominican Republic, El Salvador, India, Malaysia, Mauritius, Mexico and Tunisia, derived more than 20 per cent of their exports from such schemes.

Policies in services

Conceptual and measurement issues

There are no comparable international data that permit a systematic examination of policies on restrictions on trade in services in developing or developed countries. The reasons for this are well known: because many of the modes of delivery of services are intangible, there are no barriers that take the form of tariffs. Rather barriers take the form of quantitative restrictions, sometimes involving complete bans, and often government regulation.

Some instances of the latter may explicitly discriminate against imports of services or foreign providers, others may be of a general regulatory nature and apply equally to national and foreign service providers. And to date no general description of the barriers to trade in services that cuts across all four modes of delivery (cross-border supply, consumption abroad, commercial presence and temporary entry) and all sectors has been attempted, and may not be feasible given the present state of data collection.

Some general impressions can be obtained of the actual policy situation by examining the commitments developing countries have made in the GATS, assuming that these reflect the *status quo*. There are serious problems with this approach. First, it is known that in certain cases, for example in financial services, the commitments made are more severe than they actually are in practice (Mattoo, 1998).

Second, it is impossible to judge the degree of restrictiveness – or whether there are any restrictions at all – in the many sectors in which developing countries have made no binding commitments. Third, even if the commitments fully reflect the *status quo* there is a problem with evaluating the nature of the liberalization undertaken under GATS. Unless there is complete freedom and adherence to MFN and national treatment (except for non-discriminatory legal provisions), it is difficult to evaluate commitments as there is no information on the restrictiveness of the policies maintained or the relative importance of different modes of supply on a sector-by-sector basis (Hoekman, 1996).

The only kind of information available involves numerical exercises on which countries have made how many commitments in each sector and the strength of commitment, based on some or other index that evaluates the commitments by assigning different values to each, depending on whether they involve full liberalization, no liberalization at all or something in between. In the light of the weaknesses noted earlier and the crude nature of the quantification, the conclusions from this type of analysis are far less robust than conclusions on the state of developing countries' merchandise trade, and they should only be used to form general impressions and ascertain tendencies in various groups of countries.

Impressions of developing-country policies that affect services

The first impression gained from the existing data is that many developing countries have liberalized little of their service sector under GATS. Using data from Hoekman (1996) and applying them to the country classification used in this volume, it seems that on average developing countries made commitments on 16.5 per cent of the sectors and modes of delivery compared with 57.8 per cent for developed countries. Assuming that the GATS commitments reflect the *status quo*, this would suggest that the service sectors in many developing countries continue to be very protected.

This has serious implications for efficiency and growth: protection results in high-cost service inputs, which in turn results in wasted resources and adverse effects on the export performance of both goods and services. A protected and inefficient banking sector can be as damaging to the profitability of exportables as the imposition of high tariffs on the imported components used in the production of these same exportables. Despite the measurement difficulties noted above, there is some indication that countries with fewer GATS service trade commitments have been experiencing lower GDP growth rates, just like countries with more restrictive policies on goods (Mattoo, 1999).

If, on the other hand, the GATS commitments do not reflect the *status quo* and involve far more liberal policies, developing countries are confronting themselves with serious danger, just as they are in the context of unbound tariffs or ceiling bindings. They are allowing the future development of protectionist pressures and increasing the degree of uncertainty for foreign suppliers and investors. Thus binding, even if it is only implemented in the future, is of value in that it increases the

Table 4.12   Developing-countries services liberalization commitments (number of commitments as per cent of maximum possible)

	UR	Financial services
LDCs	3.0	15.0
Low income	14.7	27.6
Lower middle income	14.4	27.8
Upper middle income	25.5	26.4
High income	18.9	23.4
Total developing	16.5	24.0
Developed	57.8	
Total	21.7	

Notes: For the Uruguay Round this is the unweighted average as a percentage of the maximum possible (Hoekman, 1996); for the financial sector, the same approach is used but weights are used to estimate partial liberalization. Thus maximum liberalization for both insurance and banking services and for all three modes of supply (cross-border supply, consumption abroad, commercial presence) equals six; partial liberalization is assigned lower weights (0.25–0.50) per mode, per service, depending on whether limitations are imposed on commercial presence on either the number of suppliers or foreign equity, or both.
Sources: Hoekman (1996); Mattoo (1998).

certainty of access. Making commitments for liberalization in the future has been accepted in GATS and has been used in both the financial services agreement and the telecommunications negotiations.[15]

Second, looking at the Uruguay Round commitments by range of commitment and degree of development, a similar pattern emerges to that observed for trade policy on goods: the degree of liberalization appears to increase with the level of income, as shown in Table 4.12. Lower-income countries appear to have committed themselves to liberalization far less than higher-income ones. The same conclusion can be drawn by looking at the commitments of the 42 developing countries whose trade regimes were analyzed more systematically. Indeed the pattern shown in Table 4.12 is strikingly similar to that in Table 4.3 above: the lower the developing-country income, the lower the number of commitments and hence the higher the remaining protection. The basic justification used by low-income countries for not liberalizing their service sector is the same infant-industry argument used for so very long in merchandise trade. There are obvious dangers and limits to such a strategy, as many developing countries have realized in respect of goods. These dangers have to be seriously assessed by low-income developing countries that continue to protect their service sectors.

On the other hand Table 4.12 shows that the relationship between extent of liberalization and level of development does not hold true for the financial services sector, which includes banking and insurance. In this case there is no discernible pattern, with most groups of countries liberalizing at about a quarter of the maximum possible, if one weighs partial restrictions in each of the modes of supply. Again the LDCs made the fewest commitments. Only nine of the 29 LDCs made any commitments. But on average those which did made greater liberalizing commitments than other developing countries.

Third, the analysis suggests that the liberalization index for African developing countries' commitments under the financial services agreement was higher than that for Latin America and Asia in both banking and insurance. In turn Latin America's liberalization commitments were stronger than Asia's in banking, but the reverse was true in insurance. Again these findings need to be interpreted with care because they reflect the *status quo* only to the extent that commitments exist. But if they are correct they are encouraging signs that African countries are moving towards more liberal regimes in sectors that are very important for their future development (Mattoo, 1999).

Another interesting point about Mattoo's analysis is that it suggests, in respect of commitments on commercial presence in this sector, that Latin American countries tend to limit the number of suppliers, while Asian economies limit either the percentage of equity, or both equity and the number of suppliers; and that they are both more restrictive than African countries in this respect. This is actually an encouraging sign for African countries, especially if the pattern is repeated in other sectors, because of the implications it has for attracting FDI in general.

Finally, it seems that developing countries are generally moving towards a more liberal regime in services. Again there has been no systematic evaluation of this, but a strong impression is conveyed by the large number of developing countries that have made forward commitments in both financial services and telecommunications. Many of these commitments involve significant regime liberalization, some of which started in 2000.

Regional preferential trade agreements

In tandem with global integration, many developing countries have made intensive integration efforts at the regional level. Two types of measure can be distinguished in this regard: regional PTAs with other developing countries, and (for the first time) similar PTAs with developed countries. Examples of the former include the MERCOSUR customs union, which involves several South American countries, and the SADC, a free trade area of 14 developing countries. Examples of North–South regional integration include the NAFTA and the various Mediterranean agreements involving PTAs between the EU and several developing countries in the region (World Bank, 2000c).

Agreements focus in the first instance on trade in goods as opposed to services, but most envisage extending the integration effort to include cooperation in spheres such as trade-related environmental measures and investment. Some, such as NAFTA and MERCOSUR, started with commitments that went beyond cooperation in merchandise trade. The expansion of regional PTAs during the 1990s was so extensive that it is estimated that more than one third of world merchandise trade was subject to PTAs by the end of the decade (World Bank, 2000c). This fraction is likely to increase in the future, as the EU is planning to convert the unilateral preferences it has been extending to the ACP countries to regional PTAs over the next decade.

The main motivation for increased regional integration appears to stem from political/security considerations; but frequently the political economy of liberalization makes it easier to move forward through a PTA rather than multilateral negotiations. The trend towards more PTAs raises the question of their consistency with the broader multilateral efforts to liberalize trade under the WTO. The question of consistency has two aspects: a narrow (and less interesting) one that has to do with the consistency of the multitude of PTAs with Article XXIV of GATT and the Enabling Clause provisions; and the broader one of whether the spread of PTAs will benefit or harm global welfare, and whether it will undermine future efforts to liberalize trade on a multilateral basis.

The WTO has set up a committee to review the very large number of PTAs that have been reported to it in order to determine their consistency with the WTO provisions. More than 100 PTAs have been reported and over 75 have been reviewed, but the committee has been unable to reach a definitive conclusion on whether any of these agreements are consistent with Article XXIV provisions and the Enabling Clause. The problem here derives from the fact that the WTO provisions are broad enough to give considerable latitude of interpretation, and the committee's work is bogged down by an inability to agree on any specific tightening of the interpretation of the provisions. The lack of consensus is due primarily to the desire of many members, including developing countries, to retain as much flexibility as possible in the conclusion of such agreements. There is thus a danger that the multiplicity of agreements will yield welfare-reducing results for both the participants and the rest of the world (Panagariya, 2000).

At the same time, there is little evidence so far that the increase in PTAs by developing countries has undermined the global liberalization efforts. Indeed it has been argued that such agreements may strengthen the future participation of developing countries in international negotiations by permitting them to get used to regional competition first, and that these agreements are useful training grounds for developing countries that wish to deepen their integration into other spheres of economic cooperation beyond trade. A good test of the validity of these arguments will be the progress made in launching a new Round of multilateral negotiations.

Integration into world trade and the continuing debate on trade policy

The integration of the developing countries into the multilateral trading system was substantially advanced by the Uruguay Round, which contributed to the liberalization of developing countries' trade regimes and improvements in the conditions affecting access to the major markets for their export products. The integration process has been especially impressive for a group of 15–20 middle- and higher-income countries in Latin America and Asia. For many others, progress has been slower.

One of the interesting findings of the study is that following the Uruguay Round, protection through tariff and non-tariff measures appears to have become greater in low-income than in middle- and higher-income developing countries. While this conclusion is subject to a number of methodological caveats it is indicative of the many challenges and opportunities that low-income developing countries face in their effort to achieve fuller integration into the international trading system.

There is continuing debate on whether lower protection promotes faster development, especially with regard to the direction of causality. A number of studies (Dollar, 1992; Edwards, 1993; Sachs and Warner, 1995; Frankel and Romer, 1999; Dollar and Kraay, 2001) have found that trade openness is associated with more rapid economic growth. On the other hand Rodrik has argued that these studies have not adequately controlled for other economic policies; that there is a strong association between exports and growth, but that we are unable to be sure whether this association is a consequence of exports causing output growth, or of the two being jointly determined by the strength of countries' institutions, which are the main determinants of overall growth performance (Rodrik, 1992; Rodriguez and Rodrik, 1999).[16]

At the same time, although there are strong links between export growth and GDP growth, as well as between overall openness to trade and GDP growth, there appears to be a less robust (though still positive) cross-country relationship between indicators of trade policy (such as average tariff levels, coverage ratios of NTM) and GDP growth. The reason for this is that several groups of countries with different trade policy regimes have experienced large changes in their trade to GDP ratios. First, countries such as Hong Kong, Singapore and Chile have very liberal trade regimes and their integration into the international economy needs little further discussion. Second, some of the very successful exporters that experienced rapid growth in trade and GDP did so in the context of trade regimes characterized by significant import controls on the domestic market: Korea is a classic example, and India and China are more recent examples of successful integration despite a very strongly protective regime. Third, in the absence of generally effective trade institutions, the benefits of free trade regimes can be partially obtained by means of EPZs. As stated above, while numerous countries have introduced EPZs, few have actually succeeded in stimulating their exports substantially and on a sustainable basis through this mechanism. There are examples, however, such as El Salvador (which also has a fairly liberal trade regime) and the Dominican Republic and Mauritius (whose overall trade regimes include considerable protection) where EPZs have been successful. Finally, there are several major oil exporters such as Saudi Arabia, Kuwait and others whose trade to GDP ratios vary substantially over time, depending primarily on the price of oil, and have little link to their trade regime.[17]

The key to understanding the experiences of countries that have integrated their economies into international trade while retaining substantial protection, has to do with the variety of factors that affect competitiveness and the incentives to produce and sell to the domestic versus the export market. Protection strengthens the incentive to sell domestically and creates a serious handicap to selling abroad, especially when it includes intermediate products and services, which raises the costs incurred by potential exporters to levels higher than those of their competitors in international markets. But these increased costs can be offset by export subsidies and effective drawback systems, or avoided through an EPZ.

The problem, as we saw above and will be discussed further in Chapter 5, is that low-income developing countries have weak institutions and the implementation of drawback systems has been ineffective, resulting in additional costs to exporters. Nor do they have the budgetary resources to subsidize exports – even assuming that such subsidization is appropriate.

The main conclusion from this discussion is that for many low-income countries with high protection and weak trade-related institutions the most practical way of stimulating trade and opening up to the international economy is through liberal trade regimes, rather than through a complex structure of protection and export incentives.

The debate about appropriate trade policies, especially for low-income countries, appears to have become increasingly academic. While the importance of institutions is receiving increasing recognition with regard to the specifics of trade policy, developing countries are revealing their preferences through their practices: very few countries have actually increased their degree of protection in recent years, and those that have (Mexico and the Philippines) appear to have done so on a temporary basis for balance of payments reasons. Bhagwati and Srinivasan (1999, p. 6) point out that the many in-depth country analyses conducted between the 1960s and 1980s showed plausibly, and taking into account numerous country-specific factors that trade does seem to create, even sustain higher [economic] growth. Moreover there is no evidence of countries managing to achieve sustained development behind highly restrictive trade barriers.

Recently the debate has shifted to the impact of trade liberalization on poverty and income distribution. Supporters of liberal trade regimes have pointed out that – to the extent that more liberal trade regimes have a positive effect on economic growth and the latter is essential to poverty alleviation – more liberal trade policies have a beneficial effect on poverty. Indeed there is evidence that growth helps alleviate poverty and there appears to be no systematic evidence (based on regression analyses) that trade openness (defined as the ratio of total trade to GDP) is correlated with income inequality (Dollar and Kraay, 2001). But the link between trade policy and poverty is very complex (Winters, 2000a) and there is very little empirical analysis at the country level on the impact of trade reform on the income and welfare of the poor.

It is clear that trade liberalization needs to be accompanied by an effort to strengthen domestic factor markets and by the establishment of appropriate safety nets to mitigate the short-term adjustment costs (Stiglitz, 1999). Yet the evidence from a review of developing-country institutions (see Chapter 5) suggests that very few such safety nets exist. Moreover where markets are not functioning properly – for example in rural areas of low-income countries – appropriate government interventions and support may be needed to stimulate agricultural production and rural incomes, which would have implications, for example, for the maintenance of the provisions dealing with the issue in the Agreement on Agriculture.[18]

Implications for a new multilateral round of trade negotiations

The findings and analysis in this chapter have the following implications for developing countries' policies and their position in future WTO trade negotiations.

Tariffs on manufactures

Given the current situation with tariffs on manufactures, developing countries have an opportunity to pursue further tariff reductions in the context of a new WTO negotiating Round. If tariffs are included in a future Round it is likely that developing countries will be expected to make a contribution in the form of reciprocal reductions in barriers. There will be pressure for developing countries to take considerable action in this area because their bound tariff levels are quite high (much higher than those in developed countries, see Chapter 6). They will also be under pressure to reduce ceiling bindings as well as to bind a significant portion of the tariffs remaining unbound in many countries. They should take advantage of any opportunities offered by a new WTO negotiation to seek reductions in developed-country tariffs on manufactures. Such an exchange would be generally beneficial: it would permit them to reap the benefits from their own trade liberalization and policy stability that binding closer to the applied levels entails; it would provide better market access for their exports; and as trade in manufactures is rapidly expanding among the developing countries themselves, it would result in significant benefits from mutual reductions in those tariff barriers that affect their exports in other developing-country markets.

Non-tariff measures

Some developing countries continue to impose non-tariff measures on manufacturing imports. These have been shown to be very damaging to their economies for a variety of reasons, including – because of a lack of transparency – the generation of rents and corruption. NTM are also a suboptimal means of addressing balance of payments problems. There is no difference in this regard between LDCs and other developing countries. These measures should be eliminated at the earliest possible opportunity, or, where appropriate, converted into tariffs that will be subject to reduction over time, possibly as part of multilateral WTO negotiations involving tariffs in agriculture and/or manufactures.

Agriculture

There is continuing controversy on whether the existing WTO provisions on agriculture unduly limit developing countries' flexibility. There is a considerable difference between the applied and bound tariff rates in agriculture for these countries: simple (unweighted) applied tariffs in agriculture averaged 25 per cent compared with 66 per cent for bound rates for 31 developing countries (excluding the Cairns group members), which suggests that there is considerable scope for increased protection of their agriculture, should they wish to do so. On the other hand it might be argued that the exclusion of the investment and input subsidies provided to poor rural households from the calculation of the AMS is subject to the 'Peace Clause' (Article 13 of the Agreement on Agriculture) (Kwa and Bello, 1998). This may result in an unreasonable constraint being put on low-income developing countries that over time may wish to increase their support for the rural poor. To eliminate this ambiguity, such subsidies could be included in the 'green box' of measures that are permitted under all circumstances.[19]

This is an important issue on which developing countries need to focus in the recently restarted negotiations on agriculture. In this connection 11 developing countries have proposed the creation of a 'development box' of measures that would exempt developing countries from WTO discipline measures in order, *inter alia*, to enhance food security and production capacity, and sustain employment for the rural poor (WTO, 2000d). The US proposal on agriculture echoes the same theme, suggesting the establishment of 'additional criteria for exempt support measures deemed essential to the development and food security of developing countries to facilitate the development of targeted programs to increase investment and improve infrastructure, enhance domestic marketing systems, help farmers manage risk, provide access to new technologies promoting sustainability and resource conservation and increase productivity of subsistence producers' (WTO, 2000e).

Trade remedies

The experience of the last few years strongly suggests that antidumping action has become the remedy of choice for developed and higher- and middle-income developing countries. Many developing countries, consistent with their WTO obligations, have abandoned the use of non-tariff measures to protect their manufacturing sector, and are in effect emulating developed-country practices in respect of trade remedies that are consistent with WTO rules and procedures: in this regard they can be considered to have become more effectively integrated into the international trading system. Their example is likely to be followed by other developing countries in the future.

Although antidumping action carries the potential of shielding inefficient domestic producers, its proliferation in developing countries – and especially against developed-country exporters – could well provide the impetus needed for a longer-term reconsideration and tightening of the WTO antidumping provisions. Such a reconsideration should aim at reducing the flexibility all countries have in granting relief through this instrument, and induce governments to rely more on safeguard actions, which tend to be more transparent and time-limited.

Export policies

The above analysis shows that over time developing countries have reduced their interventions aimed at controlling or taxing primary exports, while bringing their practices in promoting manufacturing exports more into line with the overall disciplines of the WTO, for example with regard to the use of export subsidies. A number of developing countries put forward a proposal in advance of the Seattle ministerial meeting to relax the disciplines on export subsidies. There is very little evidence to suggest that the provision of export subsidies is a priority use of scarce budgetary resources, especially for low-income developing countries where severe budgetary constraints are common, or a useful tool for sustainable export development.

At the same time export controls on primary products continue to be imposed in a number of countries. Such controls and taxes have two adverse effects. First, they act as a disincentive to export production and can therefore reduce export earnings. Second, export controls, including taxation, result in the domestic prices of exportables being lower than the international prices. This could lead to the establishment of inefficient domestic processing industries, which can only survive because of the protection afforded by the artificially low domestic input prices. A better set of policies would include (1) instruments of taxation that were neutral in respect of income derived from exports and income derived from domestic sales, and (2) the provision of support to domestic processing activities that would not rely on artificially depressing the domestic prices of exportable primary commodities and raw materials.

Regional PTAs

There is a real danger that unrestrained PTAs could reduce global welfare and possibly undermine the multilateral trading system. But it is important to appreciate that this is not an issue driven by the developing countries. Much of the impetus comes from the developed countries, especially the EU and the US. At the same time the threat would tend to reduce with increased outward orientation of the agreements. Interestingly enough, PTAs between developing and developed countries are likely to be more beneficial to the participants and the rest of the world than agreements among developing countries. This is chiefly related to the dynamic effects accruing to developing countries from technology transfers through increased imports and investment, as well as to smaller trade-diversion costs (World Bank, 2000c). While it would be useful to try to reach agreement in the WTO on measures that will promote more outward-oriented PTAs, there is little evidence at the moment that there is any political support from either the developed or the developing countries for doing so.

Notes

1. A full list of the countries can be found Appendix 1, Table 1.1.
2. In cases where the TPRs are outdated, the analysis draws on other databases for example, on safeguards and antidumping actions.
3. The main source of the data is the WTO Integrated Database which is based on country notifications. In a few cases where the TPRs contain more up-to-date information on countries' applied rates than those notified, these later estimates have been used and are noted with an asterisk in Tables 4.1 and 4.2. Applied tariff information is sometimes available for the two-digit HS classifications.
4. This average needs to be viewed with caution as it refers to applied rates in different countries in different years, and some countries have subsequently reduced their tariff schedules. Unfortunately the data do not permit calculation of the applied tariff average for the group of countries for given years since the Uruguay Round.
5. WTO database, cited in Finger and Schuknecht (1999).
6. Table 6.3 (p. 115) suggests that the product groups that are the focus of antidumping actions in both developed and developing countries tend to be somewhat different and include especially basic metals and chemicals.
7. It should be recalled, however, that as a result of the Uruguay Round agreements and previous negotiations there have been significant reductions in the tariffs on horticultural and floricultural products of interest to developing countries.
8. See Nogués *et al.* (1986) and OECD (1997) for the definition of core non-tariff measures. The definition used is similar to the one used by the OECD but trade remedies are treated separately.
9. In the case of three countries (Brazil, Singapore and Turkey) where there were small increases, it is unclear whether the motivation was protection. In Turkey, for example, the increases resulted from the imposition of tariff quotas on agricultural products.

10. The notifications for 1998 suggest that the number is increasing. In addition to the countries mentioned above, Guatemala, Trinidad and Tobago, Nicaragua, Equador and Panama have initiated investigations since 1996, the last three for the first time in 1997–98 (WTO Anti-Dumping Database).
11. As with all other aspects of this study, no inference should be drawn about the compatibility of the measures taken with GATT provisions. It should be noted, however, that the antidumping measures taken by Mexico and several other countries have been increasingly directed against imports from non-WTO members.
12. The broad theoretical point is covered in the so-called Lerner symmetry theorem on the equivalence of import and export taxes (Lerner, 1936).
13. As with the estimates of non-automatic licensing affecting imports, the analysis excludes licensing that authorities state they undertake in order to meet health, environmental and safety standards, for reasons of national security, in conformance with voluntary export restraints negotiated with developed countries or the implementation of the Agreement on Textiles and Clothing (ATC).
14. The only economies in which such a programme did not exist were Hong Kong (which has no import duties), three African countries (Benin, Cameroon, Ivory Coast) and the Dominican Republic, where the export incentives are focused on the EPZ.
15. In this regard liberalization under GATS is analogous to commitments to reduce tariffs under GATT, where implementation would take place over a period of time, as was done during the Uruguay Round.
16. Even if we were to accept this agnostic view, the resulting policy prescription is a relatively comprehensive approach to development that includes improvement of a range of institutions, including trade liberalization.
17. This should not be taken to imply that trade policy is not relevant for oil exporters: Nigeria is now almost wholly dependent on oil exports, virtually all other exports having been wiped out by earlier weaknesses in its trade-related policies and institutions.
18. In a submission made during the preparations for the WTO's third ministerial meeting, Venezuela asked for 'policy spaces' involving market-oriented supply policies to be imbedded in the WTO rules; but the proposal did not fully specify the policies in question (WTO, 1999b).
19. An alternative would be exemption from challenges under the subsidies agreement.

5
Developing-Country Trade-Related Institutions

Introduction

As progress is being made by many developing countries to introduce more liberal trade policies, increasing attention is being paid to the capacity of their institutions to implement such policies and support their fuller integration into world trade. This increased emphasis on institutions partly reflects a more general shift in priorities in development thinking and practice. It also reflects specific concerns about the increased burdens placed on developing-country institutions by their commitments under the Uruguay Round agreements.

There are several kinds of institution whose operations affect developing countries' participation in world trade and the WTO. First, there are various institutions that are generally linked to the operation of a market economy – such as the banking system, accounting services and contract enforcement – but which also have a bearing on trade. Second, there are institutions that are more narrowly focused on international trade links, some of which may be related to exports and others to imports, for example export/import finance and insurance, and marketing. Third, there are governmental institutions that are specifically charted with the design and implementation of trade policy, including the Ministry of Trade and the customs administration body, and some, such as those dealing with standards or intellectual property rights, that were previously perceived as domestic in nature but have become 'internationalized' under the Uruguay Round agreements. In addition, of course, developing-country participation in international trade depends on the supply and quality of key inputs, such as those for transport and telecommunication, as well as the availability of a broad range of specialized human skills.

Weaknesses in the very wide range of institutions, infrastructure and skills that are needed for effective integration into international trade define the very essence of underdevelopment, and exist to some or other degree in practically all developing countries. They are obviously most pronounced in the LDCs. This very wide definition of institutions that are important for foreign trade is not helpful, however, in defining priorities for governments or the international community, because it suggests that virtually anything that is done to help strengthen skills, the transport infrastructure or development in general will benefit developing-country integration into international trade. Thus a somewhat more narrow definition of trade related institutions is the focus of this analysis. Even this more narrow definition covers many institutions, especially since the broadening of the mandate under the WTO of what is deemed to be 'trade related'.

It was because of the recognition of widespread weaknesses in a number of these new areas that the WTO agreements included extensive transition periods and developed-country commitments to provide technical assistance to developing-country members, as noted in Chapter 3. The purpose of this chapter is twofold: to review the challenges developing countries face because of weaknesses in their trade-related institutions generally, as well as those linked to specific requirements imposed by the Uruguay Round agreements; and to review the international community's provision of technical assistance, especially to the LDCs.

Institutional development and constraints

There is little systematic information on the existence or effectiveness of the operations of trade-related institutions in developing countries. Most of the available information pertains to LDCs and suggests that strengthening these countries' integration into international trade means addressing a great variety of supply-side constraints, including those deriving from trade-related institutions.

A WTO report based on needs assessments of the LDCs concludes that their trade is constrained by the following:

- Infrastructural deficiencies such as erratic power supplies, under-developed telecommunication networks and poor terrestrial, sea and air transport links.
- Weaknesses in technological capacity.[1]
- Underdeveloped financial and banking systems.

- Shortfalls in a broad range of skills and the institutional capacity needed to participate in international trade and implement effective trade policies.
- Deficient regulatory regimes that are unable to cope with weakness in the operation of markets.[2]

The focus of this discussion is primarily on the third and fourth of the above constraints, but it is important to keep in mind that these are not the only nor perhaps the most important constraints existing in many of the LDCs and other low-income developing countries.

There are various trade-related institutions, usually in the public sector, on which some relatively comprehensive information is available: (1) government institutions charged with designing or implementing trade-related policies, including those for the so-called 'new areas'; (2) activities – usually with some public sector involvement – aimed explicitly at promoting exports; and (3) the public institutions and policies needed to cope with the potential costs of closer integration into the international economy.

The increasing range and complexity of issues handled by the WTO, some of which are very technical, means that the capacity of developing countries to participate effectively in the work of the WTO depends very heavily on the analytical capacity and strength of the developing-country institutions charged with handling WTO issues. This is all the more so because the WTO is a member-driven organization with a very small secretariat, so a great deal of the analysis of issues and development of positions is done by the members.

Developing countries face a variety of challenging tasks in this regard: the drafting of appropriate legislation and regulations; the meeting of procedural notification requirements; the staffing of government institutions with technical personnel able to implement the policies and commitments undertaken; and the monitoring of trading partners' implementation of WTO obligations to assess whether market access has been unfairly denied or trade rights infringed, and to prepare an appropriate response (UNCTAD and WTO, 1996).

Weaknesses in these areas have been clear for some time, especially in the case of Africa (Oyejide, 1990). But they have become an even greater constraint in the light of the heavy burden of reporting and implementation entailed by the Uruguay Round agreements. They are amply documented in the assessments of technical assistance needs prepared by LDCs in the context of the Integrated Framework. Practically all of the more than 40 needs assessments completed by the LDCs in 1997–99 requested help in strengthening domestic institutions connected with international trade, including the training of staff at Trade Ministries and Customs Offices, the preparation of legislation and regulations, and the development of a local capacity to enable countries to participate more effectively in future discussions and negotiations, especially in respect of the new issues handled by the WTO.

Institutions related to 'new areas'

These include a variety of institutions whose task is to ensure proper classification and valuation of products entering trade, as well to ensure that such products meet technical and sanitary and phytosanitary standards, and institutions that deal with the implementation of the TRIPS agreement.[3]

The importance of Customs institutions in developing countries cannot be overstated – they are vital to the implementation of trade policy. Proper valuation and classification of products is also important in these countries because they rely to a much greater extent than industrial countries on tariffs as a source of budgetary revenue.[4] At the same time the existence of regulations on technical and other standards and the effectiveness of domestic institutions entrusted with the implementation of these regulations is of importance not only to the health of the population and the performance of firms but also to their capacity to export abroad. Weak domestic institutions and non-adherence to international standards can result in developing-country exports being denied access to foreign markets.

While the developing countries made an effort to bring their customs valuation procedures into conformity with the WTO valuation system by the year 2000, as required by the WTO Agreement on Customs Valuation, many were not able to do so. In the meantime the designated transition period has expired, and while a number of countries have contacted the WTO to request an extension, others have not, even though they have not made the necessary changes.

In many countries the changes required are significant because the valuation of goods for customs purposes is frequently based on the Brussels definition of value. It involves the enactment of new legislation, changes to the relevant rules and procedures, the issuance of new documentation, the adoption of new software and the training of officials in the new procedures and documentation requirements. Many LDCs have requested technical assistance for this purpose in the context of the needs assessments they have prepared. While it is clear that LDCs have significant needs in this area, it is likely that other developing countries also have needs that have not been assessed, and will have difficulty meeting their commitments without technical assistance.

The cost of making the customs valuation changes may be substantial (Finger and Schuler, 2000), and hence where budget and aid resources are scarce the question of the priority to be attached to the changes is of importance. In countries where customs administration is generally weak, should the highest priority be given to changing the customs valuation system, or should it be given to strengthening the customs administration more generally?

Practically all the developing-country Members of the WTO have institutions that deal with the maintenance of technical standards and enforce the health, sanitary and phytosanitary regulations, as reported in the TPR. However there is serious doubt about the capacity of many of these institutions to implement regulations. For example most developing countries have legislation on national standards that are based on those of the International Standards Organization (ISO), of which many are also members. But in some countries, for example Zambia, there appear to be no governmental testing facilities. Most countries report that they have concluded numerous formal bilateral mutual recognition agreements on technical standards. But it is not clear whether these agreements provide adequate information to producers on the standards applicable in countries where they may consider marketing their products.

The situation with sanitary and phytosanitary measures appears to be quite similar. Countries have established regulations requiring sanitary or phytosanitary certificates for imported food, drugs, agricultural and veterinary products. Again the standards used are supposed to be based on those laid down in international agreements such as the Codex Alimentarius. But it is difficult to judge the adequacy of the regulations or the effectiveness of the institutions entrusted with their implementation. In addition the certification costs can be particularly taxing for small firms. For example ISO 9000 certification for a small company plant can cost up to $250 000, with additional auditing costs being incurred after approval (World Bank, 2000d, ch. 3).

The existing standards have been designed by industrial countries to reflect their technology mix and preferences, which may or may not be appropriate for developing countries. While a country may apply other standards at the border, it has the burden of proving their scientific merit. Upgrading existing standards or developing new ones and performing risk assessments is also a costly and difficult procedure, and is neither technically feasible nor affordable for most developing countries.

Thus it is not surprising that the technical-assistance needs assessments of the LDCs have revealed many weaknesses in the institutions entrusted with the enforcement of technical or sanitary and phytosanitary standards. The areas in which assistance has been sought range from the preparation of appropriate TBT and SPS legislation and regulations, the setting up of standards institutions, testing facilities and inspection services, to staff training in all aspects of standards monitoring and implementation. Most of the assessments revealed an urgent need to increase the general dissemination of information on (1) bringing standards into line with the WTO regulations and (2) setting up 'enquiry points' in respect of the standards used by major importers to enhance access to their markets. Effective compliance with the requirement to establish enquiry points can be costly, and formal compliance with the requirement is less than 60 per cent for the SPS Agreement and 75 per cent for the TBT Agreement (WTO, 1999l).

There is little to suggest that other low-income countries do not suffer from similar institutional weaknesses in these areas, if to a smaller degree. Again the cost of establishing an appropriate set of institutions can be quite substantial for these countries; and again the question of the priority that a developing country should attach to the establishment of such institutions has to be raised. Yet in the absence of suitable institutions a country's exports may be penalized.

Perhaps in no other area are the institutional weaknesses so glaring as in international legal matters that involve the use of the Dispute Settlement Mechanism (DSM). The legal aspects of the WTO agreements are very complex and require specialist knowledge in international law, which in most developing countries is absent in both the private and the governmental sector. Governments often also lack the necessary expertise to make the initial case assessment and direct the case during its preparation, whether in defence or as a complainant.

Engaging international lawyers with the necessary knowledge and expertise is an extremely expensive proposition, with costs ranging from $250–1000 an hour, raising the total cost of prosecuting a case to a level that cannot be supported by a developing country's budget. Trying to pass on these costs to the industries affected is also a problem. A legal system that relies totally or predominantly on the participants' capacity to pay for the legal costs involved introduces inequities and distortions, and may result in the DSM being primarily seen as the locus of adjudication of the interests of large and/or wealthy companies and countries (Michalopoulos, 1999a).

Export support institutions

As shown in Table 4.11, many countries have introduced programmes or institutions aimed at ensuring the availability of trade finance (as well as insurance) for both imports and exports. Roughly half of the countries with such programmes offer concessional credit terms. In some countries, for example Bolivia, concessional terms are reserved for small and medium-sized enterprises in others, for example Fiji, they are not. It is interesting to note that some of the countries (Bolivia, Fiji) that have no explicit export subsidy programme do have concessional export finance facilities. Finally, practically all countries have established some kind of export promotion agency to help market their exports abroad.

But while countries may have established institutions in name, their effectiveness in practice is often questionable: for example the needs assessments of the LDCs suggest that weaknesses in trade-related financial institutions, quality control and marketing are important constraints to export development.

Adjustment assistance

The trade liberalizing policies pursued by developing countries since the early 1990s have undoubtedly generated significant benefits, but they have also imposed costs on firms and individuals that are adversely affected by import competition. The private costs of trade liberalization take the form of reduced employment and income in industries affected by increased competition from imports. They are not the same as social costs, which are likely to be lower than private costs because of the benefits – in the form of employment and income – that accrue to workers in export industries, whose output is likely to increase after import liberalization (Matusz and Tarr, 1999). But whatever their size, private costs are likely to exist and influence the political economy of trade reform. It could be argued that the prospect of further liberalization could be influenced by whether or not developing countries have institutions that can effectively mitigate the costs to firms or individuals of increased competition resulting from trade liberalization.

The TPR showed that only seven of the 42 developing countries have trade-related adjustment assistance programmes. In some countries, for example Mexico, the programmes focus on providing assistance to firms facing increased competition from imports. In others, for example Egypt, the focus is on providing a safety net for affected workers. In still others, trade-related adjustment assistance has been offered in the context of programmes with the wider objective of raising productivity or strengthening the profitability of small and medium-sized enterprises. In none of the cases is it possible to estimate the private costs associated with trade reform or the role that adjustment assistance programmes have played in addressing them. In a few countries, for example India, it appears that assistance programmes have had little impact on firms affected by import competition. There is very little information to suggest that developing countries more broadly have the institutional capacity to cope with the adjustment costs associated with trade reform, especially the private costs incurred by displaced workers.

It may not be optimal or even necessary to design adjustment assistance programmes that focus narrowly on adjustment linked to increased competition from imports. More broadly based programmes and/or a broad and effective social safety net may be a better way of dealing with adjustment costs. The point is that whatever the optimal instrument may be, few countries appear to have the institutional capacity to deal with the problem of adjusting to increased competition from abroad.

International assistance efforts

The main burden for strengthening institutional capacity has to be borne by the developing countries themselves. However, as noted in Chapter 3 the WTO agreements refer extensively to technical assistance being provided by the developed-country members to all developing countries that need it, and especially to LDCs. Systematically reviewing the assistance efforts by the international community to support trade development in developing countries is a very difficult task that falls beyond the scope of this analysis. Assistance to the LDCs, however, which has been a focus of the international community's efforts in recent years, is of considerable importance in its own right and will be discussed here.

The Integrated Framework for assistance to the LDCs

Based on the conclusions reached at the first WTO ministerial meeting in Singapore, the high-level meeting on trade-related technical assistance to the LDCs was held in Geneva under the WTO's auspices in October 1997 to develop an assistance programme (as well as to discuss improved market access) for LDCs. An important conclusion of the meeting was that it was not the lack of assistance *per se* that was the problem, but that it had been supply driven rather than effectively coordinated, and the reforms supported were not 'owned' by the recipient countries.

The meeting adopted an Integrated Framework for trade-related technical assistance to LDCs. The framework envisaged that the LDCs would conduct their own needs assessments, which would then be discussed at roundtables with the six agencies involved in the effort (the IMF, ITC, UN Development Programme, UNCTAD, World Bank and WTO), plus other interested donors, in order to develop an integrated programme of technical assistance activities aimed primarily at institution building.

This initiative took place at a time when there was little support from the major financing institutions for trade-related assistance. Such assistance had declined significantly in both the UNDP and the World Bank. The latter had shut down its Geneva office in the early 1990s, and the share of its trade-related operations relative to the total operations approved in the 1996 fiscal year was half of what it had been in fiscal year 1991 (Nogués, 1998).[5] On the other hand, the WTO had increased its technical cooperation activities. But the bulk of the financing for these activities, over 90 per cent in any given year, was obtained from Trust Funds provided by two or three bilateral donors, while the WTO itself typically allocated less than 1 per cent of its total annual budget to technical cooperation activities.

Several references have been made to the information contained in the more than 40 needs assessments that have been conducted. But progress in actually meeting these needs by means of coordinated assistance programmes has been slow, for a variety of reasons. According to the WTO (2000a), developing countries expect the process to result in both improved delivery of assistance and increased amounts of funding, while the donors focus on the efficiency gains and synergies resulting from better coordination. Difficulties with coordination by the recipients and among the agencies have also emerged; and the very problem of institutional weaknesses in LDCs that the initiative is designed to address appears to have contributed to implementation delays.

A review of the Integrated Framework by the six international agencies concerned, under the leadership of the World Bank, was conducted by independent consultants in mid 2000. The review recognized many of the difficulties noted above and made the following recommendations:

- The Integrated Framework should focus solely on technical assistance activities, and not on overall policy and the development of human resources and infrastructure.
- Trade-related technical assistance in the World Bank's operations should be 'mainstreamed' (that is, it should actively incorporate trade concerns in the project and programme design at the country level) and coordinated

through the Property Reduction Strategy Papers (PRSP) prepared by low-income countries for consideration by the IMF and the World Bank.
- The LDCs should be given greater ownership and oversight of framework activities.
- The procedures and coordination mechanisms of the six agencies should be simplified and strengthened.
- A trust fund for projects conducted under the framework should be established.

Following the issuance of the report, in a joint statement the six agencies announced a number of steps to implement some of its recommendations. In particular the agencies accepted the recommendations on 'mainstreaming' and strengthening the LDCs' ownership of the activities. In this connection they proposed the establishment of a steering committee representing the LDCs and the six agencies. It is unclear whether they accepted the report's recommendation to narrow the assistance programme to technical assistance activities. And their proposed trust fund was not intended to fund projects, but essentially to fund project feasibility analyses. At the time of writing the future of the framework is unclear. Some funds have been committed to the Trust Fund, and the linking of the framework to the PRSP process has started; but little has happened in respect of channelling more resources to the LDCs.

Helping the LDCs to strengthen their institutional capacity may require not only technical assistance but also financial assistance, *inter alia* for infrastructure, human resource development and trade finance. Hence there is little justification for limiting the framework's scope to technical assistance only; but it should be recognized that assistance activities in this area should have a direct trade focus and should not be aimed at general private sector or infrastructural development. It would be advisable to provide such assistance in the context of an overall poverty-reduction strategy developed jointly by the LDCs, the Integrated Framework (IF) bodies and other organizations active in providing trade-related assistance. But the question arises as to what will happen to countries that have not yet prepared a poverty-reduction strategy. Should they be excluded from receipt of assistance under the framework?

There are no guidelines on this issue. Putting the framework in the context of an agreed poverty strategy with the World Bank and other international finance institutions is a good thing insofar as it provides greater assurance that it will receive the proper priority and adequate resources. But it would seem that certain aspects of trade-related institutional capacity could be strengthened and receive international support if they are deemed to be of priority to a particular country, even if that country does not have a World Bank/IMF programme. For example many LDCs are not even members of the WTO. Framework assistance to such countries may well need to focus on helping them to become WTO members – not a simple task, as we shall discuss in Chapter 9.

At the same time there is no reason for setting up a trust fund along the lines proposed by the six agencies. Helping the LDCs to integrate more effectively into the international trading system is a priority that the international community articulated several years ago. It would seem that such a priority should already be reflected in the six institutions' budget allocation.

Broader trade-related assistance issues and policies

The institutional weaknesses and problems of the LDCs are common to many other low-income developing countries, and any differences are primarily a matter of degree. There is a more general question, therefore, as to what the international community will do to assist them, as it has promised it will do in the context of the WTO agreements.

The WTO, despite a significant increase in 2001, provides a very small amount of assistance from its regular budget, just in excess of US$1 million per annum, or slightly more than 1 per cent of its total budget. But, as noted above, most WTO technical assistance is financed by trust funds provided by two or three bilateral donors. Despite the fact that the WTO is not a development assistance institution, it still appears desirable for the WTO to increase the resources it allocates from its own budget to the provisions of (1) staff to analyze issues of interest to developing-country members, and (2) technical assistance to developing countries to enable them to discharge the obligations entailed in membership of the WTO. Dealing with issues of interest to developing countries and strengthening their institutional capacity involve many parts of the WTO and its secretariat. It is important that the secretariat be adequately staffed to handle these matters, while preserving the neutrality of its staff and the character of the WTO as a member-driven institution.[6]

The provision of assistance in the legal area raises complex issues. Many governments dislike the idea of providing bilateral aid to developing countries that could be used to do legal battle with their own commercial interests or Trade Ministry. The WTO is required by Article 27.2 of the Dispute Settlement Mechanism to provide legal advice and assistance to developing countries. Accordingly the WTO secretariat has engaged the consultancy services of two legal experts to assist developing countries with their cases. But the support they can offer is extremely limited: their services are available for a total of four working days a month or roughly 400 hours a year, which is usually not enough time to deal with one case. Although the secretariat could use additional resources to provide basic technical assistance, such as training courses on dispute settlement procedures and general advice on the meaning of legal provisions, its staff or consultants cannot, by their very nature as neutral civil servants, provide much-needed case-by-case assistance.

The developed countries' commitment to provide technical assistance to the developing countries is neither concrete nor specific, and hence it is difficult to establish whether it has been met. A more explicit linkage is needed between the developing countries' binding commitment to implement the WTO rules and the developed countries' equally binding commitment to provide technical assistance to help them do so. One way of doing this is substantially to increase the WTO's budget for technical cooperation.

The European Commission is considering a so-called 'milestone' approach, which could be viewed as a complement rather than an alternative to an increased WTO budget.[7] The idea is that developing countries would commit themselves to implementing new WTO agreements within defined (but not necessarily uniform) periods, subject to receiving agreed (but individually tailored) packages of implementation assistance. The idea would apply in the first instance to regulatory agreements, but could be extended to market access commitments where developing countries need to tackle domestic adjustment problems. It is not envisaged that the assistance commitments would be legally binding; rather that the members' implementation record in that respect would be subject to the TPR process.

While this approach would go some way towards dealing with the issue, it has three shortcomings. First, it would deal only with new agreements, hence it would do nothing about the existing problems facing developing countries as a result of their Uruguay Round commitments. Second, if there is no legal commitment to provide assistance, then the developing countries should be assured that they will not be subjected to complaints under the DSM for failure to comply. Third, it does not specify how the assistance packages would be put together or who would be eligible. Addressing these shortcomings can only be done effectively if there is greater coherence between trade and assistance policy – a topic that will be discussed in Chapter 11 and should be on the agenda of any new Round of multilateral trade negotiations.

While capacity-building assistance should focus on the strengthening of developing-country institutions, it is worth noting that the international community has established a number of initiatives with a special focus on assisting low-income countries' Geneva delegations and overall representation in the WTO. Most notable of these are the AITIC and the Advisory Centre on WTO law. AITIC assists less-advantaged countries (such as low-income countries, LDCs and economies in transition) to participate more effectively in the WTO through individually tailored assistance to delegations, and the conducting of workshops and other education and training activities in Geneva. The AITIC, which was originally sponsored by the Swiss government and focused on strengthening the capacity of the Geneva delegations, has recently obtained wider donor support. It has also established a unit for non-resident members and observers of the WTO and is taking steps to increase the information flow to capitals. In addition the Advisory Centre on WTO Law has been established in Geneva to provide assistance to developing countries in matters relating to specific cases involving the DSM, be this as complainant or plaintiff. The centre, which is legally separate from the WTO itself, is partly funded by nine developed-country donors and partly by developing-country users. There are currently 32 members, of which 23 are developing countries.

The resources required for trade-related capacity building are so large that none of the above efforts will go very far without the support of the World Bank, which is the institution with the largest potential to provide assistance in this area. As noted in Chapter 3, the commitments made in the WTO agreements by the trade negotiators, mostly at the last moment in order to obtain developing-country consent, were not coordinated with the rest of their governmental bodies in the developed and developing countries alike. Hence there was no serious link between the commitments made and the agendas of the national or international institutions that would be implementing them. More recently members of both the WTO and the World Bank have been quite clear in their message to the Bank that it should increase the resources it devotes to trade. The Bank was told fairly explicitly by its Board to 'mainstream' trade in its operations as early as the summer of 1999 (World Bank, 1999) but it failed to do so, even in its budget for 2000–1. As a result the Integrated Framework remained an unfunded initiative and the six agencies had to try to set up another bilateral-donor trust fund in order to finance activities they would normally finance from their regular budget.

Trade agreements involving developing-country commitments and other aspects of strengthening their integration into international trade need to be carefully analyzed in terms of the additional technical and financial assistance requirements they create, and a coordinated approach involving all the interested aid donors should be put in place to implement them – with clear signals being sent by governments to all institutions about the priority attached to the task. Finally, the World Bank management needs to be more responsive and attach greater priority to trade-related assistance in its programmes than has been the case in recent years.

Transition periods

Many developing countries, including LDCs, have found it difficult to implement the WTO agreements on safeguards, subsidies and counter-vailing measures, antidumping, technical barriers to trade, sanitary and phytosanitary measures and TRIPS, despite being given additional time to do so. Developing countries with fiscal constraints often have few resources to direct towards the institutions responsible for overseeing and coordinating the implementation of WTO agreements, which is quite costly. The difficulties were supposed to have been overcome through technical assistance and longer transition periods. But these appear to have been negotiated without much involvement by developing-country officials familiar with how long it takes to build institutional capacity where it is inadequate or absent. A very careful look at the transition periods is needed in all the areas in which they have been extended on the ground of institutional weakness.

A number of the transition periods expired at the end of 1999 and many developing countries claim to have experienced difficulty with establishing the required institutions. Developed countries have declared in the WTO that they are prepared to consider waivers, but on a case-by-case basis. On the face of it this should not cause problems as different developing countries have different institutional capacities. However if each of the, say, 80 or 90 developing countries that truly has a problem meeting the timetable for its commitments were to have its case considered individually, this would tie up the proceedings of the WTO for months. At the same time a blanket extension for all developing countries – including the most advanced, which may not need them – does not appear appropriate. Clearly an approach is needed whereby not all developing countries are treated the same but the process will not bog down the work of the whole organization.

Both developed and developing countries need to move from their present positions: the developing countries should abandon the myth that all of them are equally incapable of meeting their WTO commitments; while the developed countries should abandon their request for case-by-case determination. One possibility would be to extend the transition period for all low- and lower-middle-income countries (based on the World Bank definition) while considering the rest on a case-by-case basis. The review of the transition period needed should involve panels of experts from governments and appropriate international institutions who are knowledgeable about capacity building and requirements in the respective areas.

Notes

1. The GATS attempted to address the question of technology deficiencies by providing, through Article IV(1), for the strengthening of domestic service capacity efficiency and competitiveness by, amongst other things, the provision of access to technology on a commercial basis, and improvement of access to distribution channels and networks. LDC members maintain that this provision has not been sufficiently implemented.
2. Based on the responses to a needs assessment questionnaire, as recorded in WTO (1999i).
3. The latter is discussed separately in Chapter 7.
4. Developing countries have faced problems with the undervaluation of products more broadly, which gives rise to a requirement for preshipment inspection. According to the most recent information from the WTO, 16 of the countries investigated had a preshipment inspection programme (WTO, 1999e; see also Low, 1995). And there were a further 18, mostly small, low-income countries or LDCs, using such services for which TPRs were not conducted.
5. Nogués notes in this connection that 'It would be a historical error of major proportions for the Bank to conclude that because so much has been achieved (in trade reform), there remains no significant progress to be expected from investing additional intellectual and financial resources in this area' (Nogués, 1998, p. 94).
6. The Development Division (with only about 2.5 professional staff, excluding the director, working on strictly development issues) is only one of several divisions working on issues of actual or potential importance to developing countries; the others include trade policy review, trade and environment, agriculture and textiles. Many developing countries also believe that greater progress is needed in staffing the WTO secretariat with developing-country nationals in order to improve the staff's understanding of developing-country problems (Michalopoulos, 1999a).
7. Statement by Commissioner Pascal Lamy, 6 March 2001, Brussels.

6
Developed-Country Policies

Introduction

In the 1990s mixed developments in the external environment affected developing countries' trade. On the one hand developed countries' GDP, an important determinant of the overall demand for developing-country exports, increased at a slightly lower rate than the long-term growth trends in these countries – just under 2.0 per cent for 1990–99 compared with 2.2 per cent in the 1980s and 3.0 per cent in the 1970s (OECD, 2000). On the other hand, the market access conditions for developing countries improved, partly as a result of standstills and subsequent liberalization linked to the Uruguay Round agreements and reductions in tariffs following the information technology agreement.

The actual implementation of the Uruguay Round agreements, including the information technology agreement, had not been completed by the end of the period examined, but there is evidence that access to developed-country markets was improving in many respects. Nevertheless access continued to be impeded by high trade barriers in certain sectors, such as agriculture and textiles; and while progress was made on issues such as tariff escalation, the problem persisted in certain sectors, for example textiles and leather products. Finally, as part of the Uruguay Round agreements the WTO members committed themselves to take additional steps in favour of developing countries in areas such as antidumping, the implementation of which is important to review.[1]

Tariffs

Overall averages

The effects of the Uruguay Round agreements on the MFN tariffs of developed countries have been extensively considered in other studies, whose main findings will be summarized here (Martin and Winters, 1996; UNCTAD/WTO, 1997; OECD, 1997). Broadly speaking the tariffs on imports of manufactures into the major industrial countries were reduced by an average of 40 per cent, from a trade-weighed average of 6.3 per cent to 3.8 per cent, with the reductions to be phased in over five years and the first instalment to be put in place on 1 January 1995.[2] Countries have reduced their tariff rates accordingly since then. Moreover in 1997, in accordance with the information technology agreement, the duty on a number of products in this sector was reduced to zero on an MFN basis (Finger and Schuknecht, 1999).

The tariffication of various measures of support and protection in the agricultural sector resulted in substantial increases in the initial tariffs on a wide range of agricultural products in some major markets. Thus the average applied MFN rate for agricultural commodities (production weighted) in 1996 ranged from 7.9 per cent in the US to 10.7 per cent in the EU (OECD, 1997, table 3.1). Subsequently, developed countries were to reduce their agricultural tariffs by 36 per cent across the board, and at the same time access for agricultural products would be enhanced by reductions in domestic support measures.

The problem was that developed (and developing) countries chose to bind their tariffs at higher rates than the actual tariff equivalents during the years just before the conclusion of the Uruguay Round agreements (1989–93). For example the final bindings for the EU were almost two thirds higher than the tariff equivalents for 1989–93 (Binswager and Lutz, 2000 p. 9), and for the US they were more than three quarters higher. Binding the tariffs at such high levels allowed countries to vary their actual tariff rates according to the results they wished to achieve in protecting their domestic markets – much as the EU used to do with variable levies, which have been prohibited since the Uruguay Round. The result of this so called 'dirty tariffication' has not been improved market access, merely that protection has become more transparent.

In most developed-country markets the applied MFN tariffs on other products are on average lower than in agriculture. In accordance with the liberalization measures in the Uruguay Round agreements the applied MFN tariffs on non-agricultural products range from an average of 0.8 per cent in Japan to 3.7 per cent in the US and 4.0 per cent in the EU

(UNCTAD/WTO, 1997, Annex Table 1). But the rates are higher on products of interest to developing countries (Hertel and Martin, 1999). At the same time, for the Quad countries (Canada, the EU, Japan and the US), one third of all MFN tariff lines are duty free, involving a large range of products of export interest to developing countries.

Preferences

The actual tariff rates applied to imports from individual developing countries tend to be even lower than the above MFN rates, however. There are two main reasons for this: because the generalized system of preferences (GSP) further reduced the tariffs on selected commodities and countries; and because of the existence of preferential arrangements for particular countries in specific developed-country markets, for example the preferences afforded to the ACP countries in the EU market, the ones enjoyed by Mexico as part of NAFTA, and the Caribbean and Central American countries' preferential treatment in the US market as a consequence of the Caribbean Basin Initiative. In addition, individual developed countries granted preferential treatment to LDC imports following the high level meeting on trade-related measures for LDCs in 1997. For example the EU extends to the LDCs the same duty-free treatment it extends to all the ACP members, the benefits of which tend to be greater than those of the GSP.

Given the complexity of the various preferential systems, it is very difficult to assess their overall effect on the average tariffs applied to eligible developing countries. One study suggests that the GSP 'remains a valuable tool for promoting developing country exports' (UNCTAD/WTO, 1997, p. 9) despite the erosion of preferences associated with the MFN tariff reduction and the increasing limitations imposed on product and country eligibility by the 'graduation' features of various pro-grammes. This is because, when the GSP is taken into account, the average applied tariff rates decline further in major markets as the frequency of items on which duties are set at zero increases substantially – doubling, for example, in the US. Notwithstanding such benefits, the GSP and other unilateral preferential schemes may offer the wrong types of 'dependency' incentives to developing countries and retard rather than promote their integration into the international trading system (Finger and Winters, 1998; Srinivasan, 1998).

Peaks

Despite the overall decline in the average applied MFN tariffs since the Uruguay Round, there are a number of sectors and product groups in various developed countries where tariffs are substantially higher, thus limiting market access. The Uruguay Round agreements increased the tariff dispersion in some developed-country markets and reduced it in others (OECD, 1997, p. 18; Daly and Kuwahara, 1998, p. 223). But in all countries there are many products and product groups in which the average MFN applied tariff level currently exceeds 12 per cent, or roughly three times the average MFN applied tariff level of developed countries. These products and groups can be defined as having tariff 'peaks'. They exist in both agriculture and manufacturing in a number of developed-country markets. But the very high rates are typically the consequence of tariffication in agriculture. The main products in which such tariff peaks can be observed are the following:

- Major staples such as meat, sugar, milk, dairy products and cereals, where the tariffication of quantitative restrictions has resulted in tariff rates frequently exceeding 100 per cent and rising, for example, to 550 per cent for rice in Japan.[3]
- Cotton and tobacco: for similar reasons, similarly high rates are applied to these products, with the rate on tobacco reaching 350 per cent in the US.
- Fruit and vegetables, including 180 per cent for above-quota bananas in the EU, and 550 per cent and 132 per cent for shelled groundnuts in Japan and the US respectively.
- Processed food products, including fruit juice, tinned meat, peanut butter and confectionery, with rates exceeding 30 per cent in several markets and rising to 230 per cent for grape juice in the EU.
- Textiles and clothing: tariff rates are in the 12–30 per cent range for a large number of products in Canada, the EU and the US, although developing-country exports of these products are at present being restrained (but on a declining basis) under the ATC.
- Footwear and leather products, with tariff peaks in excess of 35 per cent for 10 per cent of products in Japan (rising to 160 per cent for shoes) and 17 per cent of products in Australia (Smeets and Fournier, 1998).
- Selected automotive and transport sector products (lorries in the US and the EU, ships and boats in Canada), with rates exceeding 20 per cent.

The GSP and other preferential schemes operated by the various developed countries tend to reduce, in some cases significantly, the tariff rates on imports of the above products from developing countries. However in almost all cases where tariff peaks are present, the sensitivity of the domestic industry to imports has resulted in the exclusion of various products from the schemes or in some type of limitation being imposed either on the amount that can be imported under the preferential rates or on the number of countries that are eligible. For example the US excludes most textile products from its GSP scheme, and the EU limits preferential margins and imposes country/sector quotas. Quota limitations also exist for non-traditional suppliers of various fruits and vegetables to the EU and in Japan's market for leather goods and footwear.

Escalation

Tariff escalation is a matter of concern for developing countries in the context of market access because it tends to increase the rate of effective protection at higher stages of processing, thereby making market access more difficult for finished manufactured products, which in turn can adversely affect developing countries' industrialization efforts. There is little disagreement that as a consequence of the Uruguay Round agreements the degree of overall escalation has decreased. But evidence from a number of sectors suggests that it is still a matter of concern.

Under the agreements the tariffs on agricultural products tended to rise. As a consequence, if one includes the tariffs on raw materials and unprocessed agriculture products in the calculation of primary products, in 1996 they were no higher than those on semimanufactures in a number of developed-country markets (the US, the EU, Canada and Norway). But this simply means that the pre-Uruguay Round calculations of tariff escalation – which did not include the non-tariff barriers present in agriculture – were biased upwards and the apparent improvement was less significant. At the same time, whereas the degree of overall escalation declined in all the countries studied the tariffs on finished manufactured products continued to be higher than those on semimanufactures in the developed countries, apart from the US, Japan and Australia (OECD, 1997). Furthermore, various studies of specific product chains in a number of developed countries point to continued tariff escalation in such products as processed foods (wheat flour, orange juice, vegetable oils, dairy products), clothing, leather and wood products (Lindbland, 1997; UNCTAD, 1997a; WTO 1998c). These findings should be treated with caution because data limitations and the continued existence of non-tariff measures in some of these product chains make it difficult to calculate the effective rates of protection. But they do suggest that tariff escalation – as with tariff peaks – in certain products, though reduced by the Uruguay Round agreements, continues to be an area of concern in respect of market access for developing-country exports.

Non-tariff measures

Since the Uruguay Round it is probably fair to say that the pervasiveness of core non-tariff measures in developed-country trade regimes has fallen to its lowest point in more than 50 years. By core non-tariff measures we mean the use of non-automatic licensing, quotas and tariff quotas and voluntary export restraints, as well as price control measures such as variable charges, minimum prices and voluntary export price restraints.

Non-tariff measures have been drastically reduced in agriculture, where only tariff quotas continue to exist for a number of products in some of the major developed markets. At the same time the use of non-automatic licensing has reduced in all major developed-country markets, and is now primarily linked to the maintenance of sanitary and phytosanitary standards, technical standards or environmental protection.[4]

Finally, voluntary export restraints were due to be phased out by the end of 1998, and the remaining restraints in developed countries appear to be directed in significant measure against non-WTO Members.

The total frequency ratios for core non-tariff measures in developed-country markets are presented in Table 6.1. This ratio is the same frequency measure used in the context of developing countries in Chapter 4, but relates to the ratio of tariff lines affected by a core non-tariff measure relative to the total tariff lines.[5] As can be seen from the table, there was a decline in the frequency of non-tariff barriers in all developed countries for all measures between 1993 and 1996. In two countries – Australia and Switzerland – the markets became virtually free of non-tariff barriers. In the Quad countries the total frequency ratio of border non-tariff measures ranged from a low of 1.2 per cent in Canada to 3.8 per cent in the EU. A comparison with Table 4.8 (keeping in mind the methodological limitations of some of these measures) strongly suggests that non-tariff measures are much more pervasive in developing-country than in developed-country markets.

The decline in the pervasiveness of NTM reflects several factors:

- The tariffication process in agriculture, which reduced quantitative controls as well as price-related measures such as variable charges though, of course, it also increased tariffs.
- The termination of voluntary export restraints. Some restraints, for example that on sardines in the EU, have already been terminated; others were due to expire at the end of 1998. Presumably this will lead to further declines in the frequency ratios reported in Table 6.1.
- Other *ad hoc* reductions of NTM.

Table 6.1 Non-tariff measures and trade remedies, selected major developed-country markets, 1993–1996 (tariff line frequencies in per cent)

	Australia		Canada		EU		Japan		Norway		Switzerland		US	
	1993	1996	1993	1996	1993	1996	1993	1996	1993	1996	1993	1996	1993	1996
NTM – Total	0.3	0.3	1.4	1.2	9.4	4.2	3.8	2.6	24.0	3.8	3.5	0.2	10.3	2.9
Licensing, non-automatic	0.0	0.0	0.0	0.0	1.7	0.8	1.3	1.3	3.5	2.6	0.45	0.0	0.0	0.0
Export restrictions	0.0	0.0	1.4	1.2	5.6	3.0	0.0	0.0	13.8	1.2	0.0	0.0	10.1	2.7
Other QRs	0.0	0.0	0.3	0.0	0.0	0.1	1.7	0.6	0.2	0.0	1.4	0.2	0.2	0.0
Variable charges	0.0	0.0	0.0	0.0	1.5	0.1	0.8	0.7	5.4	0.0	1.6	0.0	0.0	0.1
Other PCMs	0.3	0.3	0.0	0.0	0.6	0.3	0.0	0.0	1.1	0.0	0.1	0.0	0.0	0.1
Trade remedies														
AD/CV and VEPRs	0.4	0.4	0.8	0.7	1.3	0.2	0.0	0.0	1.9	0.0	0.0	0.0	7.3	5.0

Source: OECD (1997), Table 5.1.

Agriculture

The reduction of NTM in agriculture after the conclusion of the Uruguay Round does not seem to have resulted in significant improvements in market access for developing countries, for a variety of reasons. First, there were problems with the way tariffication was implemented, as discussed earlier. Second, the reduction of AMS has not affected the significant support given to products of interest to developing countries, such as sugar and dairy products. Third, despite the commitment to reduce export subsidies, these have been maintained at such high levels as to undermine the incentives provided to developing-country producers. Examples abound of the adverse effects of export subsidies on developing country-producers: subsidies in dairy products have damaged production in a large range of countries, including Brazil, Jamaica and Tanzania; subsidies on tomato concentrate have especially affected West African countries such as Burkina Faso, Mali and Senegal; support for beef has undermined efforts to increase livestock production in some of the same countries; and EU beef has come to dominate the markets of Benin and Côte d'Ivoire, for which Burkina Faso and Mali were once important suppliers. In effect, there has been far less 'real' improvement in the agricultural sector than was anticipated.

Perhaps because the agricultural agreement has not changed things as much as expected, some of the fears of net-food-importing developing countries (NFIDCs) about the possible adverse effects of the agreement have not been realized. Recall in this context the 'Decision on measures concerning the possible negative effects of the reform program on the least developed and net food importing countries'. This called for a study by the World Bank and the IMF on the implications of the agriculture agreement on food import prices for these countries and the provision of appropriate compensatory finance to deal with the problem. At the time it was considered a prime example of how 'coherence' between the WTO and the international financial institutions could be strengthened (see Chapter 11). In the event there was little evidence that the export subsidy reductions laid down in the agreement led to an increase in the import expenditures of the poorer NFIDCs, and there was no need to provide financing over and above what could be obtained through their regular facilities.

The same decision also called for the problems of the NFIDCs to be taken into account in the context of the Food Aid Convention. This convention, negotiated in 1999 (International Grains Council, 1999), stipulates that when food aid is being allocated, priority should be given to LDCs and low-income countries. Other NFIDCs can be provided with food aid 'when experiencing food emergencies or internationally recognized financial crises leading to food shortage emergencies or when food aid operations are targeted on vulnerable groups'. But there is nothing in the agreement (nor, as will be argued below, should there be) to suggest that the NFIDCs should be compensated with food aid for problems caused by trade liberalization in the developed countries.

While some of the fears about new problems proved unfounded, others were realized. These had to do with the implementation of the new SPS agreement. We discussed earlier the problems that have arisen in respect of the capacity of developing countries to develop the necessary institutional arrangements to meet their SPS-related WTO commitments. Conforming with the set standards, along with testing and certification, account for between 2 per cent and 10 per cent of overall product costs. Hence they impose a burden on developing-country exports, even when the standards are used for legitimate reasons and the countries are able to meet them.

It has been argued of course that the SPS agreement makes developed countries' actions more transparent and ensures a degree of accountability for their actions. But the agreement may serve to legitimize developed-country actions that result in substantial problems for developing-country trade, even if the action appear to be justified, for example on health grounds. Otsuki *et al.* (2000) have found that a 1998 EC regulation that raised the maximum permissible level of certain types of aflatoxin (a toxic substance) in foodstuffs and animal feed to a higher level than that required by the Codex Alimentarius, is estimated to have resulted in close to $700 million in lost revenues to African exporters of groundnuts.

At the same time fear has been expressed that developed countries may be using the SPS agreement as a form of disguised protection. This has been claimed in respect of several products: meat (Burkina Faso), fresh fruit and vegetables (Kenya), tinned tuna (Papua New Guinea) and fish (Uganda). In this regard it may not be the SPS agreement as such that is at fault, but rather its potential use to legitimize continued protection of agricultural and fishery products.

Manufactures

While the vast majority of manufactured products enter developed countries free of non-tariff controls, such controls are pervasive in a few sectors, including clothing in the US, EU and Canada, and silk and man-made fibres in Japan (OECD, 1997, p. 61). This largely reflects the continuing influence of the ATC, which at present constitutes the main remaining NTM impeding access to developed-country markets.

Under the terms of the agreement the integration of the textile and clothing sector into GATT (for example the elimination of quantitative restrictions that would otherwise not be permitted by GATT) is taking place in stages. Stage 1 involves the integration into GATT of 16 per cent of products (in volume of 1990 imports) in four specific categories upon the entry into force of the WTO agreement. Stage 2, involving the integration of another 17 per cent by volume, started on 1 January 1998. Stage 3, involving 18 per cent, will start on 1 January 2002, and the balance will be integrated on 1 January 2005. In parallel, specific quotas are being eliminated as a consequence of the integration process, and the remaining ones are being enlarged at specified rates.

In 1997 the Textile Monitoring Body, set up to monitor the implementation of the ATC, conducted a review of the liberalization steps members had taken during the first stage of the implementation of the agreement, the plans for the further liberalization of textiles and clothing[6] during the second stage of implementation and other aspects of the implementation of the agreement including the use of a transitional safeguard mechanism, and special provisions for least-developed countries and cotton-producing exporters.

The Textile Monitoring Body's review (WTO, 1997c) revealed that the four major developed country-members that maintained restrictions (the US, the EU, Canada and Norway) had met their commitments in terms of liberalizing 16 per cent of their 1990 imports by volume (of the appropriate textile and clothing categories) during the first stage and their planned integration of another 17 per cent of 1990 imports by volume during the second stage. However they had done so by including low-value products (which they had the right to do to under the ATC). As a consequence the liberalization of textiles during the second stage (that is, by 31 December 2001) will only amount to between 18 per cent and 29 per cent (in value terms) of the 1990 imports, leaving the bulk of the liberalization for the end of the period. In addition the review suggested that the quotas would actually be eliminated on only a few products in stages 1 and 2 and the annual growth rates for the remaining quotas would be small. Thus while implementation of the ATC can be viewed as being consistent with the legal requirements, the manner in which it has been implemented raises the question of whether developed countries will find it possible to honour their commitment to integrate all of their textile and clothing sector into the mainstream GATT rules by 2005.[7]

As the value of textile and clothing imports liberalized in countries with quotas under the agreement had been small, the review expressed concern about the likelihood of subsequent elimination of trade barriers by the developed countries (ibid.). As the liberalization of clothing and textiles was an important aspect of the overall commitments and concessions made by developing countries in the Uruguay Round agreements, doubt about the willingness of the developed countries to undertake the adjustment steps needed for the further integration of the textile and clothing sector into GATT is tending to cloud the atmosphere for negotiations in other areas.

Trade remedies

The evidence shows that the frequency of antidumping and counter-vailing actions (as well as other price-related controls) in developed countries declined significantly during 1994–97. Several developed countries (Japan, Switzerland and Norway) used no such measures at all; while in other countries (the EU and Canada) the frequency of their use fell to less than 1 per cent of the total tariff lines.

This evidence is corroborated by a detailed analysis of antidumping actions by developed countries (based on the WTO Antidumping Database). Table 6.2 shows that the annual average number of antidumping investigations initiated by developed countries fell from 160 cases in 1989–93 to 95 in 1994–97, although they increased in 1997 after declining for four consecutive years. It is too early to say whether this marked the beginning of a series of actions. It is also worth noting that the share of developed countries in antidumping investigations fell to less than 50 per cent of total investigations in the later period – that is, in the

Table 6.2   Developed and developing economies: antidumping investigations by WTO reporting members, 1989–97 (number of cases)

	Developed Members	Developing Members	Developed as % of total
1989	66	30	69
1990	147	18	89
1991	184	44	81
1992	261	65	80
1993	141	158	47
1994	115	113	50
1995	73	83	47
1996	73	148	33
1997	118	115	51

*Includes Poland (25 investigations) and Israel (15 investigations).
Source: WTO Antidumping Database.

later period it was developing rather than developed countries that initiated the majority of antidumping investigations.

Most of the developed-country antidumping investigations and definitive measures against developing countries have been directed at higher- and middle-income developing countries (often the same countries that have themselves made increasing use of antidumping measures) and non-WTO members (see below). Bangladesh is the only LDC to have been subjected to antidumping investigations and definitive measures on three occasions (in 1992, see Miranda *et al.* 1998).

The major product groups that are the object of anti-dumping investigations are much the same for developed as for developing countries. Table 6.3 shows that basic metals, chemicals, plastics, and machinery and electrical equipment account for the bulk of antidumping investigations in both developed and developing countries, although the emphasis naturally tends to differ from country to country. These four

Table 6.3 Sectoral distribution of anti-dumping investigations by developed and developing countries, 1987–97 (number of cases)

		Developed	%	Developing*	%
I	Animal products	8	0.6	17	2.2
II	Vegetables	11	0.8	18	2.3
III	Fats and oil	4	0.3	13	1.7
IV	Prepared foodstuff	52	3.7	9	1.2
V	Minerals	41	2.9	11	1.4
VI	Chemicals	210	15.0	157	20.2
VII	Plastics	147	10.5	102	13.1
VIII	Leather	8	0.6	1	0.1
IX	Wood	16	1.2	8	1.0
X	Pulp and paper	65	4.6	47	6.0
XI	Textiles	95	6.8	55	7.1
XII	Footwear	24	1.7	9	1.2
XIII	Glass	59	4.2	15	1.9
XV	Base metals	374	26.7	178	22.9
XVI	Machinery and electrical equipment	212	15.1	83	10.7
XVII	Vehicles	27	1.9	7	0.9
XVIII	Instruments	19	1.4	21	2.7
XIX	Arms	3	0.2	0	0.0
XX	Other Manufactures	27	1.9	27	3.5
	Total	1402	100	778	100

*Includes Poland (25 investigations) and Israel (15 investigations).
Source: WTO Antidumping Database.

sectors together accounted for more than two thirds of all antidumping investigations world-wide over the decade 1987 to 1997.

Finally, it is important to recall that during the Uruguay Round, and in the context of the Agreement on the Implementation of GATT Article VI on antidumping, the developed countries committed themselves to giving special regard to the special situation of developing-country members when considering antidumping measures under the agreement (Article 15). The possibility of using the constructive remedies provided for in the agreement should be explored before applying antidumping duties that will affect the essential interests of developing-country members.

There is little guidance on how this article should be implemented, particularly in respect of the way in which the special situation of developing-country members should be taken into account. The article does not appear to commit developed countries to do anything more than make use of the constructive remedies mentioned in the agreement before applying antidumping duties. But presumably they would have to do this in all cases, not only those involving developing countries. In practice the results have been mixed. On the one hand the overall use of antidumping action by developed countries and the total number of cases brought against developing countries have declined since the Uruguay Round. On the other hand the proportion of investigations in which developing countries have been affected has been much higher than the share of developing countries in world exports (Table 6.4).

The ratio of the two shares, R_{ad}, should be interpreted with care because the proportion of investigations may not accurately reflect the actual quantities of exports affected. Nevertheless it would be difficult to conclude anything other from the data in Table 6.4 than the fact that the developing countries suffered a disproportionate number of anti-dumping investigations in 1987–97. The R_{ad} for investigations of developing countries had a value of 1.6 compared with 0.6 for the developed countries in that period. This means that developing countries were more than twice as likely to have their imports affected by an antidumping investigation (relative to their share in international trade) than developed countries.

The situation has not changed since the WTO came into being. Table 6.4 shows that the R_{ad} values have basically remained the same for both developed and developing countries, but the values for the former have continued to be much lower than those for the latter. The table also shows a very large incidence of antidumping actions against non-WTO members, especially the so-called 'non-market economies', whose share

Table 6.4 Antidumping: share of affected economies in total cases relative to share of world exports

Affected economies	Share of world exports (%)		Share of total antidumping investigations (%)		Share of total definitive measures (%)		Ratio investigations*		Ratio definitive measures	
	1989–1997	1995–1997	1987–1997	1995–1997	1987–1997	1995–1997	1987–1997	1995–1997	1987–1997	1995–1997
WTO Members	88.2	87.7	77.8	73.4	73.9	63.9	0.9	0.8	0.8	0.7
Developed	63.5	62.5	38.1	34.1	34.9	21.7	0.6	0.5	0.5	0.3
Developing	21.6	22.0	34.5	34.4	32.9	36.1	1.6	1.6	1.5	1.6
Transition and other	3.0	3.2	5.0	4.8	6.2	6.1	1.7	1.5	2.1	1.9
Non WTO Members	11.8	12.3	22.2	26.6	26.1	36.1	1.9	2.2	2.2	2.9
Non-market	6.3	6.9	16.4	20.8	21.4	32.1	2.6	3.0	3.4	4.7
Other	5.5	5.4	5.8	5.8	4.7	4.0	1.0	1.1	0.8	0.7

*Ratio of share in investigations (measures) to share in world exports.
Sources: WTO Integrated Database and Antidumping Database; J. Miranda et al. (1998).

of antidumping investigations was disproportionate to their share of world trade. Indeed, controlling for the value of total exports, an antidumping investigation over the decade in question was at least four times more likely to be directed against a product from a non-WTO, non-market economy than a product from a developed-market economy. In this regard the situation of non-WTO, non-market economies (essentially China and the countries of the former Soviet Union) deteriorated after the establishment of the WTO. In the period 1995–97 their exports were targeted for antidumping investigations six times more frequently than exports from developed countries.

The differences between country groups become even more pronounced when R_{ad} values are calculated for definitive antidumping measures (shown in the last two columns of Table 6.4). In the 1995–97 period, definitive measures were five times more likely to be taken against developing-country compared with developed-country exports; and they were even more likely to be taken against non-WTO members, especially countries classified as non-market economies. These countries, which accounted for less than 7 per cent of world exports, were affected by about a third of the definitive antidumping measures taken in 1995–97.

It has been argued that the reason for the disproportionate share of investigations against transition economies and developing countries is that 'the latest arrivals in the world markets tend to price their exports competitively, because otherwise they cannot capture market share from incumbents' (Miranda *et al.* 1998, p. 67). Table 6.4 suggests that other factors may also be at play: the very high incidence of antidumping actions against non-WTO members that are classified as non-market transition economies by the EU and the US, as compared with the incidence of investigations and definitive actions against transitional economies that are already WTO members, suggests that countries may feel less constrained about taking action against non-WTO countries. And with respect to so-called non-market economies, there is evidence to suggest that the procedures used tend to be more opaque and may well lead to a greater incidence of definitive findings than those used against other economies (Michalopoulos and Winters, 1997).

What can be concluded from this analysis of the prevalence of antidumping actions against developing countries as an indicator of market access to developed-country markets? There appears to have been an improvement in recent years because in general fewer antidumping actions have been taken by developed countries, but the developing countries' share of these actions, taking account of the value of their exports, has not changed and tends to be disproportionately high for investigations and even more so for definitive actions. This reflects a somewhat mixed response by the developed countries to their commitment to give special regard to the situation of developing countries. Similarly, there is no evidence that the Article 15 provision on using constructive remedies before applying antidumping duties on imports from developing countries has been employed.

Least developed countries

The international community has made a special effort to address the market access problems faced by the LDCs. For example, as noted above, only one LDC has been subjected to antidumping action by a developed country. Since the 1997 high level meeting on LDCs, developed countries (and other developing countries) have made additional preferential market-access commitments to LDCs.

Given the attention that the international community devoted to the question of integrating LDCs into the international trading system, it is worth noting that – partly as a result of the composition of their exports and partly as a consequence of the special preferences these countries typically enjoy in developed countries – the average tariff rates they face in developed-country markets are generally much lower than those levied on other countries.

Overall it is estimated that 80–90 per cent of the value of LDC merchandise exports have duty free access to the main developed-country markets. It has also been estimated that in 1995 the average unweighted tariff applied to the LDCs' main exports to seven developed-country markets (the Quad countries plus Australia, Norway and Switzerland), taking account of all the preferences they enjoy, was 1.8 per cent, substantially less than the average tariff of 3.6 per cent faced by all developing countries. The average is set to decline further as a consequence of improvements since the high-level meeting. At the same time the tariffs levied in other developing-country markets on LDC products are much higher – 14.5 per cent (WTO, 1997b).

The main reason why the tariff rates for LDCs are so low is that the bulk of their exports are primary commodities on which tariffs are low or absent, and because of the extensive preferences they enjoy in major markets. Even so, about 10 per cent of LDC exports to developed countries face tariffs of more than 5 per cent and there is some tariff escalation. The main product sectors in which high tariffs are charged are agriculture, clothing and footwear, that is, much the same sectors that are important to other developing countries. For a number of products (beef, asparagus, cigarettes, processed wood, clothing and footwear), amounting to about 10 per cent of the LDCs' total exports, tariffs in the seven developed-country markets noted above range from 5 per cent to 15 per cent (WTO, 1997b).

The incidence of non-tariff measures against imports from LDCs is difficult to measure. The only available estimate is based on a frequency distribution of controls on 112 leading LDC export products. This shows that LDCs face a probability that about 6 per cent of the 112 products will be subject to some type of formal non-tariff measure or control such as licensing, quotas, tariff quotas and so on in developed-country markets, and 16 per cent in developing-country markets (WTO, 1997b). These 'formal' non-tariff barriers do not include barriers or limitations that are less formal but may be of even greater importance in constraining LDC exports because of the acute institutional inadequacies in these countries. These include the necessity of meeting the SPS requirements for food and fish products, eco-labelling requirements and the difficulty of taking advantage of preferential arrangements because of complex rules of origin.

In sum the market access problems for LDCs mainly concern a few particular products and tend to be greater for developing-country than developed-country markets. At the third WTO ministerial meeting there were indications that developed countries might be prepared to go further in extending voluntary preferences to these countries, perhaps even commiting themselves to duty-free access for all LDC exports as part of new round. Such commitments are relatively easy to make in political economy terms, as LDCs account for a very small faction of developed-country imports in most product categories. As a consequence LDCs may not have to offer any new liberalizing commitments in order to obtain improved market access. On the other hand, as noted in Chapters 4 and 5, an evaluation of the LDC needs assessments prepared under the Integrated Framework suggests that the main constraints to LDC export expansion primarily derive not from market access problems, but from weaknesses in institutional capacity and other supply-side factors (WTO, 1998c).

Services

As is the case with developing countries, there are no systematic investigations of developed-country policy on trade in services and the implications of the restrictions they impose on potential exports from developing countries. The impression is that their overall policies on service imports are more liberal than those of the developing countries because they have made more commitments on liberalization under GATS. But when it comes to the movement of natural persons they tend to be more restrictive than developing countries regardless of sector. Liberalization in this area would be of considerable benefit to developing countries because of the latter's comparative advantage in labour-intensive services across all modes of supply. In addition, in maritime services international competition is extremely limited and there are serious constraints deriving from national legislation that actively discriminates against foreign suppliers, as in the US.

The movement of natural persons

While some progress has been made with regard to the movement of qualified professionals to work abroad, developed-country restrictions inhibit increased service earnings for developing countries through this mode of supply. The commitments on trade in services tend to emphasize the regulation of commercial presence, which is important for foreign direct investment, rather than 'mode four' involving movements of natural persons.

There are quantitative restrictions on the number of visas issued per year, and the qualification and licensing requirements of professional organizations formally discriminate against foreign qualifications. Still other barriers involve wage-matching requirements – whereby the wages paid to foreigners must be the same as those paid to nationals – and the provision of local training.

The commitments on the movement of natural persons primarily involve intra-corporate transferees, business visitors and, to a lesser extent, independent professionals, including those providing services under a service contract. A large number of countries impose an economic needs test. This typically involves judgements by government agencies, based on non-transparent criteria (market conditions, the availability of local service providers and so on), as to which foreign service providers to permit and which to refuse. Indeed, of the 54 countries that have made their commitments subject to a needs test, only three have revealed their criteria for the test. Frequently the result is to nullify access commitments involving 'mode four' service supply.

There are many sectors in which developing countries have a comparative advantage, usually based on labour costs, and would benefit from developed-country liberalization, particularly in respect of software development and construction services. The former is an area where developing-country exports, for example from India, have been expanding very rapidly in recent years. Many of these exports involve onshore delivery because of the need for continuous contact between client and programmer. While technological and managerial innovations may cause the share of onshore delivery to decline, with increases coming mainly from cross-border trade, the increased software demand by developing countries may be so high as to necessitate the further liberalization of 'mode four' restrictions. Similarly, several developing countries, especially in Asia, have the capacity to export construction services, based on their comparative advantage in labour-intensive activities, but are constrained by developed-country restrictions on the movement of persons.

Maritime services

Efforts to reach agreement on this sector during the Uruguay Round failed in 1995–96, and the negotiations were suspended with a view to resuming them in the wider context of the negotiations starting in 2000. This should be a major area of interest for developing countries in the service negotiations.

Shipping continues to be dominated by cartels known as shipping conferences. These cartels fix prices and pursue other collusive activities in the substantial proportion of maritime services they control and they are often exempt from antitrust law in developed countries (Francois and Wooton, 1999). The effect they have had in raising transport costs to poorer developing countries, especially in the case of low-volume, long-distance shipping to Africa and poorer island economies, would not even be offset by further tariff liberalization: the shipping margins on merchandise trade in Sub-Saharan Africa exceed 6 per cent compared with the OECD tariffs (after preferences are taken into account) of less than 2 per cent (ibid.). Liberalization in this sector, which would lead to increased competition and reduced margins, would be of great importance to many of the small WTO Members.

Implications for market access negotiations

Despite the many complaints by developing countries about the market access conditions they face in developed countries, it is clear that the situation has improved since the Uruguay Round. However a number of problems remain. Some of them relate to how the Uruguay Round commitments have (or have not) been implemented by developed countries. Others relate to issues that the Uruguay Round did not address fully or well and need to be taken up in a new Round of multilateral negotiations.

Agriculture

While the Uruguay Round provided a major step forward by bringing the agricultural sector under the disciplines of GATT, very substantial protection continues to exist in the form of controls and interventions that encumber international trade. The above analysis suggests that the different developing countries face different situations and challenges in their agricultural sectors, which may well result in different groups of developing countries emphasizing different issues in the ongoing WTO negotiations. First, a number of developing countries (members of the Cairns group) have relatively low agricultural protection but are major exporters of agricultural commodities. These countries face two major challenges in expanding their agricultural exports: the continued presence of high tariffs and substantial AMS by developed countries, which restrict market access; and developed-country export subsidies, which make it difficult for them to compete in third-country markets.

A second group of countries includes the traditional net-food-importing developing countries (NFIDCs) and others with substantial agricultural protection. These countries are concerned that the reduction of export subsidies by the developed countries will increase their import bills. However there is little evidence that these countries have been harmed by the reductions implemented so far. Indeed the main problems they face derive from the fact that the continuation of large subsidies and protection in the developed countries is undermining production incentives in these developing countries.[8]

Even so, it is appropriate to consider what will happen if developed-country export subsidies do decline in the future, and what the proper international response should be. The main problem concerns the adverse short-term effects that the elimination of trade-distorting measures may have on poor NFIDCs, although these are likely to be outweighed in the longer term by world-wide efficiency gains. Actually the short-term effects are likely to spread out over time as the distortions are bound to be phased out rather than eliminated at once. And it would be very difficult to isolate the impact of the resulting price increases from other factors, including the developing countries' own policies. It is for this reason that the IMF did not provide automatic financing from its Compensatory Finance Facility (CFF) for cereals, but drawings from the CFF were included in the IMF programmes for individual countries. But there is nothing – nor should there be – automatic about the assistance provided. Indeed if a need is shown to exist the international response should not be limited to food aid but should extend to general purpose financing on appropriate terms. The latter would be better than food aid, which is frequently tied to procurement from a particular donor and determined by food stock availability in the donor country rather than by the needs of the recipient.

The new Food Aid Convention should prove of great assistance to developing countries as a whole, and could help in a small way with some of the food security problems many face, but it is not a substitute for the further liberalization of agricultural trade – indeed it should be viewed as a supporting element of such liberalization. Reduced protection in developed-country markets will improve the market access prospects of both existing and potential exporters; while reduced developed-country export subsidies will lessen the international market distortions that impede the expansion of developing-country agricultural production, and reduction of their own agricultural protection (as part of a broader reduction of protection) will stimulate efficiency through improved allocation of domestic resources.

Manufactures

The policy issues surrounding the protection of trade in manufactures can be divided into three distinct areas: tariffs, non-tariff measures and trade remedies.

Tariffs

There is mounting support by several countries – both developed and developing – for tariff reduction (outside agriculture) to be made part of future WTO multilateral negotiations. Developing countries have been concerned about tariff peaks and escalation in developed-country markets for some categories of manufactures. The above analysis shows that there are peaks in agricultural commodities and processed foodstuffs (which should be a subject of the negotiations in agriculture), textiles and clothing and a few other sectors, including leather products and cars. The analysis also shows that applied tariffs for manufactures are on average higher in developing countries than in developed countries. This is even more the case when bound rates are compared, and many developing countries have not bound a significant proportion of their tariffs on manufactures.

Further tariff reduction in manufactures would benefit all countries because of the efficiency losses caused by the protection of the country imposing it. As noted, this is likely to involve pressure for the developing countries to take considerable action in this area because their tariff levels are much higher than those of developed countries. They will also be under pressure to reduce ceiling bindings, as well as to bind a significant portion of the tariffs that remain unbound in many countries. The developed countries have already reduced their tariffs on most manufactures, and those which remain are concentrated in a few sensitive sectors. There will be opposition by some major developed countries for tariff reductions in these areas, especially in the case of textile and clothing, since with the implementation of the ATC, tariffs will be the sole means of protection available to this sector.

As there are few such sectors outside agriculture, developing countries will need to seek a formula for reducing tariffs that will permit them to exchange reductions in their tariffs on a broad range of products for reductions in the peaks that occur in the manufacturing sector of developed countries. Finally, as trade in manufactures between the developing countries is rapidly expanding, they would benefit significantly from mutual reductions in those tariff barriers which affect their exports to other developing-country markets.

Non-tariff measures

As there are few remaining formal NTM in the developed countries, the key issues for developing countries are for the commitments under the ATC to be implemented and for NTM not to be imposed under the guise of any other rules or arrangements. One way in which this might occur is through the application of discriminatory rules and practices under the agreements on SPS and TBT. The way to guard against this development is to scrutinize the actions of developed countries to ensure appropriate implementation of the relevant agreements. But while textiles and clothing actions are being monitored systematically by the Textile Bureau, there is no similar agreement for SPS measures and TBT – areas in which many developing countries have a limited institutional capacity, which may constrain their ability to scrutinize the consistency of developed-country actions.

Trade remedies

Many developing countries have decried the fact that developed countries have done next to nothing to implement the 'best efforts' provisions of the Uruguay Round agreement on antidumping. Instead of providing developing countries with more favourable treatment, developed countries have taken proportionately more antidumping actions against developing countries than is warranted by their share of world trade. At the same time, as noted above, many developing countries have abandoned the use of non-tariff measures to protect their manufacturing sector and are using antidumping and to a lesser extent safeguard measures instead. The only way forward on this issue is for developed and developing countries to agree to a tightening of the WTO antidumping agreement provisions in the context of a new Round of multilateral trade negotiations. It is difficult to say whether the political will exists to move forward in this area in either group of countries.

Services

The main way in which developed-country restraints are damaging developing countries is through 'mode four' limitations on the movement of natural persons. This is adversely affecting developing country interests in all sectors, but especially in software development and construction. In addition, developed-country restrictions on maritime services are imposing a severe burden on a number of developing countries, especially small island economies and others located far from the main markets.

On the other hand the developing countries have not liberalized their own services trade in many sectors; or if they have, they have not made binding commitments. As in tariffs, this again appears to be an area in which negotiations on further multilateral liberalization may yield large dividends for developed and developing countries alike.

Least developed countries

The international community – especially the developed world – has devoted an extraordinary amount of attention to the problem of market access for the LDCs. This attention is out of proportion to the contribution that concerted action in this area is likely to make to the integration of these economies into the world trading system. This is because access for these countries' exports is largely free already, and the main constraints on integration derive from institutional capacity and other supply-side factors. Moreover the major problem is gaining access to the markets of other developing countries, not those of developed countries.

Nonetheless attention to LDC market access issues has become symbolic for developing countries that seek evidence of developed-country support for developing-country issues in the context of a new Round of negotiations. The issue has become a symbolic gesture of a different kind: in developed countries market access is already relatively free and the products in which LDCs account for even an identifiable share of developed country markets are few and far between. Thus, it would be relatively easy for developed countries to make this symbolic gesture as it would not have significant impact on major domestic protected interests.

Nevertheless it is symptomatic of the developed countries' reluctance to open up their markets in sensitive areas that the several efforts to reach agreement on providing the LDCs with completely duty-free and quota-free access have failed. The main difficulties arise in agriculture and textiles, the same sectors identified as posing problems for all developing countries. In late 2000 the European Commission proposed duty- and quota-free access for all but three commodities (bananas, rice and sugar), phased in over three years. The proposal ran into predictable protectionist opposition by EU farming interests as well as non-LDC exporters from the ACP countries, which would lose some of the preferences they enjoy in the EU market. This resulted in a modification of the original proposal and extension of the phase-out of the quotas to 2006–8.[9] It is important for the international community to agree to a similar gesture as that made by the EU. This would be as important for the improved atmosphere it would create during negotiations as it would for the new producers of the few products that would gain access to developed-country markets as a result. But it is also essential that this gesture be accompanied by action on the part of other developing countries to facilitate LDC access to their markets. Such liberalization might actually prove even more important than other measures aimed at boosting LDC exports.

Notes

1. See Article 15 of the Uruguay Round Agreement on the procedures for implementing GATT Article VI.
2. The EU brought forward from 1 January 1997 to 1 January 1996 its schedule for implementing the third stage of tariff reductions for most non-agricultural products as part of its compensation for EU enlargement through the accession of Austria, Finland and Sweden (WTO, TPR, EC, 1997, p. 15).
3. Estimates reported in UNCTAD/WTO (1997) and UNCTAD (1997a). It is difficult to estimate accurately the *ad valorem* tariff equivalents for many agricultural commodities where tariffication involves the adoption of specific duties, often combined with quotas.
4. Some concern, however, has been expressed about whether the implementation of WTO agreements in these areas has been motivated by the protection of domestic industries, and a number of disputes has arisen regarding the compatibility of certain measures implemented by some countries with these agreements.
5. As with the developing-country data, the information assumes that measures apply across the board to imports from all countries, and is not based on transaction-by-transaction data.
6. The precise words were the 'integration of a volume of textile and clothing products in GATT 1994', which implies the elimination of the quantitative restraints permitted under the ATC.
7. Some developing countries also feel that neither the commitment on consultations with cotton exporters nor the special consideration to be given

to the interests of LDCs when implementing the transitional safeguards were fully honoured.

8. A third group, mainly small islands and others frequently with uncompetitive agriculture sectors, also fear further liberalization in agriculture.

9. See European Commision (2001).

7
The TRIPS Agreement and Developing Countries

Introduction

Intellectual property rights (IPRs) have been the subject of a number of international conventions and agreements administered under the auspices of the World Intellectual Property Organization (WIPO). Many developing countries are party to these agreements and members of the WIPO; but many others are not, and the enforcement mechanisms for the agreements are weak.

The inclusion of IPRs in the Uruguay Round represented a major extension of rule making into a policy area not covered by GATT. It was motivated by the desire of developed countries to raise the standards and strengthen the enforcement of IPRs worldwide. Thus the Uruguay Round negotiations had a clear North–South dimension. The developed countries argued that the benefits of increased IPR protection would accrue to developing countries as well, since it would strengthen their incentive to engage in research and development, promote foreign direct investment and encourage the transfer and dissemination of technology. Most developing countries saw little benefit in committing themselves to basic global standards for increased IPR protection, which was better suited to developed countries' interests and might be inappropriate for their own socio-economic and technological needs. They only agreed to participate as part of a 'grant bargain' that involved the developed countries phasing out controls on textiles and clothing and the inclusion of agriculture in the GATT disciplines.

For developing countries, the conclusion of an agreement on trade related aspects of intellectual property rights (TRIPS) was one of the most controversial outcomes of the Uruguay Round. The concerns voiced about TRIPS have focused not only on the inequitable distribution of benefits to developed and developing countries, but even more fundamentally on whether the agreement will actually result in net losses for many if not most developing countries (Deardorff, 1990; South Center, 1997; Third World Network, 1998).

Several developing countries proposed changes to the TRIPS agreement during the run-up to the Seattle ministerial meeting. But the failure of the meeting meant that the issues they raised remained unresolved. Many of the same issues were again raised in the context of a review of the implementation of the agreement, initiated by the TRIPS Council in 2000. But to date no significant progress has been made in addressing the developing countries' concerns.

The developing countries' trade interests do not always coincide with each other, either in the TRIPS or in other agreements.[1] The one IPR issue on which most developing countries coalesce is that of patents, possibly the most contentious topic of discussion in the Uruguay Round negotiations. Within patents, the particular area where much concern is centred is biodiversity and the provisions of Article 27.3(b). Other areas of general interest for developing countries include technology transfer, geographical indications, compulsory licensing and the transition periods for the implementation of the agreement.

This Chapter examines developing-country concerns about the TRIPS agreement and possible strategies for addressing them. The next section examines the economic dimensions of IPR protection in developing countries, focusing especially on the question of patents. The third section considers various aspects of the implementation of the agreement. The fourth section analyses the key concerns of developing countries with regard to the TRIPS agreement and examines the proposed means of addressing them. The last section discusses the implications of the analysis for dealing with TRIPS in the context of a future Round of WTO multilateral negotiations.

The economic dimension of TRIPS

Transitional arrangements

Under the TRIPS agreement a one-year period of grace was allowed to developed Members of the WTO to implement its provisions (1 January 1996). Developing and transition countries were given four extra years from the entry into force of the agreement (1 January 1995) to begin to apply its provisions. The LDCs were granted an additional six years, or 11 years in total.[2] Under a separate provision, an additional five years were allowed to countries that would have to introduce product patent protection in areas of technology that lacked such protection at the time of general application of the agreement.[3]

Notwithstanding the existence of IPR protection in developing countries before the TRIPS agreement, there is little systematic empirical evidence on the impact of IPR protection on development either in general or for individual developing countries. Given the varying transitional periods allowed under the TRIPS agreement, all the analyses conducted on its costs and benefits are theoretical and based on broad assumptions and generalizations rather than on actual developing-country experience. These analyses tend to focus on the economic costs and benefits of protecting IPRs through patents and copyrights, as these are the areas in which developing-country interests appear to be mainly at stake.[4]

Costs and benefits

Patents

Industrial countries account for the vast majority of patents worldwide (about 95 per cent). Similarly they account for the lion's share of worldwide expenditure on R&D (Braga *et al.*, 1999). In theory, better IPR protection should encourage more R&D and hence innovation. But even in the case of industrial countries with a long history of strong IPR, there is limited empirical evidence of a positive link between IPR protection and R&D (World Bank, 1998, p. 34).

Innovation in most developing countries is concentrated on minor adaptive changes that are not likely to be captured by the patent system (Correa, 1998). Other innovations and forms in which knowledge is held and utilized, for example indigenous communities' knowledge and utilization of plants and herbs for medicinal and other purposes, are not protected under the TRIPS agreement. And the less developed the country, the more likely that such innovations will be the dominant form of invention. Thus, developing countries with limited inventive and innovative capabilities will be net importers and users of technology generated by foreign inventions. And the more stringent the IPR protection, the more it will deter the imitation and adaptation of foreign inventions to domestic needs.

In agriculture, a sector of great importance to developing countries and especially the LDCs, IPRs have traditionally played a limited role as most agricultural research has been conducted by public sector institutions in developed and developing countries alike. Recently, however, public sector R&D has declined in comparison with R&D by private firms in developed countries. Consequently an increasing share of new seeds and farming technology of importance to poor countries is owned by developed-country firms, sometimes based on biological and genetic material that originated in the developing world (World Bank, 1998; Braga *et al.*, 1999).

IPRs tend to be culture specific, and the incentives needed for innovation to occur vary between economic sectors and between countries. Hence there should be no presumption that IPR protection should be of the same duration for all forms of intellectual property and economic activity or for all countries (Deardorff, 1990). While the developing-country WTO Members did provide patent and copyright protection prior to the TRIPS agreement, many (25) did not provide explicit patent protection for pharmaceuticals[5] and a somewhat smaller number (13) did not provide it for chemicals, while more than 50 per cent provided general patent protection for shorter periods (Braga, 1996). The underlying rationale for not extending protection in these areas was to promote the establishment of competitive markets with lower prices, so as to enhance the availability of drugs and healthcare to the poor, vulnerable and less-advantaged sections of the population, and to reduce the cost of fertilizers and other chemical inputs for low-income farmers. The shorter periods of protection were designed to make the technology generally available sooner, thereby reducing the rents accruing to producers and patent holders.

The purpose of the TRIPS agreement on patents, copyrights and related IPR issues is to standardize minimum IPR protection worldwide, and thereby extend it to sectors not previously covered in developing (and some industrial) countries. The agreement seeks to extend and standardize the period during which IPR protection is afforded. It lays down rules and procedures on the acquisition, maintenance and enforcement of IPRs, as well as providing a dispute settlement mechanism. And, as is the case with so many other Uruguay Round agreements, it requires developed-country members to provide technical and financial assistance to help strengthen developing countries' institutions and enforcement capability, as well as to provide incentives to enterprises and institutions in their territories to encourage technology transfers to LDCs.

The agreement allows flexibility in the implementation of its terms: implicitly by establishing minimum standards but leaving their enforcement to the discretion of national legal bodies, and by ambiguous provisions that permit alternative interpretations; and explicitly by sanctioning, in certain circumstances, compulsory licensing and permitting the use of a *sui generis* regime of protection for plant varieties.[6]

The main potential costs of TRIPS to developing countries are the economic losses that might be suffered by their consumers and producers, and the so-called 'deadweight' efficiency losses from reduced competition. These result from the introduction of patents held by producers in industrialized countries and the consequent monopolization of the sectors and industries in question by the patent holders, or by increasing the time frame over which patents are valid in all sectors (Deardorff, 1992).

As the overwhelming proportion of all patents is likely to continue to be owned by producers in developed countries, the developing countries' losses will only be slightly offset by the gains obtained from their own inventions, stimulated by the introduction of more secure property rights in the context of TRIPS. In short, developing-country losses will be transferred as gains in rents by patent holders in developed countries. These gains, however, will be less than the developing countries' losses because of overall deadweight efficiency loss resulting from the creation of monopolies based on patent rights. A recent estimate puts the rent transfer from developing to developed countries at $8.3 billion (Maskus, 2000). To put this estimate in perspective, it is equivalent to about 40 per cent of the total developing-country gains from the Uruguay Round agreements (Harrison *et al.*, 1996) and twice as much as the annual concessional assistance that poor developing countries receive from the World Bank.

The actual costs incurred by developing countries will depend on market structures that prevail in the absence of patent protection (Subramanian, 1995; Braga, 1996): the more competitive the market structure adopted as an alternative to patent protection, the larger the costs. An extreme case is where a previously competitive industry is substituted by a foreign monopoly. At the other extreme, if a foreign monopoly exists before the patent protection, economic welfare will not be affected by the introduction of patents. But many in-between situations are likely to arise in which developing countries incur losses. For example if a duopoly exists before patent protection, consisting of one domestic and one foreign firm, patent protection for the foreign firm might not affect prices significantly, it will simply result in transfers from the developing-country producer to the industrial one (Nogués, 1993). On the other hand, if the market is characterized by numerous fringe domestic firms offering significant competition to a foreign firm – a situation that might conceivably arise in the more advanced developing countries – the introduction of patent protection for this firm might result in greater losses than it would in less-advantaged countries where the same foreign firm would face less competition. As a consequence the competition policies of developing countries have an important role to play in determining the magnitude of the costs of stronger IPR protection.

Because the pharmaceutical industry has not previously enjoyed patent protection in many developing countries, it is the main sector for which the potential losses from TRIPS have been estimated. The estimates vary widely between countries and depend on the assumptions made about market conditions as well as the share of patentable drugs in each market (Subramanian, 1995). In some other sectors, for example computer software and integrated circuits, better protection of intellectual property may result in gains to individual developing countries that are at the forefront of research and development.

No estimates are available on the effects of extending the time for which patents are made available in developing countries for all sectors. There is a theoretical assumption, however, that such costs may well be substantial, as they are likely to include pure rents to industrial-country patent holders. This is because developing-country markets account for only a small proportion of the world market for most products, and inventions usually occur in industrial countries, irrespective of whether protection is provided in a developing country for 10 years or 20.

In sum, developing countries as a group are certain to suffer increased costs with the introduction of patents involving stronger IPR protection for both their and developed-country producers. The total magnitude of these costs is uncertain, as estimates are based not on empirical evidence but on assumptions about issues on which there is little information, including market structure, the effectiveness of competition policies and the fundamental link between stronger IPRs and the creation of new technology. Furthermore the costs will vary substantially from country to country, and those with very strong innovation potential might conceivably make gains.

Against these costs, stronger IPR protection for developing countries was expected to lead to increased technology transfers and technological diffusion from developed countries, which would result in increased developing-country productivity and reduced costs. It was thought that the publication of patents would make information available for use in adaptations and inventions; that the owners of technology in industrial countries would be more willing to transfer proprietary knowledge to developing countries through licensing or foreign direct investment; and that the private sector in developed countries would have a greater incentive to devote resources to the development of drugs against tropical diseases endemic to developing countries (World Bank, 1998). However there is only weak evidence that technology transfers have increased as a result of these mechanisms.

In certain industries, including pharmaceuticals, agricultural chemicals and software, reverse engineering and imitation can result in technology transfer irrespective of patents or the incentives provided to patent holders in industrial countries. However in other sectors reverse engineering is not possible, hence the increased information offered through the patent regime is basically irrelevant. The same is true of technology transfer through foreign direct investment. Stronger IPR protection appears to be pertinent only in cases where technology is copied after a foreign patent owner has established production in a developing country. The empirical significance of such cases is unclear. In support of increased IPR protection the World Bank (1998) referred to the findings of a report prepared before the TRIPS agreement. According to this report, 25 per cent of pharmaceutical and chemical firms in the US, Germany and Japan felt that IPR protection in a number of developing countries was too weak for them to consider investing in joint ventures or transfering advanced technology to a wholly owned subsidiary. A somewhat smaller proportion of machinery and electrical equipment manufacturers in these countries felt the same.

The above argument, however, can be looked at conversely: if 75 per cent of firms in the industries clamouring for the strengthening of IPR protection felt that more stringent IPR protection would make no difference to their investments or technology transfers, this suggests the limits of the argument and the importance of increased rent-seeking as a motive for strengthened IPR protection. China offers a clear illustration: its IPR protection is weak and it is not a member of the WTO, yet it has attracted huge foreign direct investment inflows since the early 1990s.[7]

Similarly, the expectation that increased IPR protection would enhance pharmaceutical companies' effort to develop drugs against diseases that are endemic to developing countries has, sadly, also not been realized. Sachs (1999) shows how little has been done in this regard in respect of diseases such as malaria and certain strains of AIDS. It is ironic that the international community has had to put together a major new initiative – the Global Alliance for Vaccines and Immunization – to provide an assured market for such drugs, when only a few years ago it was argued that if only the TRIPS Agreement were put in place the private sector would take care of their research and development, given the enhanced incentives offered by strengthened IPR protection.

Trademarks and geographical indications

The strengthening of developing-country IPR regimes on trademarks and geographical indications is unambiguously serving to increase the rents that accrue to their holders/producers, which are mostly located in developed countries. Both trademarks and geographical indications involve producer efforts to establish product differentiation by claiming superior quality or standards and hence product value, which permits the owner/producer to charge a higher price than that on similar competitive products. 'Pirates' that illegally use trademarks are typically able to undercut the official licensees with products whose quality may or may not be inferior to that of products made under license.

There is little doubt that trademark piracy causes significant losses for producers, usually located in developed countries. The issue here is primarily one of ethics and legal enforcement. By using false trademarks pirates are able to secure higher prices – and hence higher rents – than they can without the trademarks. The tightening of enforcement lowers the rents accruing to pirates, offers gains to developing-country consumers (to the extent that they have been paying higher prices than the quality of the products warrants) and increases the transfers to the owners of the trademarks.

Geographical indications are important in the food, wine and spirit industries. In this case a product from a particular location is claimed to possess superior qualities (and hence can command a higher price) due to unique vegetative, climatic and/or soil conditions. With some exceptions in wines and spirits (for example Mexican tequila), such product differentiation is of significance primarily to the developed countries.

Under TRIPS the treatment of wines and spirits is not identical to that of other products: whereas the former have explicit additional protection for geographical indications (Article 23), the general protection provided to other goods (Article 22) is less rigorous. Some developing countries have become aware of the possible benefits to be had by extending the additional protection granted to wines and spirits to products of interest to them, for example foods and handicrafts.

In summary, IPRs 'are a compromise between preserving the incentive to create knowledge and the desirability of disseminating knowledge at little or no cost' (World Bank, 1998, p. 33). Whether the TRIPS agreement *per se* represents a good compromise for the developing countries is very much an open question. The agreement is probably unique among those negotiated in the Uruguay Round in that its implementation may well result in long-term net economic losses for the developing countries as a group. By contrast, agreements involving the liberalization of trade in goods and services may result in short-term adjustment costs, but there is a strong presumption, based on extensive experience and empirical evidence, that more liberal trade regimes tend to be conducive to longer-term development (Harrison *et al.*, 1996). The key issue in mutually liberalizing trade negotiations is the share of the overall gains that accrue to developed countries relative to developing countries and to each country individually.

Some argue that the developing countries' losses, though potentially considerable, will only be short term (Fisch and Speyer, 1995, p. 69). The empirical evidence, however, is unconvincing and insufficient to over-turn the conclusion of theoretical analyses that greater IPR protection will result in long-term net costs for many, if not the majority, of developing countries (Deardorff, 1990). Moreover a sound evaluation of the effects of IPR protection on developing countries would have to include factors on which there is little information and which are inherently difficult to measure, such as the assumed market conditions, including the effective-ness of the prevailing competition policies, the capacity to imitate technology and the degree of inventiveness.

Given this conclusion, why did the developing countries sign the TRIPS agreement? The answer lies partly in the pressure exerted by developed countries concerned about rent losses from trademark piracy and copyright infringement. It was one of the areas in which developed countries were expected to obtain concrete benefits in exchange for gains by developing countries in other areas, such as the general lowering of tariffs or the liberalization of developed countries' textile trade. To a certain extent, developing countries also felt that the agreement was of symbolic importance: their adherence to international IPR norms would demonstrate to foreign investors that they were 'open for business'. Some countries felt that they should strengthen their IPR protection in order to share in the development of the new technologies of the future. Irrespective of what one thinks about the Uruguay Round compromise, the question facing developing countries at present is what to do about implementing the agreement, and what changes to seek in the ongoing review and the possible new Round of multilateral trade negotiations.

Implementation

In implementing the TRIPS agreement, developing countries have to consider two issues: how to utilize the flexibility allowed under the agreement to pursue their development objectives; and what steps are needed to strengthen their institutional capacity to meet their commit-ments when their transition period expires.

There are various aspects of flexibility that developing countries need to consider. Some pertain to the legal interpretation of specific provisions.

For example in Article 27.3(b) important terms that are open to interpretation are 'micro-organisms' 'essentially biological processes', 'microbiological' and *sui generis* plant protection (Tansey, 1999). It may be to their advantage to limit the obligation to grant patents on micro-organisms to genetically modified ones (Correa, 1998). Another aspect of flexibility involves the use of alternative policies – permitted under TRIPS – to pursue development objectives, such as price differentiation, parallel imports or compulsory licensing, which rigid IPR protection would impede.

On the granting of patents for pharmaceutical products, for example, one of the more serious concerns of developing countries is that this will result in significant increases in the price of medicines that are essential for improving the health standards of the population as a whole, but particularly the poor and vulnerable segments. However the flexibility allowed by the TRIPS agreement means that this can be prevented by the imposition of price controls, which are not prohibited under the agreement and have been used in the past by several European countries.

Similarly, compulsory licensing will allow countries to compel the owner of a patent to license it to others for general social and other policy objectives, and will have the effect of limiting the monopoly power of the patent holder. Finally, as the agreement does not formally address the issue of global IPR 'exhaustion', parallel imports are permissible. If a patent holder charges a lower price in one country than in another, countries may be able to take advantage of the difference and obtain the product from the source with the lowest price (Correa, 1998).

In this connection, the South African Medicines Act of 1997 permits compulsory licensing, parallel imports and domestic production of generic drugs against AIDS as a means of combating the very high cost of such drugs under the existing arrangements, even though patents on the brand-name drugs are still in effect. Initially, the US and the multinational pharmaceutical companies objected to the terms of the Act. The US administration stated that, while in its view the Act did not conform to the TRIPS provisions on compulsory licensing, it would 'raise no objection to compulsory licensing or parallel importing of pharmaceuticals on the part of South Africa as long as it is done in a way that complies with TRIPS'.[8] Since then, faced by widespread public concern about the threat that AIDS poses to Africa, the US has stopped harassing South Africa on the issue. However the Act has been challenged in the South African courts by 39 pharmaceutical companies, most of which are subsidiaries of multinationals, only to have this challenge also fizzle in early 2001, when, under pressure from public opinion, the drug industry dropped its suit (IHT, 2001)

Because the developing countries were not required to implement most aspects of the TRIPS agreement until 2000, attention was focused on the preparatory institution-building process that would permit them to meet their obligations under the agreement on a timely basis. Notwithstanding the transition arrangements for developing countries, Article 70.8 stipulated that all Members that did not currently provide patent protection to pharmaceutical and agricultural chemical products in line with Article 27 should establish 'a means by which such patents can be filed' and apply to them 'the criteria of patentability as laid down in the agreement'. Moreover, under Article 70.9, where products were subject to a patent application under the above procedures, Members were required to grant exclusive marketing rights for five years, after obtaining marketing approval in the member country.

The US and the EU lodged complaints against India over this matter in 1996 and 1997 respectively. These concerned the absence in India of patent protection for pharmaceutical products and agricultural chemicals, and of any formal system for filing patent applications and providing exclusive marketing rights on pharmaceutical and chemical products. India was thus accused of failing to meet its obligations under Article 70. To deal with the complaints the WTO set up dispute settlement panels, which found for the complainants on the grounds that India had violated Article 70.8 by failing to a establish a legal basis for the preservation of novelty and priority in respect of applications for product patents for pharmaceutical and chemical inventions; and Article 70.9 for failing to establish a system for granting exclusive marketing rights (WTO, 1997a, 1998e).

The broader institutional requirement for developing countries was to enact the necessary legislation and establish the necessary rules, regulations and implementation capacity to enable them to meet their commitments under the agreement. Implementation of the provisions under Article 27.3(b) was of special interest to developing countries for a number of reasons. First, this article was important to agriculture, a sector of prime social and economic significance in most low-income countries, where a large proportion of the population live in rural areas and where subsistence farming coexists in varying degrees with commercial agriculture. Second, developing countries feel they have a proprietary stake in biodiversity resources, most of which are located in their territories. Third, issues of biodiversity and agricultural research are central to the development prospects of many developing countries, especially low-income countries and LDCs.

Establishing the proper institutional arrangements to meet the requirements of the TRIPS agreement proved a very difficult task for many developing countries. The best evidence of the difficulties encountered, especially by LDCs, was the high demand for technical assistance under the Integrated Framework and other programmes.

The international community put in place a number of assistance efforts aimed at helping developing countries and LDCs to strengthen their capacity to meet their overall WTO commitments, including those on TRIPS. Most of these efforts were initiated and led by international organizations, but individual developed countries also offered assistance. In particular the WTO worked closely the World Intellectual Property Organization, with other intergovernmental organizations and with WTO Members to respond to the developing countries' requests.[9] The modalities of the technical assistance were varied, including seminars and workshops to help developing countries to understand the TRIPS agreement and to review the relevant national legislation necessary for implementing it.

Technical assistance aside, Article 66.2 of the TRIPS agreement specifically stipulated that developed countries should provide incentives to their enterprises to promote technology transfers to the LDCs, but it appears that no action by developed members in this regard took place.

Many developing countries, especially the low-income ones, found themselves in a major quandary. On the one hand they lacked the capacity to set up the necessary institutions to implement the provisions of the TRIPS agreement, and they perceived that international assistance for this purpose was inadequate. At the same time they were worried about the apparent willingness of the US and the EU – as evidenced by the India cases and several subsequent ones – to use the WTO dispute settlement mechanism to enforce the agreement. This situation led several WTO Members to propose extensions of the transition period allowed for the implementation of the agreement.

Review and modification of the TRIPS agreement

Negotiating strategy options

A formal review of the implementation of the agreement started in 2000. It would be in the interest of developing countries to develop strategies for the kinds of change they would like to see in the TRIPS agreement and the setting in which to pursue them. Some basic options are probably closed to them, for example it would be very difficult to open up the issue of allowing the early expiry of patents in developing countries as a form of special and differential treatment, even though it might make eminent economic sense to do so. Others, however, that would have the effect of delaying the costs that they will eventually have to incur – for example various extensions of the transition period – could well be worth pursuing. Another possible course would be to seek non-action in the event of their non-compliance with the TRIPS agreement for an agreed period (Correa, 1999). Other issues of interest to them may require modification of specific aspects of the agreement, as they have already stated in the proposals so far submitted.

At the same time developing countries will have to confront the proposals and positions developed countries are putting forward. In the run-up to the Seattle meeting developed countries stated that the TRIPS agreement *acquis* should be used as a basis for further development of IPR protection and would not contemplate the possibility of 'lowering of standards or granting further transitional periods'.[10] Moreover it is certain that developed countries will demand an increase in the level of IPR protection within the framework of the TRIPS agreement. Their proposals, if accepted, could result in further reducing developing-country flexibility, for example by defining specific *sui generis* regimes for the protection of plant varieties, tightening the use of compulsory licensing and limiting the time frame under which it is allowed, and seeking firmer discipline on parallel imports and pipeline protection.

A fundamental question is whether it would be in the developing countries' interest to seek to amend the agreement in specific, substantive ways, and if so, which of these changes should be given the highest priority – recognizing that the developed countries will probably want to move in the opposite direction. Alternatively, if there is sufficient flexibility in the existing provisions to permit developing countries to minimize the costs inherent in complying with the agreement, it might be more expedient to avoid seeking substantive changes (Correa, 1999). For some developing countries, especially those with a more developed institutional infrastructure, this may be a pragmatic option. If the majority of developing countries do choose this option, they may wish to propose specific ways in which the agreement could be modified to their advantage. Tactically, this would be necessary in order to fend off the developed countries' likely demand for tightened IPR protection.

Another important procedural question is whether developing countries should pursue their proposals in the context of the review of TRIPS or during the course of a new Round of multilateral trade negotiations.[11] The more significant the issue on which they want amendments, and the more drastic the changes they seek, the more difficult it will be to pursue their interests in the context of the TRIPS review. If they feel they can live with the degree of flexibility that the TRIPS agreement affords them, then they probably will not need to include specific negotiations on TRIPS in a new Round of negotiations. In such a Round, however, developing countries may be faced with increased pressure to liberalize their service industries or reduce ceiling bindings on manufactured products, as seems likely from the proposals on industrial tariffs tabled so far. These concessions and other areas where developed countries might demand further trade liberalization and more rigorous discipline could be traded against changes that developing countries wish to be made to the TRIPS agreement.

Developing-country proposals

In the run-up to the Seattle ministerial meeting, developing countries tabled a number of proposals for changes to the TRIPS agreement. These fell into five main areas: the transfer of technology; greater protection for geographical indications of goods; exemptions and alternatives to patents (Article 27.3(b); compulsory licensing; and extension of the transition periods.

Transfer of technology

Developing countries have drawn attention to the TRIPS declaration (Article 7) that IPR protection should contribute to the promotion of technology innovation and the transfer of technology. In their view, not only has technology transfer not advanced significantly since the signing of the agreement, but they are increasingly forced to pay exorbitant prices for the use of foreign technology. Developing countries and LDCs have repeatedly complained that developed countries have failed to implement Article 66.2, which requires them to provide incentives to their enterprises and institutions to promote technology transfers to LDCs. This failure, they argue, casts doubt on the effectiveness of one of the prime objectives of the agreement, namely the promotion of technology transfers.

To address this deficiency, developing countries have proposed that the reviewers of the TRIPS agreement consider ways to put into practice the principles relating to technology transfers and the dissemination of technology to developing countries, particularly to LDCs. The African group has called for a regular and full review of the implementation of the provisions of Article 66.2 by developed countries (WTO, 1999g). The developing-country proposals did not include specific recommendations on how technology transfers should be accomplished and what kinds of incentive would be useful to induce firms to transfer technology to LDCs. Some specific suggestions on this matter are discussed below.

Exclusions and alternatives to patents – Article 27.3(b)

The patentability of plants, animals, genetic materials and micro-organisms is one of the most controversial aspects of the TRIPS agreement. It relates to matters of great importance to developing countries, such as sustainable agriculture, food security, access to plant genetic resources and the rights of indigenous peoples. Although in principle there should be no incompatibility between the objectives of conservation, access to and sustainable use of plant genetic resources for food and agriculture, and stimulating investment in plant development through IPRs (FAO/AITIC, 1998), the issue has given rise to much controversy in connection with Article 27.3(b).[12]

The general developing-country concern is that certain companies, particularly from developed countries, will be able to monopolise and secure a lawful claim on genetic information from plant varieties obtained from farmers in developing countries, which would then be sold back to them with added royalties.

They are also concerned about the discrepancy between some provisions in the TRIPS agreement and the UN Convention on Biological Diversity (CBD) and other related multilateral agreements, such as the FAO's International Undertaking on Plant Genetic Resources.[13] An example of apparent incongruity is that whereas the TRIPS agreement recognizes IPRs as private rights in such areas as micro-organisms and microbiological processes, the CBD affirms that a nation has sovereign rights over (implicitly all) its biological resources. Furthermore the CBD explicitly espouses the equitable sharing of any benefits arising from the use of these resources and recognizes the usefulness of traditional knowledge, innovations and practices related to the conservation of biological diversity and its sustainable use.

Some developing countries also see a discrepancy between the TRIPS agreement and the FAO's International Undertaking on Plant Genetic Resources. The latter defines and recognizes farmers' rights, such as those to do with the past, present and future contribution of farmers to conserving, improving and making available plant genetic resources. At the same time the International Undertaking recognizes that plant breeders' rights, as provided for in Act of the Union for the Protection of New Varieties of Plants (UPOV), are not inconsistent with farmers' rights (FAO/AITIC, 1998).

Others wish to ensure that developing countries will retain the flexibility they now have in choosing a *sui generis* regime for the protection of plants and animals. They would be concerned, for example, by attempts to narrow the choice of regimes to that provided in the UPOV (1991), which is seen as appropriate for developed-country agriculture.

In keeping with these concerns, a number of developing countries (the African Group, India and Venezuela) had proposed that since the provisions of the TRIPS agreement, the CBD and the International Undertaking are intrinsically linked, they should be reexamined in order to reconcile any contradictions. Presumably such reconciliation would favour the developing countries, whose interests are more fully reflected in the provisions of these treaties. In view of the fact that the reconciliation of the TRIPS agreement, the CBD and the International Undertaking is a vital factor in the protection of biodiversity and is strongly associated with IPR protection, these countries also argue that the *status quo* in respect of Article 27.3(b) should be maintained in the interim.

At the same time, a number of countries have tabled specific proposals for the modification or amendment of Article 27.3(b), and numerous other changes have been suggested at developing-country meetings and in individual reports. The proposed amendments have two main objectives: to broaden the range of items/products/processes that countries can exclude from the provision of patents; and to strengthen the protection of or increase the returns to holders of traditional knowledge.

In pursuit of the first objective, some proposals are aimed at the addition of micro-organisms and micro-biological processes to the list of items that do not require patents, on the ground that they are not scientifically different from items and processes already on the list (WTO, 1999g). This of course would cover a large number of products and processes involving seeds and drugs that are of great interest to patent holders in developed countries.[14] Venezuela has proposed that all essential drugs on the WHO list should also be exempt (WTO, 1999f), and similar proposals are being considered by African countries.

The main proposals aimed at strengthening the protection of traditional knowledge call for the following changes to the TRIPS agreement:[15]

- Explicit legal protection of traditional knowledge and the innovations introduced by farmers and indigenous communities in developing countries.

- Explicit recognition of protection for traditional farming practices, including farmers' right to save and exchange seeds.
- The restriction of patents on items that are already available to the public by virtue of use, written description and so on.
- Prohibition of plant materials obtained from international germoplasm banks and other deposit institutions.
- Assurances that if a patented item is derived from the resources of a particular country, the patent holder will share the economic benefits of the patent with that country.

This is a large number of recommendations and support for them among the various groups of developing countries will obviously vary according to the level of institutional development, the importance of agriculture and biodiversity to the economy and so on. But they constitute a wide 'menu' of alternatives that can be used by developing countries as the basis of a strategy for participating in the TRIPS review and/or future negotiations.

Extension of the transition periods

There are two main proposals on extension of the transition periods – one narrow and one general. The narrow one, which would apply to all countries, involves extension of the five-year suspension period laid down in Article 64.2 on dispute settlement. This subparagraph pertains to non-violation of the nullification or impairment provisions in Article XXIII (c and d) of GATT 1994. This extension has been proposed by a number of developing countries, transition economies (WTO, 1999k) and even a Quad member (Canada). Hence it is not a purely developing-country issue. It can be argued that there has not been enough experience with dispute settlement under TRIPS, or of non-violation complaints within the WTO, which would justify prolonging this suspension. Developing countries can ally themselves with other members to recommend the maintenance of the suspension on non-application indefinitely, or until a specified time in the future when members judge that sufficient experience has been gathered to justify lifting it.

The broader proposal relates to extension of the transition period for the implementation of the overall TRIPS agreement by developing countries (Article 65.2). There is no doubt that many developing countries still lack the institutional capacity to implement their obligations under the TRIPS agreement and would like an extension of the transition period, which ended in 1 January 2000, but only a few countries have argued for such a general extension. A proposal by the African group – which includes many countries that are likely to have serious implementation difficulties – calls for a more modest extension that focuses on deferring the implementation of Article 27.3(b). The African group maintains that additional time is needed for the review of the article in order to consider the consistency between this article and the CBD, the UPOV and the International Undertaking, and that an additional five years will be needed after the review is completed to establish the appropriate institutional arrangements (WTO, 1999g).

Compulsory licensing

Under Article 31 of the TRIPS agreement a country can demand, under certain circumstances (states of national emergency, or extreme urgency or in cases of public non-commercial use) that patent holders license their patent to other companies as a condition of selling the patented product. This can result in less favourable conditions for patent holders than those prevailing under strictly commercial conditions. Compulsory licensing is particularly pertinent when a new drug is developed to treat a disease or health problem of epidemic proportions or otherwise requiring urgent treatment, as in the case of the AIDS epidemic in Africa and other countries for whom it is important to obtain AIDS drugs at affordable prices.

In the past pharmaceutical companies in developed countries, through such bodies as the Pharmaceutical Researchers and Manufacturers of America, sought to tighten the rules on this provision through more explicit restrictions on parallel imports and compulsory licensing.[16] However their attitudes changed recently as a consequence of the worldwide concern that patents on pharmaceuticals were making it difficult to combat AIDS and other diseases in developing countries. As a consequence, in early 2001 many pharmaceutical firms started to offer their AIDS products to developing countries at considerably discounted prices.

While this is a move in the right direction, it is probably not enough. Developing countries would like to extend the provision of compulsory licenses and to have no time limits on them. Brazil has introduced legislation, which has been challenged by the US, that imposes local production of a patented invention as a condition for enjoying exclusive patent rights over it. Many African countries feel that there is a need to relax the exclusive rights of patent holders in respect of drugs listed as essential by the WHO, and to permit countries to use automatic compulsory licensing for the essential drugs on the list so that they can be supplied at reasonable prices. Questions have also been raised about countries' ability to pay for drugs even when they are offered at discounted prices.[17]

Protection of the geographical indications of goods

Many WTO members, including the Central European Free Trade Area (CEFTA) countries,[18] and several developing countries,[19] including the African group, wish to extend the protection provided by geographical indications to products other than wine and spirits. A number of agreements in which developing countries participate (the Cartagena Agreement for the ANDEAN Community, the Bangui agreement on a possible African intellectual property organization) provide protection on a wider range of products, including beverages, dairy and other food products, such as basmati rice, Darjeeling tea, alphonso mangoes and Amazonian nuts, as well as handicrafts.

Nothwithstanding these examples, it is unclear whether an extension of geographical indications to other products would be of net benefit to developing countries as a group. It could also result in increases in such designations for products originating in developing countries for which other developing countries are consumers. In addition, developing countries with a comparative advantage in imitating these products, or producing like-products, may not wish to go along with a broader definition of geographical indications, which would result in higher protection. On this issue the divide does not seem to be North-South and individual countries need to think carefully about what position to take and to find suitable allies among other WTO members, developed or developing.

The TRIPS review

The TRIPS Council initiated a review of Article 27.3(b) in 1999 and an overall review of TRIPS in 2000. To date discussions have focused on Article 27.3(b) and geographical indicators. They have been inconclusive on both issues. The developing countries have reiterated some of the proposals they put forward in the run-up to the Seattle meeting. In particular they have pushed the points on biodiversity, traditional knowledge, benefit sharing, farmers' rights with regard to seeds and the compatibility of WTO commitments with the UN Convention on Biological Diversity (CBD). The developed countries, on the other hand, prefer to leave the article as it is and wish to discuss only the procedural and technical aspects.

Discussions have also continued on geographical indications, but there is no agreement in sight. A mixed group of developing and developed countries, ranging from Switzerland to the Czech Republic and India, have proposed that protection be extended to more products, but this has been opposed by the US, Canada and others. In addition, concern about the implications of TRIPS for the price of pharmaceuticals has raised the profile of questions on licensing and parallel imports.

As noted above, it is unlikely that the review of either Article 27.3(b) or the TRIPS agreement as a whole will result in substantive changes to the agreement. Such changes will probably only occur in the context of a new Round of multilateral negotiations.

Implications for a new Round of multilateral negotiations

The TRIPS agreement poses serious problems for many developing countries and should be an important priority in a new Round of trade negotiations. It is an agreement that, while in some respects flexible, contains many potential hazards. It is important for developing countries to exert considerable effort to try to improve the agreement and redress the present imbalance between producer/consumer and developer/user interests. The TRIPS agreement should be viewed as a bargaining chip to obtain concessions in the negotiations in exchange for agreeing, for example, to liberalize further their trade in services or industrial products, which would probably be beneficial to them in any case. This will not be easy because developed countries are likely to seek changes that will serve to tighten the disciplines under the agreement, which would not be to the developing countries' advantage.

The main objectives of developing countries should include, in order of priority, the following:

- Maintenance of the existing flexibility within the agreement. To this end, they must try to ward off efforts by developed countries to limit flexibility on *sui generis* systems or expand the basic provisions on IPR protection already included in the agreement.
- Securing developed-country support for concrete and effective ways to render operational TRIPS provisions that involve technology transfer to developing countries, and in particular to LDCs. This could be done by establishing concrete financial targets for developed-country compliance with Article 66.2, or more generally, technology transfers to developing countries should be agreed upon, with developed countries being given a choice between alternative modes of meeting their obligations.[20] This could include purchasing patents and granting them to developing countries (for example gene donations

in the case of biotechnology or environmentally sound technologies) or contributions to the Global Alliance for Vaccines and Immunization; purchasing drugs to issue on a grant basis to needy developing countries; and providing fiscal incentives, such as tax reductions or exemptions for firms transferring technology in priority areas.

- Ensuring that benefits from patents based on animals, plants and micro-organisms originating in developing countries are shared between patent owners and the country of origin by insisting that explicit provisions for the sharing of royalties and/or other economic benefits derived from such patents be added to the TRIPS agreement. The formula for benefit sharing should be flexible, with the agreement between Merck & Co. and INBio of Costa Rica serving as a useful model.[21]

- Obtaining reasonable time extensions for the implementation of the agreement. It would probably be unrealistic to seek a general extension of the transition period, but as few developing countries have introduced suitable *sui generis* legislation it may well be reasonable to argue strongly for (1) examination of the means to ensure compatibility between Article 27.3(b) and the CBD and International Undertaking, and (2) additional time to implement Article 27.3(b) in light of the findings of the review and the need to structure laws and regulations compatible with all the agreements on biodiversity. Alternatively the implementation of Article 27.3(b) could be put off until a specific time after the conclusion of the next Round. Developing countries could also join other WTO Members in seeking an extension of the moratorium on application of the non-violation provisions of GATT – but this is not an issue on which they should expend negotiating capital.

- Increasing, where possible, developing-country flexibility under the agreement. Some specific amendments of Article 27.3(b) that developing countries might wish to pursue include exempting naturally occurring substances (including genes), naturally occurring micro-organisms and essential drugs on the WHO list from the patent requirement. But when considering whether to press specifically for these amendments, or any others, they need to evaluate whether they can accomplish this without losing flexibility or incurring costs through the further tightening of IPRs in this area, which may be sought by developed countries.

In parallel with negotiating changes in the TRIPS agreement, developing countries need to take steps domestically to implement aspects of the agreement in ways that are both consistent with the existing provisions and do the least damage to their development prospects. There are three areas in which work is needed:

- Adoption of *sui generis* regime – under Article 27.3(b) – that is appropriate for each country's needs.
- Adoption of legislation and regulations that exploit the flexibility offered by the agreement with regard, for example, to price controls, compulsory licensing and parallel imports. These must be consistent with the TRIPS provisions or they will face the unpleasant prospect of developed-country complaints raised under the WTO dispute settlement mechanism.
- The design and implementation of suitable competition policies that will limit opportunities for the monopolization of domestic markets by foreign firms.

They should also try to secure as much technical assistance as possible from international organizations and bilateral donors in the design of the legislation, regulations and other institutional arrangements needed for this purpose.

In order both to negotiate effectively and to implement the TRIPS provisions, countries need to place high priority on the development if national policy coherence. This will involve the establishment of mechanisms for information sharing and consultations between the public sector and its constituent parts, as well as with the private sector and elements of civil society that are involved directly or indirectly with IPR protection. This will not be an easy task because TRIPS involves a variety actors, for example ministries or other institutions dealing with international trade, agriculture, industrial development, competition policy, science and technology, public institutions of higher education and/or research, private entrepreneurs in industry and agriculture, the legislative branch and other elements of civil society.

Notes

1. The agreement covers copyright and related rights, trademarks, geographical indications, industrial designs, patents (including IPRs in the case of micro-organisms and plant varieties), integrated circuits and trade secrets.
2. Except for obligations pertaining to most-favoured-nation (MFN) and national treatment.
3. But the WTO Members agreed to accept patent applications and exclusive marketing rights for pharmaceutical and agricultural chemical products from the date the agreement entered into force.

4. The economic analysis on the protection of industrial designs and integrated circuits is analogous to that involving patents.
5. Four developed countries also did not.
6. Under Article 27.3(b) countries may exclude essentially biological processes, as well as plants and animals other than micro-organisms and microbiological processes, as long as they 'provide for the protection of plant varieties either by patents or by an effective *sui generis* system, or any combination thereof'.
7. The evidence on the effects of stronger IPR protection on trade flows also appears to be ambiguous, although there is some evidence that the IPR market-expansion effects may dominate the market restriction ones (Braga, 1996), but much more work on developing-country aspects of this issue is needed.
8. US Congress, 1999. In May 2000, however, the US brought a complaint against Brazil on a related TRIPS issue (WTO, 2000c).
9. The WTO and the WIPO signed an agreement in 1998 to strengthen their technical cooperation in this area.
10. WTO (1999c).
11. The failure of the Seattle meeting left unresolved the extension of the non-violation provision, which had been needed before 1 January 2000.
12. The Council on TRIPS has gathered information on the ways in which countries are implementing patent or *sui generis* protection of inventions involving plants, animals and biological processes for the production of plants or animals. Several of the countries have reportedly based such protection on the principles of the 1991 Act of the Union for the Protection of New Varieties of Plants (UPOV) Convention, under which parties are free to protect plant varieties by means plant breeders' rights.
13. The CBD agreement has been signed by 175 countries. An important exception is the US.
14. A somewhat less drastic version of this proposal would extend the exclusion to 'the gene sequence and essentially biological process for the production of plants, animals and their parts' as well as to 'naturally occurring micro-organisms' (Das, 1998a).
15. These proposals can be found in various reports and analyses (for example Das, 1998a; Tansey, 1999; Correa, 1999). Some of the proposals have been put forward as recommendations for changes by individual or groups of developing countries.
16. *Inside US Trade*, 28 August 1998.
17. Venezuela has made a similar proposal (WTO, 1999f).
18. The CEFTA countries include the Czech Republic, Hungary, Poland, the Slovak Republic and Slovenia.
19. Cuba, the Dominican Republic, Egypt, Honduras, India, Indonesia, Nicaragua, Pakistan, Turkey and Venezuela.
20. The combining of specific financial targets with flexibility in the means of achieving them has been used by the international community to raise funding in other priority areas, for example debt relief.
21. Some details of this agreement can be found in World Bank (1998).

8
Developing-Country Participation in the WTO

Introduction

The capacity of the developing countries to promote changes to the system of rules governing international trade that will benefit their development depends very much on the effectiveness of their participation in the WTO. Such participation has two main aspects: involvement in the ongoing activities of the organization, including the reviews of the various agreements and the DSM; and participation in the multilateral trade negotiations organized under the WTO's auspices, including the preparatory processes leading up to the negotiations.

As noted earlier, throughout the 1960s and 1970s developing countries did not view GATT as an institution through which they could promote their interests in international trade. Their representation in GATT reflected the low priority they attached to it: many developing countries were not members, and of those that were, a large number did not maintain official representatives in Geneva, but instead used representatives based in other European capitals to cover GATT matters – in the case of the ACP countries, usually their missions to the EU in Brussels. Moreover their participation in GATT negotiations prior to the Uruguay Round was passive in that they did not engage in a significant way in the mutual exchange of concessions on a reciprocal basis (Whalley, 1987).

Subsequently, however, their attitude towards participation in GATT (and later the WTO) changed significantly. Many developing countries played a very active role in the Uruguay Round negotiations, and a large number decided to become Members of the WTO. This attitude change was the result of a number of complex and interrelated developments. Developing countries in general became more effectively integrated into the international trading system, and several became major exporters of manufactures. The trade policies of many countries were liberalized, favouring outward orientation and lower protection. And there was growing appreciation of the importance of observing international rules in the conduct of trade as well as the need to safeguard trading interest through effective participation in the activities of the new organization.

The establishment of the WTO has resulted in further changes that place additional demands on developing countries for their effective participation. First, the WTO covers a variety of new areas, such as services, standards and intellectual property rights, all of which require additional institutional capacity in member countries, both for more effective representation in Geneva and in their home capitals. Second, the WTO, unlike GATT, has been engaging in a number of negotiations on the liberalization of various sectors, which requires continuous active involvement by member countries. Negotiations on Basic Telecommunications, Information Technology Products and Financial Services were concluded in 1997 and more have been in progress since 2000, as part of the built-in agenda of the Uruguay Round. Third, the new dispute settlement mechanism offers increased opportunities for developing countries to address grievances, but poses tremendous challenges because of their very limited institutional capacity in the field of international trade law.

A key question at present is whether developing countries' representation at the WTO is adequate for effective participation in WTO activities and promotion of their interests in the expanding range of issues being addressed. This question is of particular importance because the WTO, like GATT before it, is a member-driven organization, meaning that the bulk of the analytical work, the development of proposals and the negotiation of agreements and handling of disputes falls on the member countries and their representatives. The WTO secretariat primarily performs a support function for the effective consideration of topics at the various meetings. It does not normally initiate proposals or interpret rules (Blackhurst, 1998). A related question has to do with WTO decision-making processes in general and, in the context of multilateral trade negotiations, whether these processes permit effective representation of developing-country interests.

This chapter analyses the participation of developing countries at the WTO from mid 2000. The focus is on three main issues: (1) representation, as reflected in the existence or otherwise of a Mission of adequate size in Geneva to deal with WTO matters; (2) participation in the affairs of the WTO, both in the formal and informal processes that characterize WTO governance and decision making on day-to-day issues, and in WTO ministerial meetings and the preparation for and conduct of multilateral trade negotiations; and (3) participation in the DSM. Based on this analysis, the last section in the chapter draws a number of conclusions and recommendations for the more effective participation of developing countries in the WTO.

Membership

Developing countries now account for 73 per cent of the WTO membership, compared with 66 per cent in 1982 (Table 8.1). Another 28 countries are applying for accession, most of which are developing countries or countries in transition (see Chapter 9).

During the period 1982–2000 almost all of the 48 new members were developing countries or, most recently, countries in transition. Only one of the new members, Liechtenstein, was a developed economy. Table 8.1 shows the GATT/WTO representation at different points in time, each associated with a distinct period in the organization's activity: 1982, before the start of the Uruguay Round; 1987, a year after the Uruguay Round was launched; and 2000, several years after the establishment of the WTO and when the Round was in full swing. The membership increased slightly – by seven countries – in the period 1982–87, notably with the addition of large developing countries such as Mexico, and subsequently exploded with the addition of 41 new Members (Table 8.1).[1]

At present the WTO Members account for over 90 per cent of world exports, compared with slightly more than 75 per cent in 1982. The largest exporting countries/territories that are not yet Members are China, Chinese Taipei, Russia and Saudi Arabia – all of which are at various stages of the accession process (see Chapter 9).

During the same period the proportion of world exports accounted for by developing-country Members increased even more, from 11 per cent in 1982 to 21 per cent in 1999 (Table 8.1). This was because of the increase in developing-country membership, and because of the rapid expansion of developing-country exports in the 1990s. Overall developing countries continue to constitute a much larger proportion of the WTO membership than their proportionate share of international trade. Contributions to the annual WTO budget are assessed on the basis of shares in international trade, with a minimum of about 19 000 Swiss Francs in 2000. Thus the overall share of developing-country contributions to the WTO budget is not significantly different from their share of international trade.

Table 8.1 GATT/WTO membership and world trade 1982–2000

| | GATT/WTO membership | | | | | | World exports | | | | | |
| | Number | | | Per cent | | | Value in US $billion | | | Per cent of world exports | | |
	1982	1987	2000	1982	1987	2000	1982	1987	1999	1982	1987	1999
Developed	24	24	25	27	25	18	1,168	1,734	3,754	63	70	67
Developing	58	65	99	66	68	73	211	348	1,168	11	14	21
Transition	6	6	12	7	6	9	57	84	140	3	3	2
Total GATT/WTO Members	88	95	136	100	100	100	1,436	2,166	5,062	77	87	90
Non-members							434	322	545	23	13	10
Total world							1,870	2,488	5,607	100	100	100

Sources: GATT/WTO.

The data on membership disguise the fact that a significant number of developing countries have been formally designated as 'inactive' for failing to pay their contribution to the WTO budget for more than three years.[2] At the beginning of 2000, 15 developing countries/territories were so designated (down from 23 in 1997). Such a designation means that they were not able to receive technical assistance from the organization or have their representatives chair WTO bodies, and had lost their right to a number of other privileges, such as the distribution of documents.[3] A further seven developing countries were more than one or two years in arrears and consequently were barred from chairing WTO bodies. Thus 22 developing countries – that is, about a fifth of the total membership – were barred from chairmanships. Sixteen of these were LDCs, most of which had no mission in Geneva and many others had only token representation.

Representation

Location of Missions

It is difficult for a country to represent its interests effectively in a member-driven organization such as the WTO without a significant presence in Geneva. Today, 27 of the 99 developing countries, or a little over a quarter, do not maintain WTO Missions in Geneva, 24 continue to be represented by Missions or embassies elsewhere in Europe (mainly Brussels, but also Bonn, London and Paris) and three are represented by people located in ministries in their own capitals (Table 8.2, top section).

The proportion of developing-country Members of GATT and then the WTO actually represented in Geneva increased only slightly between 1982 and 2000, from 69 per cent to 72 per cent respectively, mostly because a number of countries – such as Uganda, Zambia and Zimbabwe – moved their representatives from elsewhere in Europe to Geneva (Michalopoulos, 1998, annex). By contrast all developed-country Members and all the transitional economies have a Mission in Geneva.

There are two main reasons why many developing countries continue to be represented from outside Geneva. First, many of the smaller ACP countries consider that their main international trade policy concerns involve the EC rather than the WTO, and thus locate their representatives in Brussels, from where they also are supposed to follow WTO issues. Second, a number of the new Members are very small island economies with very few representatives abroad, and simply cannot afford separate missions in Geneva. Of the 29 LDC Members, 17 had representatives in Geneva, representing a substantial increase of five since 1997.

Table 8.2 Country membership of and representation in GATT/WTO, by location, 1982–2000

	1982 Geneva		Europe		Capitals		1987 Geneva		Europe		Capitals		1997 Geneva		Europe		Capitals		2000 Geneva		Europe		Capitals	
	No.	Staff	No.	Staff	No.	Staff	No.	Staff	No.	Staff	No.	Staff	No.	Staff	No.	Staff	No.	Staff	No.	Staff	No.	Staff	No.	Staff
Developed	24	99					24	120					24	166		1	1	2	25	179		1		2
Developing	40	120	14	15	4	5	45	147	15	21	5	5	64	277	26	60	7	7	72	331	24	73	3	4
Latin America	11	33	3	3			12	43	4	4	1	1	21	99	8	18	2	2	22	118	9	19	1	1
Transition	6	16					6	18					9	25					12	40				
Total	70	235	14	15	4	5	75	285	15	21	5	5	97	468	26	61	8	9	109	550	24	74	3	6

	1982 No.	Staff	Staff/country	1987 No.	Staff	Staff/country	1997 No.	Staff	Staff/country	2000 No.	Staff	Staff/country
Developed	24	99	4.1	24	120	5.0	25	169	6.8	25	182	7.3
Developing	58	140	2.4	65	173	2.7	97	345	3.6	99	408	4.1
Latin America	14	36	2.6	17	48	2.8	31	119	3.8	32	138	4.3
Transition	6	16	2.7	6	18	3.0	9	25	2.8	12	40	3.3
Developing (Geneva)	40	120	3.0	45	147	3.3	64	280	4.4	72	320	4.4
Total	88	255	2.9	95	311	3.3	131	539	4.1	136	630	4.6

*For a few developing countries (Barbados, Central African Republic, Mauritania and Mozambique) and in one developed country (Lichtenstein) where there is representation both in Geneva and in European Missions and or capitals, only the Geneva representative is shown but all staff working on WTO matters have been included.

Source: GATT/WTO, *Directory* (1982, 1987, 1997, 2000)

There is little doubt that representation from Brussels or another Mission in Europe can cause difficulties, delays and sometimes confusion. The limitations to and constraints on effective participation in the WTO that derive from lack of representation in Geneva have been noted many times, and they have recently been documented in the case of Sierra Leone, an LDC whose representatives in the WTO are based in Brussels.[5]

Size of Missions

In mid 2000 there were 630 Mission staff working on WTO matters in Geneva (plus developing-country representatives working in other European capitals), of whom 408 represented developing countries, 182 developed countries and 40 other, mostly transition economies. This was more than double the number that worked on GATT issues in 1982, with most of the increase occurring after 1987.[6] In 1997–2000 there was a very sizable increase (18 per cent) in the number of staff developing countries devoted to WTO matters, reflecting in many cases the decision to increase the effectiveness of their representation at the WTO.

The increase in the total head count was partly due to the increase in WTO membership but largely because of an increase in the average size of missions dealing with WTO matters: from 2.9 persons per Mission in 1982 to 3.3 in 1987 and 4.6 in 2000, an increase of over 40 per cent, with most of the growth occurring after 1987.[7]

The average Mission size increased for both developed and developing countries. For developed countries the increase was from 4.1 persons in 1982 to 6.8 in 1997 and 7.3 in 2000. For developing countries the average rose from 2.4 in 1982 to 4.1 in 2000, with a large proportion of the increase occurring after 1997 (see Table 8.2, bottom section).[8] Thus the difference between the average size of the developed- and developing-countries' Missions actually increased between 1982 and 2000.[9]

The fact that the average size of developing-country Missions continues to be substantially lower than that of developed countries and the difference is growing should not necessarily be taken as an indicator of the capacity for effective representation at the WTO by the developing countries as a whole. This is because, as in so many other areas, the average disguises very large variations. At the one extreme is a group of LDCs or small low-income countries and a large number of small island economies with little trade and basically only nominal representation, for example St Kitts and Nevis, St Lucia, St Vincent and Grenadines, and so on. The average Mission size for these countries is only 1.2 persons. At the other extreme are economies such as Korea, Thailand and Brazil, whose

WTO Missions in Geneva are reported to be larger than those of Canada and the US and almost as large as that of the EC. The Latin American countries average about six persons per Mission – which is close to the figure for developed countries – but drops to 4.3 when the large number of smaller Caribbean countries are included.

A large number of developing countries are represented in Geneva by relatively small joint Missions that also deal with a variety of UN institutions headquartered there. In such cases, even if some of the staff are listed as dealing with WTO matters, there is a strong likelihood that they have to deal with other international institutions and issues as well, and hence their capacity to deal with WTO matters is diluted. This is also likely to be the case for countries whose representatives are based in other European capitals.

Discussions with Mission staff from both developed and developing countries suggest that they are hard pressed to cope with the increased number of WTO meetings and activities. According to Blackhurst (1998), in the first half of 1996 there were approximately 46 scheduled WTO meetings in the average working week, rising – according to some informal staff estimates – to nearly 60 in 2000. To this one must add all the informal consensus-gathering meetings among delegations that take place outside the formal settings.

Based on informal estimates developed in consultation with a number of Missions, just to follow the topics of the various WTO bodies and attend their meetings requires a staff of at least four or five people, and the average is increasing.[10] If one uses this number as yardstick it is clear that a very large number of developing countries have been inadequately represented. Assuming that effective representation in the WTO requires the permanent presence in Geneva of least four staff (including the head of Mission), in mid 2000 27 developing countries and territories did not meet this number because they did not have a Mission in Geneva; another 29 did have a Mission (almost always as part of a joint UN Mission) but fewer than four people were assigned to WTO tasks. A further three countries, while having a nominally adequate Mission in Geneva, had arrears problems and as a consequence they were either formally designated as inactive, or their representatives were excluded from election to WTO bodies. This gives a total of 68, or close to 70 per cent of the total developing-country membership of the WTO, whose representation was handicapped in some or other fashion. Finally, a number of other countries, perhaps 15–20, had the minimum number of staff required for adequate representation, but these staff also had to deal with a number of non-WTO issues.

This leaves around 15–20 developing countries (including some already noted) that by virtue of the interest they take in the WTO, the staffing level of their Missions and the leadership shown by their representatives play a very active role in the affairs of the organization. They are also the ones that provide the bulk of the formal leadership structure of the WTO and take part in the informal consultations aimed at developing a consensus. Thus a duality is evident in developing-country representation: there are a few countries, mostly middle- and higher-income East Asian and Latin American countries but also including India and Egypt, with effective representation; but the vast majority have only weak or no representation.

Decision making

Any consensus-based institution such as the WTO, and GATT before it, must develop a variety of formal and informal decision-making processes. In principle any one member can block a decision by casting a negative vote. It was clear even in the context of GATT, where the developing countries had a majority of the votes but played a decidedly lesser role, that it would be futile to attempt to exercise voting strength to block major progress or to force developed countries to implement obligations they had not freely accepted (Evans, 1968). In practice voting rarely takes place. This puts a premium on formal and informal consensus-building consultations.

As the WTO now has more than 140 Members it is very difficult to conduct consultations, or for that matter any kind of business activity where everybody has to be consulted about everything. Thus while the General Council, the ultimate decision-making body where all Members are represented, and the various subsidiary bodies and committees meet frequently, informal consultations take place even more frequently.

Leadership positions

The following analysis of leadership positions focuses on the country distribution of chairmanships in various GATT/WTO bodies and committees. Chairs have traditionally played a fairly active role in forging consensus in GATT and the WTO – their role has not been purely cosmetic. Operating according to consensus when the countries represented are very different in terms of economic size, presents complex challenges when designing decision-making structures that will ensure equitable representation of the interests of all participants. Chairpersons play a role in the effort both to forge consensus and to maintain a reasonable balance of interests. Thus the share of chairmanships and other offices held by the developing countries should give some indication of their involvement and potential influence in the organization, especially over time.

The analysis includes not only chairs but also the vice-chairs appointed to a number of the main bodies of the organization and subsidiary committees, often in order to maintain a balance between developing and developed countries. The analysis also distinguishes between chairmanships (including vice-chairmanships) of two main groups. The 'important' chairmanships include those of the main constituent bodies, such as the GATT Council and later the WTO Council on Goods, Services and so on, as well as the chairmanships of the permanent organs of GATT and later of the committee structure of the WTO.[11] The 'less important' chairmanships include those of various *ad hoc* working groups and other entities established under a lesser authority – for example those under the multilateral codes of GATT, the plurilateral agreements of the WTO and the accession working parties. The distinction is somewhat arbitrary. During the reorganization that followed the establishment of the WTO a number of groups that had functioned under a lesser authority, such as the antidumping committee and the customs valuation group, were incorporated into the more formal committee structure of the WTO.

A breakdown will help to bring out some interesting points about developing-country representation. Table 8.3 shows that between 1982 and 2000 developing countries substantially increased the absolute number of 'important' chairmanships they held. Indeed from 1987 they held, in absolute terms, more important chairmanships than the developed countries. In all cases their proportion of chairmanships was lower than their share of the total membership of the institution but higher than their share of international trade.

The distribution of the very top leadership positions in GATT (the chairperson and three vice-chairpersons of the Council) in 1982 and 1987 seems to have been very carefully balanced: in each instance the chairmanship was rotated annually and was alternately held by a representative of a developed and then a developing country, and the three vice-chairmenships were held by the representatives of a developing country, a developed country and a country in transition (although the latter were not called that then). A similar balance existed in the very top WTO leadership positions in 2000, involving the positions of chair of the General Council (Norway), chair of the Councils of Goods (Uruguay), Services (Korea) and TRIPS (Singapore), chair of the Dispute Settlement

Table 8.3 Country composition of chairmen/vice-chairman (number)

	GATT 1982–1987 Permanent committees & organs		GATT 1982–1987 All other committees under certain arrangements, MTN codes, panels and groups		WTO 1997 General Council and subsidiary bodies, committees and WPs DSB, TPRB	WTO 1997 All other working parties and committees (plurilateral agreements, accessions, etc.)	WTO 2000 General Council and subsidiary bodies committees and WPs, DSB, TPRB	WTO 2000 All other working parties and committees (plurilateral agreements accession, etc.)
	(1982)	(1987)	(1982)	(1987)				
Developed	7	4	19	20	18	22	16	23
Developing	7	7	7	12	20	11	22	8
Transitional	1	1	1	0	2		5	0
Total	15	12	27	32	40	33	43	31

Source: GATT/WTO Directory (1982, 1987, 1997, 2000)

Body (Hong Kong), chair of the Trade Policy Review Body (Bangladesh) and the chairs of key committees. Indeed there is an informal rotation of the top positions, with the understanding that chairs (held for one year) previously held by a developed country will be succeeded by a developing country and *vice versa*.[12]

The picture that emerges in the case of the lesser chairmanships, however, is entirely different. In 1982 and 1987 very few chairmanships went to developing countries. This was partly because most of the groups in question were focusing on the implementation of the multilateral codes, in which developing-country participation was very limited. Developing countries focused their interest – and maintained the chairmanships of – groups such as the Trade and Development Committee, the group responsible for relations with the ITC and similar entities that had been mainly created to address the interests of the developing countries – not the institution as a whole.

The situation has changed little since the inauguration of the WTO – the developing countries hold proportionately fewer of the leadership positions in bodies dealing with the implementation of the two remaining plurilateral agreements and very few of the chairmanships of the many working parties set up for the accession of new Members. A number of these working parties have been in place for several years (see Chapter 9) and their chairs, mostly from developed countries, remain in office even after they have left their positions in Geneva.

At the same time there is a proliferation of committees and working groups relative to the number of high-level, experienced developing-country representatives who have sufficient time to devote to the growing range of WTO tasks. If one judges that about 15–20 developing countries are active in WTO affairs, ambassadors or senior representatives from developing countries hold the chairmanship of 30 WTO bodies or committees (Table 8.3). This is not a bad score, given that several ambassadors also have to represent their countries at other international organizations in Geneva. Fundamentally it reflects an effort by the WTO Members to maintain balanced representation in the leadership positions.

The implications of the findings on leadership positions should not be exaggerated. They do suggest that the WTO as an institution is flexible enough to accommodate increasing interest on the part of developing countries. Whether this translates into the promotion of issues of importance to developing countries is a more complex issue, however. The preparation and presentation of issues does not hinge primarily on the holding of a chairmanship or another leadership position. It is based on a lot of preparatory work and institutional initiatives in capitals, and on the development of points of common interest with similarly minded countries and delegations.

Informal consultations

When issues of importance to the WTO as a whole require consultations, these usually involve the Director General and a smaller group of Members that include the major developed and developing trading countries, and others that are judged to be representative of the views of the remaining membership. The composition of this group (called the 'Green Room Group' because it meets in the Director General's green conference room) tends to vary by issue. But on issues of general importance to the organization it can consist of upwards of 30 members. Given that in such meetings the representative of the EC speaks on behalf of all the EC member countries developing countries may actually have the majority voice in some consultations.

During the late 1970s and early 1980s an effort was made to formalize the establishment of a smaller group of countries to engage in regular consultations in GATT. This so-called 'Consultative Group of Eighteen' included 10 developing countries. Although from time to time there have been proposals to revive such a group in the context of the WTO, it has not been possible to do so, in part because of the difficulty of accommodating all the countries that would want to participate because other Members might not adequately represent their interests. As a consequence the loose and flexible consultation formula has remained in place. Neither the weighted-voting nor the related representation formula, whereby one country represents a number of others (frequently at a vastly different level of development) in the decision-making bodies of the IMF and the World Bank, has found favour in the WTO. Yet despite the disparity between trade weights and voting strength, both GATT and the WTO have been able to function properly, perhaps for the reasons discussed above and noted by Evans (1968).

Developing countries often do not have a common position on the major issues handled by the WTO. There is a WTO developing-country group that holds consultations from time to time; and the developing countries consult on trade policy issues of importance to them in UNCTAD. However establishing a common developing-country position on all issues is becoming more and more of a challenge as there are growing disparities in their income levels, trading interests, degree of integration into the international economy, institutional capacities and participation in WTO affairs. Some developing countries, for example Korea, Mexico and Turkey, are also members of the OECD, and on some issues share the outlook of the developed countries in the OECD. Others also find that, on some issues, their interests tend to coincide with those of developed-country Members and hence participate in groups with mixed developed-developing country memberships.

Agriculture is one such issue. The Cairns group, perhaps the most well known and formal of these groups, consists of a mixed membership of exporters of agricultural products, and includes countries such as Australia, Argentina and Thailand. As discussed in Chapter 4, the interests of these exporters are often quite different from those of a large number of developing countries that are net importers of foodstuffs.

Another informal group of mixed membership is worth noting: the so-called 'Invisible group' consists of officials from the trade ministries of major trading countries, with a balance between developed and developing countries (including the Quad countries and developing countries as Brazil, India and Korea). It meets in Geneva (or nearby) about twice a year to discuss (with the participation of the Director General), usually in general terms, forthcoming issues of importance to the WTO.

Prior to the Seattle ministerial meeting a number of other country groups emerged – as had been customary during the preparatory processes that took place before (and during) multilateral Rounds. Three such groups may be noted. First, the 'Friends of the Round' consists of 15 countries with liberal trade policies and includes 10 developing countries (Argentina, Chile, Costa Rica, Korea, Mexico, Morocco, Singapore, Thailand, Uruguay and Hong Kong. Second, the 'Like-Minded group' consists of six developing countries with more protectionist policies (the Dominican Republic, Egypt, India, Pakistan, Indonesia and Malaysia) whose concern is to ensure the implementation of the Uruguay Round provisions, especially the special and differential provisions, before the commencement of a new Round. The third group consists of Central American countries (including Panama but excluding Costa Rica) and the Dominican Republic. Their views are somewhat similar to those of the previous group, but their special concern is the maintainance of special and differential provisions for export subsidies. The 15–20 developing countries with active representation at the WTO are usually important participants in all of these groups.

In addition to these groups, developing countries participate in the discussions of regional groupings such as the Africa group and ASEAN, as well as in groups with a wider agenda such as the G-15 and sectorally oriented bodies such as International Textiles and Clothing Bureau, or in smaller caucuses among like-minded countries whose composition sometimes includes both developed and developing countries.[13]

Agenda setting and ministerial meetings

Prior to and during the Seattle ministerial meeting, developing countries voiced two complaints in respect of their capacity to influence the issues addressed by the WTO and ensure that the agenda of future multilateral trade negotiations would reflect their interests. First, they were concerned that – partly because of their own institutional weaknesses, and partly because of the absence of an international institution such as the one provided by the OECD for the developed countries – they were unable to undertake research and analyses or to develop proposals of interest to a large group of developing countries, which could then be presented at the WTO for consideration by its full membership.[14] As it turned out, this concern may not have been justified because developing countries submitted the bulk of the proposals for inclusion in the Seattle agenda.

But the second concern, which had to do with their perception that the processes followed in Seattle (and in Singapore) to reach consensus tended to ignore the interests of many developing countries, has proved to be a serious and lasting problem for the WTO as an organization. The problem derives fundamentally from the fact that WTO ministerial conferences (which take place at least once every two years) such as the one in Seattle, which was expected to launch a new Round of multilateral trade negotiations, put an especially heavy burden on the participants in respect of consensus building. This is because the conferences deal with a large range of issues in a very short period of time, and without adequate preparation and work towards consensus in advance of a conference, devising procedures that permit both effective negotiation and full participation at the conference itself is extremely difficult, if not impossible.

Consensus decisions are essential for any actions that affect the legal rights and obligations of governments, as they do under the WTO. No government will cede this right to others. On the other hand, serious negotiations are simply not practicable if every issue has to be discussed in a body as large as the General Council. 'Green Room' style meetings have to be small enough to allow effective negotiations to take place, but at the same time all the major developed and developing countries need to be represented if the results are to command consensus support. This means that very few of the many small developing countries are included in such consultations, prompting many to complain that their interests are not being taken into account.

After the failed Seattle meeting a variety of proposals were tabled to make the decision-making processes more fair, transparent and inclusive. Some countries advocated an UNCTAD-type system with regional groupings. Others proposed variations of the World Bank/IMF constituency groupings. Still others made proposals aimed at opening up the WTO deliberations and increasing the transparency of the proceedings.

After due consideration of the various proposals, it appears that the WTO Members are moving towards agreement on a range of reforms that will improve the participation of the smaller developing countries in decision making while increasing the information flow to all. The central principle of consensus decision making will be retained, as will the smaller negotiating groups. But an effort will be made to ensure that participation is more representative of the entire membership and of the subjects discussed. Moreover the deliberations of the smaller groups will be promptly reported in an open meeting of the full membership, providing an opportunity for all countries to express their views. Furthermore, information on the deliberations of the organization will be made promptly available to the public in order to increase transparency. Implementation of these procedures will be left to the Director General. The challenge is to put these procedures into practice during the pressure-packed ministerial meetings. The latter are unlikely to make significant progress unless they are better prepared in the sense of working towards consensus on the issues under consideration in advance of the actual meeting.

Dispute settlement

Both developed- and developing-country members have utilized the new WTO DSM far more actively than the GATT mechanism for settling disputes. By August 2000, developing countries had made 43 requests for consultations on 37 separate matters. Roughly half of these were against developed countries. Developing countries were the target of 67 complaints by developed countries on 40 different matters.[15] Developing countries also joined developed countries in lodging complaints against developed countries in another 10 cases involving four different matters (Table 8.4).[16] It appears that an asymmetry may be emerging in the use of the DSM between developed and developing countries: developing countries have been the target of far more complaints than their relative share of exports would suggest. Table 8.4 shows that by mid 2000 46 per cent of the developed countries' complaints had been lodged against developing-country WTO members, while the latter accounted for only about 25 per cent of developed-country trade. Just over 50 per cent of the developing countries' complaints, on the other hand, were lodged against developed countries, which was considerably less than the latter's share of trade with developing countries.

Table 8.4 WTO disputes* (number of cases)

Complainant	Developed countries		Complaints lodged against: Developing countries		Total	
	Distinct matter	Consultation request	Distinct matter	Consultation request	Distinct matter	Consultation request
Developed	64	79	53	67	117	146
Developing	19	23	18	20	37	43
Mixed**	4	10	0	0	4	10
Total	87	112	71	87	158	199

* As of 22 July 2000
** Combined developed and developing-country complaints.
Source: WTO.

It does not appear that the proportionately larger number of complaints by developed countries primarily reflected the difficulty that poorer or smaller developing countries were having in meeting their Uruguay Round obligations (see Chapter 5). Nineteen developing countries were the target of complaints by both developed countries and other developing countries. The developed countries' complaints were raised against only 12 developing countries that were important participants in international trade and active participants in the WTO, for example Korea, Brazil, Argentina, Chile, Thailand, Mexico, India and Indonesia. On the other hand, 15 developing countries accounted for all the complaints against developed and other developing countries. It is interesting that 10 countries appear on both lists (the countries named above plus Venezuela and the Philippines). With the exception of South Africa, no other Sub-Saharan African country and no LDC appeared on either list. Hence although the DSM was actively used by some developing countries, by mid 2000 the overall number that had been involved in the DSM (either as respondent or complainant) was only around 20, which more or less coincided with the number of developing countries actively participating in the WTO.

There is evidence to suggest that developed countries tend to coordinate their complaints against developing countries. This is shown by the substantial difference between the number of complaints (67) and the number of matters involved (53). For example in the case of India's quantitative restrictions, six developed countries lodged the same or similar complaints, and four developed countries filed complaints about Indonesian measures that were affecting the car industry. On the other hand, no more than two developing countries have made the same complaint about developed countries on any one matter.

Developing countries seem to have fared reasonably well in those cases that have been completed or were settled by consultation between the parties involved. Of the 34 cases apparently settled or otherwise inactive, 26 involved complaints by developed countries, of which seven were against developing countries; nine involved complaints by developing countries, of which five were against developed countries; and one involved a combination of developing and developed countries against a developed country (WTO, 2000c).

Of the 38 cases where legal action was completed, in the sense that panel and or Appellate Body reports were adopted by decisions of the DSB, 13 involved complaints by developed countries against developing countries, seven were complaints by developing countries against developed countries, three were between developing countries, and one involved a combination of developed and developing countries against a developed country (WTO,

2000c). It is beyond the scope of this analysis to attempt to conclude who 'won' these cases. In any case, the frequently complex rulings made it possible for all sides to claim victory. But the record shows that among the cases decided so far, a fair number of legal points have been decided in favour of developing countries (either as complainants or defendants), and both developed and developing countries have taken action to implement the decisions or to deal with the issues that gave rise to the complaints, which indicates that the DSM is in fact working.[17]

Active developing-country participation in the DSM would give them the opportunity to address trade issues of concern to them, but so far this opportunity has been seized by only a few countries. The main reason for this is probably that most developing countries lack the resources and institutional capacity to pursue complaints, so this is part of the larger question of the developing countries' institutional capacity to design and implement trade policy.

Capacity constraints and institutional integration

Effective developing-country participation in the WTO and proper representation of their interests depends crucially on their developing an adequate institutional capacity. As noted in Chapter 5, the ever-increasing range and complexity of the issues handled by the WTO, some of which are very technical, means that the capacity of developing countries to participate effectively in the work of the WTO depends very heavily on the analytical capacity and strength of the governmental and other institutions handling WTO issues in the various capitals.[18] In the previous section it was also suggested that institutional constraints probably limit the ability of developing countries to use the dispute settlement mechanism, and that only a few developing countries have actually done so. Furthermore it has been argued that only 15–20 developing countries have adequate representation in Geneva, based on the number of staff in their missions. It may be interesting to bring these strands together in order to develop a tentative list of developing countries that are effectively integrated into the WTO as an institution.

The strength of a country's institutional capacity in international trade can be measured by the following:

- Whether the country has initiated an antidumping action, a complex task requiring the implementation of complex administrative procedures (see Chapter 4).

Table 8.5   Institutionally integrated WTO developing-country members

Argentina*	Mexico*
Brazil*	Peru
Chile	Philippines*
Costa Rica*	Singapore
Guatemala	Thailand*
India*	Turkey
Indonesia	Venezuela
Korea	

* 'Globalizers' in the 1990s, according to Dollar and Kraay (2001).

- Whether it has initiated a complaint under the DSM, also a difficult and expensive task, as discussed in Chapter 5.
- Whether it has adequate representation in the WTO, as measured by the presence in Geneva of a WTO mission with at least four staff (including the head of the Mission).

Obviously, integration into the WTO is a continuum and any listing that uses discrete criteria will exclude some countries that should not be excluded or include others that might not have been included had different criteria been used. With this in mind, 15 developing countries meet the three criteria listed above and therefore can be seen as 'institutionally integrated' into the WTO (Table 8.5).

The list includes only one low-income country (India) and, interestingly, no African country. Seven of the 15 are 'recent globalizers' (Dollar and Kraay, 2001; see also Chapter 2): Argentina, Brazil, Colombia, Costa Rica, India, Mexico, the Philippines and Thailand, as marked by an asterisk in Table 8.5. Three others were early globalizers – Chile, Korea and Singapore, whose liberal trade regimes have been in place somewhat longer – and Turkey has a customs union agreement with the EU.

One can disagree about the indicators chosen to define this list and a few of the countries on it, but there is a core group of about 18 developing countries that can be viewed as effectively integrated into the international trading system, including those in Table 8.5 and a few others for example Colombia and Malaysia (excluded from our list on grounds of staff size) and Hong Kong, China (which has not yet initiated an antidumping case but is institutionally capable of doing so). In addition Egypt, Pakistan and South Africa may not meet the criteria in our list, but they are quite active in the WTO in Geneva. This brings the total to 21. One would also have to add China (a recent globalizer) and Chinese Taipei (an 'older' one) when they become members of the WTO in 2001–2 or thereabouts.

But there is a very large group of countries that clearly are not integrated, including all the LDCs (perhaps with the exception of Bangladesh) and other low-income countries. The provision of international assistance to strengthen the domestic institutional capacity of these countries, as discussed in Chapter 5, is essential to their effective participation in the WTO – there is no point to trying to strengthen the representation of a country's interests in Geneva without improving its institutional capacity at home.

Policy implications

The above analysis suggests the existence of duality with regard to the participation of developing countries in the WTO. On the one hand there are a few developing countries that have significantly increased their capacity to participate in WTO activities since the Uruguay Round and whose representatives are playing an active part in the decisions of the organization. Their participation in the formal and informal decision-making processes is substantial, although they frequently do not speak with one voice as their interests sometimes diverge, resulting in the formation of different coalitions.

This does not imply that the consultation process always results in a consensus that reflects the interests of the majority of the developing countries. For example many developing countries felt that their interests were not fully reflected at the Singapore and Seattle ministerial meetings. But the problem in this case was more to do with the decision-making process and the difficulty of reaching a consensus in a short period of time than with the absence of effective representation.

On the other hand there is a very large group of mainly small and low-income developing countries (accounting for as much as three quarters of the total developing-country membership) for whom effective representation and participation in the WTO's activities is still a serious problem. Their situation has changed little since the early 1980s. Many are not represented in Geneva and hence can not effectively participate in the consultations that precede the consensus decisions on which the WTO is based. Their staffing has not increased significantly, but the complexity of the issues and the number of meetings and obligations in the WTO have grown tremendously.

For many developing countries, especially the LDCs and some of the smaller island economies, institutional weakness severely constrains them from meeting their obligations under the WTO, participating effectively in the WTO and representing their interests. It must be recognized that institutional development is a complex process that takes a great deal of time. Consequently solving the problem of developing-country representation is not going to be easy and is not amenable to quick, stroke-of-the-pen changes in policies or rules. That said, there are a number of things that can be done, some of which should start now, although their payoff may take some time.

First, developing countries need to ensure that the effectiveness of their participation is not impaired by such matters as failing to pay their membership dues. The amounts involved are typically very small, and deliberately falling into arrears is not cost-effective even in the face of serious budgetary constraints.

Second, ensuring adequate representation in Geneva is a complex issue for which there are no general solutions. For some countries with a very small international representation in general, setting up a Mission may not be the optimal use of scarce human and material resources. The main objectives of such countries should be to ensure that they are provided with adequate information on the issues handled buy the WTO and how these affect their interests; and to identify like-minded countries or groups that do have effective representation and engage in regular consultations with them, thereby obtaining some assurance that their interests are reflected on an ongoing basis. Two of the alternatives that countries can explore in this connection are pooling their resources and representation in Geneva through the regional groupings to which they belong; and seconding one or more representatives to the Geneva Missions of like-minded countries.

For all countries, measures to increase effective representation in Geneva should be taken *pari passu* with measures to strengthen their institutional capacity at home, as part of the broader process of becoming more fully integrated into the international trading system. Likewise an adequate flow of information to the appropriate ministries and other decision-making bodies in capitals is essential and should be addressed immediately. At the same time they need to strengthen the policy-making and implementation-capacity of these institutions, seeking assistance for this purpose from international donors and the WTO itself.

It is important to recall in this context the discussion in Chapter 5 on trade-related technical and other assistance. Efforts by the international community to help strengthen developing countries' overall capacity to trade will go a long way towards helping them to participate more effectively in the WTO.

Notes

1. As noted in Chapter 3, there is no formal developing-country definition and countries follow the principle of self-selection. The definition of countries as 'developed' or 'transition' is provided in Appendix 1 and is used throughout the volume. In this chapter, of course, only the Members of GATT/WTO are included in the various groups.
2. These rules are listed in GATT (1994).
3. Since 1998, LDCs in arrears have not been barred from receiving technical assistance from the WTO.
4. An earlier version of this analysis, using data up to 1997, is presented in Michalopoulos (1999a). The basic information on representation and leadership positions comes from the GATT/WTO directories issued in 1982, 1987, 1997 and 2000. A detailed discussion of the limitations of these can be found Michalopoulos (1998). The annex to that study contains a detailed list of the location and size of each WTO Mission as of mid 1997.
5. See Chaytor and Hindley (1997).
6. This was much larger than the expansion of WTO secretariat staff over the same period, which rose from 340 in 1982, to 383 in 1987, 515 in 1997 and about 540 in 2000. The two lists are not comparable, however, as the secretariat's list includes support staff. As the professional staff in the secretariat – excluding interpreters and translators – numbered less than 200, both the absolute and the relative increase of WTO professional secretariat staff over the period was much smaller than the expansion of Mission staff.
7. Only four countries (Burundi, Gabon, Malaysia and the Democratic Republic of Congo) had fewer Mission staff working on WTO/GATT issues in 2000 than in 1982.
8. The average size of Missions in the 'other' category, mostly transition economies, did not change.
9. Recall that 'mission' includes representatives to the WTO/GATT as listed in the directories, irrespective of whether they are located in Geneva or elsewhere. The differences are actually somewhat smaller if one compares only the countries with missions in Geneva.
10. This is consistent with the minimum-size Mission estimated by Blackhurst (1997).
11. The chairmanship and vice-chairmanship of the GATT Contracting Parties are included in the list of 'important' chairmanships, although their functions were mostly ceremonial. According to GATT practice these positions were held by representatives of countries that had held the same positions in the GATT General Council the previous year.
12. Interestingly enough, very few of these top leadership positions have been held by representatives of the EU, the US or Japan. At the same time the chairmanship of the Committee on Trade and Development, which deals exclusively with developing-country issues, has traditionally been held by somebody from a developing country.
13. One such group active in the late 1990s was called the 'Beau-Rivage group', which included the Geneva-based representatives of a number of smaller

developed and developing countries that shared an active participation in WTO affairs and a commitment to the multilateral trading system. It was similar in composition and orientation to the 'De la Paix group', which was active during the Uruguay Round. The composition of these groups was sometimes supposed to be secret and was frequently unstable, changing when a particular ambassador left Geneva.

14. Many developing countries continue to look to UNCTAD as an institution in which such analyses and positions can be developed. UNCTAD had also provided a discussion forum for broader aspects of a trade policy agenda for developing countries (see for example UNCTAD, 1997b).

15. In the context of this analysis the 'transition and other' group of member countries has been added to the developed-country group.

16. The banana case, brought by several Central American countries and the US against the EC, is one example of this.

17. For example the US announced that it would implement the recommendations of the DSB in respect of the complaint by Venezuela and Brazil in the gasoline standards case. The US also announced that the measure involving restrictions on cotton and man-made-fibre underwear (which provoked a complaint by Costa Rica) had expired in March 1997; while the measure affecting imports of woven woollen shirts and blouses, which had led to a complaint by India, had expired before the panel had concluded its work. Similarly, for the complaint by Brazil against the EC on measures affecting poultry imports, the DSB found that the EC had acted inconsistently with Article 5.5 of the WTO agreement on agriculture, but found for the EC on a number of other points. On the other hand the DSB found Indonesia to be in violation of certain articles of GATT (but not all), as alleged in a complaint by several developed countries in respect of measures affecting its automotive industry; and Argentina undertook to reduce its statistical tax and specific duties on textiles following a complaint by the US.

18. In the absence of governmental institutional capacity, countries have had to rely on outside consultants to represent them at WTO meetings. This can lead to confusion and misunderstandings, as Sierra Leone's experience of representation in the WTO Committee on Trade and Environment suggests (Chaytor and Hindley, 1997).

9
WTO Accession Issues

Introduction

Previous chapters have noted how the decision of many developing countries to integrate themselves more fully into the world trading system led several of them to join GATT in the 1980s and later the WTO. There is no way of making the rules of the international system benefit a country's interests unless the country is a member of and, as stressed in Chapter 8, effectively represented in the WTO.

Accession to the WTO is a far more complex, difficult and lengthy process than was the case with GATT. At the moment 28 countries are at various stages of their membership negotiations. Of these, 11 are transition economies that applied for accession after the collapse of central planning in the early 1990s. About half of the remainder are LDCs. Two large developing countries are in the late stage of the negotiation process: China and Saudi Arabia. Indeed there are very few countries that are neither WTO Members already nor applying to accede. These include Afghanistan, Iran, Iraq, Libya, Tadjikistan and Turkmenistan, many of whom have not applied because of political considerations.

This chapter analyzes the WTO accession process. The next section briefly summarizes the main benefits that countries can expect from WTO membership. The third section discusses the process and strategies for accession, as well as the main issues that have arisen in the case of developing countries and countries in transition. The fourth section reviews the progress made on accession by the various countries, as well as the causes of the delays that have been common in the accession of most countries. The final section presents the main conclusions from the analysis and a number of recommendations aimed at facilitating and expediting the process of accession for those countries which have already applied and those which have not.

The benefits of WTO membership

Apart from the obvious benefit of participating in the activities of an institution within which the global rules for trade are set, WTO membership provides additional benefits in three main areas: (1) strengthening domestic policies and institutions for the conduct of international trade in goods and services, which is needed before accession to the WTO can be accomplished; (2) improving the ease and security of market access to major export markets; and (3) gaining access to a dispute settlement mechanism for trade issues.

Domestic policies and institutions

While there are significant differences between the institutional and policy environments of the countries applying to accede, it is remarkable how similar the opportunities and challenges of WTO membership are for individual countries or groups. When the transition economies were under central planning, the government controlled trade through ministries and state trading enterprises. The institutions governing other aspects of the international exchange of goods and services, such as intellectual property rights, standards, phytosanitary provisions and procurement were either different or non-existent. LDCs applying for accession face similar challenges in establishing the institutions needed to implement their WTO commitments. Perhaps the most important of these challenges is the introduction of laws and institutions for the operation of private enterprises and markets free from government controls, other than those explicitly provided under WTO regulations regarding, for example, health, intellectual property rights and state trading practices.

Equally important to a country's economy is the greater stability in commercial policy that comes from adherence to WTO rules and legally binding agreements. Stability is important both to domestic producers and to exporters from other countries wishing to access that country's markets. There is little doubt that adherence to the WTO provisions, for example by binding tariffs and specifying the conditions of establishment for FDI in a services agreement, improves the efficiency and productivity of acceding countries.

WTO membership also offers the opportunity for some new members to lock in their relatively liberal trade regimes. While trade regimes in acceding economies vary considerably, many have established regimes with relatively low tariffs and no significant non-tariff barriers. For these countries, membership provides the opportunity to lock in these regimes by assuming legally binding obligations regarding tariff levels. This not only permits them to enjoy the benefits of liberal trade but also gives them a first line of defence against the domestic protectionist pressures that are inevitably present in all market economies.

Market access

There are two main dimensions of market access that are important to acceding economies. The first is the extension of permanent and unconditional MFN status that comes with WTO membership. At present, economies that are not Members of the WTO enjoy voluntary MFN treatment by major trading partners. But there is no guarantee that they will continue to receive such treatment. For example the US extension of MFN to Russia and several other economies in transition is contingent on these countries' adherence to the provisions of the Jackson–Vanik amendment to the 1974 Trade Act regarding freedom of emigration.[1]

Second, there is substantial evidence, as discussed in Chapter 6, that the incidence of antidumping actions (both investigations and definitive measures) is much higher against non-WTO Members than against Members. Also, for the transitional economies, some of which are considered as 'non-market economies' by major trading partners such as the EU and the US, WTO membership could help improve market access by making the processes used in antidumping cases against them more transparent (see below).

Dispute settlement

Access to an impartial and binding dispute settlement mechanism whose decisions have a significant chance of being enforced is a very important potential benefit for the acceding economies, many of which are small and heavily dependent on international trade. The dispute settlement mechanism, in the short time since its establishment, has proven successful in providing the opportunity for a Member to satisfactorily address its grievances when the practices of other members damage to its trade. The problems developing countries face in accessing this mechanism have been noted, but membership provides opportunities that, with proper assistance, can be beneficial to new Members, especially in their relationship with large trading partners.

The accession process and strategies

The process of accession to the WTO is demanding and takes a long time for most countries. It can be divided into an introductory phase of formalities and three substantive phases. The three substantive phases involve: (1) preparation of a 'Memorandum on the Foreign Trade Regime', in which the applicant provides full details of its policies and institutions that have a bearing on the conduct of international trade; (2) the fact-finding phase; and (3) the negotiation phase. The last two phases, while conceptually separate, in practice tend to overlap. Throughout the applicant has to meet the requirements and provisions of the WTO and the demands of the existing Members. With very few exceptions the negotiations are one sided: the applicant is required to demonstrate how it intends to meet the existing WTO provisions – it cannot seek to change them. Moreover the existing Members can ask the applicant to reduce the level of protection in its markets, but the reverse is not usually possible.

The formalities

The first step taken by an applicant country is to send a letter to the Director General of the WTO expressing its desire to accede to the organization. The request is then considered by the WTO General Council, which consists of representatives of all the Member countries and meets frequently during the course of the year. The General Council routinely sets up working parties with appropriate terms of reference to consider individual accession applications. The General Council nominates the chairman,[2] but participation is open to all members of the WTO. In the case of large countries such as China and Russia, a large number of countries participate: in the case of smaller countries participation is usually limited to Quad countries, plus Australia, New Zealand, Switzerland, a few of the larger developing-country trading partners and neighbouring countries that are significant trading partners. This phase can be quite short and normally takes no longer than the time needed to find a chairman for the working party and to translate and distribute the accession request before the next meeting of the General Council.

The memorandum

The first substantive phase is the preparation of a 'Memorandum on the Foreign Trade Regime', in which the applicant explains its policies and institutions. This can be a very demanding task because of the range of issues that the memorandum has to address and the degree of detail required. The issues include much more than simply trade in goods and services – although the latter, which encompasses such issues as the financial sector, insurance, telecommunications and professional services, is a large enough task in itself. The other issues include various aspects of macroeconomic policy (especially that related to foreign exchange management and controls), investment and competition policy, the protection of intellectual and other property rights, and enterprise privatization. The preparation of this report is the responsibility solely of the applicant, as is any delay in its preparation.

The greater the extent to which the memorandum is incomplete in its details or the legislation and practices described are inconsistent with the WTO provisions, the more protracted the subsequent question and answer period becomes. On some occasions Members have asked the WTO secretariat to review draft memoranda before they are circulated so as to prevent incomplete documentation from being circulated. But the secretariat does not assume any responsibility for the contents of memoranda.

Questions and answers

Once a memorandum has been circulated to the WTO Members the accession process enters the second, often time-consuming process in which Members ask questions about and obtain clarification on the applicant's policies and institutions, based either on the memorandum or on independent evidence gathered by the Members. This typically takes several months, but in the case of Russia it took more than a year. The working party does not usually meet until the memorandum and the initial questions and answers have been distributed. The subsequent questions, answers and clarifications can occupy several working party meetings and sometimes take several years.

The purpose of this detailed review is to make sure that the applicant's legislation and institutions are in conformity with the provisions of the WTO. One of the reasons why the process is so time consuming is that the review is exhaustive in its details. The applicant is requested to submit for consideration by the working party all relevant legislation on a variety of issues covered by the WTO, which is reviewed in detail for its consistency with the provisions of WTO agreements. Delays during this phase are frequent: if a member country feels that the answers submitted to a question or the actions taken to remedy an inconsistency are inadequate, it simply returns the question for resubmission.

The issues raised in each accession process vary somewhat according to the country, but some common themes emerge in the discussions –

especially in the case of countries in transition but often more broadly – that are worth highlighting.

First, there is a general requirement for the laws and regulations of the acceding country to be in conformity with the WTO provisions. These extend far beyond the obvious, such as customs law, tariff schedules and related regulations on imports and exports. They include such items as laws on joint stock companies, the central bank and credit institutions, the licensing of economic activity, domestic taxation, regulations on food and alcoholic beverages, veterinary medicine, quarantine, patent and copyright protection, and consumer protection. The list of laws of a small country reviewed by a recent working party ran into two single-spaced pages and included than 75 laws and regulations.

Second, in the context of laws and the operation of government institutions, there are two broad issues that typically receive special attention in the case of transition economies: the degree of privatization of the economy, and the extent to which government agencies involved in the regulation of economic activity do so on the basis of transparent rules and criteria, as opposed to administrative discretion. Both of these concerns emanate from the dominant role that the state previously played in these countries' centrally planned economies. A key issue in respect of enterprises that are expected to remain state-owned is whether they operate under market conditions or enjoy special monopoly rights and privileges.

Third, there are issues that relate to the jurisdiction and capacity of national agencies to implement policies on which commitments are being made. The fundamental concern is one of governance: whether the government agencies have the authority and capacity to implement the commitments they are making in the context of WTO accession in the case of laws and regulations that concern the conduct of international trade. A related concern is the role and jurisdiction of local authorities and whether they have the right and opportunity to nullify the commitments made by the national authorities in the context of accession negotiations.

Finally, there are some issues that are particular to countries of the former Soviet Union (FSU). First, after independence most of these countries passed VAT laws under which VAT was imposed on imports from the rest of the world but not on imports from the rest of the FSU. Moreover such products were taxed at the point of origin. This is contrary to international practice and all countries acceding to the WTO are asked to change their laws accordingly. A related issue that has led to a large amount of questioning pertains to the free trade and custom union agreements signed by several FSU countries. The concern is whether these agreements are actually operative, and whether they are consistent with the WTO provisions contained in Article XXIV of GATT and Article V of GATS.

Negotiations

At some point during the question and answer phase, frequently before all the points raised by the working party have been answered, the applicant is requested to submit its initial schedule of 'offers' in goods and services. This consists of the following:

- A detailed schedule of the tariffs the applicant proposes to impose on goods and the level at which the tariffs will be bound.
- The applicant's commitments (and limitations) on maintaining access to its market for services. These include the so-called 'horizontal commitments', involving market access to and national treatment in all service sectors; and commitments and limitations in respect of the different modes of supply in the service sectors and subsectors.[3]
- The level of support it plans to provide to its agricultural sector relative to a base reference period (usually three representative years before the application for accession) and other aspects of its support for agricultural trade (for example export subsidies).

Once these offers have been tabled the accession process enters its final phase, which involves bilateral negotiations on proposed tariff levels and degree of openness in the service sector. These negotiations take place between the applicant and each WTO Member who wishes to hold them. The timing of the offers varies considerably, and sometimes they are tabled very early in the question and answer phase, as for example in the case of Georgia. The bilateral negotiations often take place in parallel with formal meetings of the working party, which continues to deal with questions and answers on the foreign trade regime. The negotiating phase can also be lengthy, depending on the degree of openness the applicant proposes and the demands made by Members for market access.

When these negotiations are in the process of being finalized and the applicant has provided assurance that the legislation and institutions that will permit compliance with the WTO provisions are in place, a draft report on accession is prepared by the secretariat for consideration by the working party. This report includes the schedule of agreed commitments on goods and services. After approval from the working party, the report is forwarded to the General Council. Following a favourable decision by the

General Council (usually a formality), the country is invited to sign a protocol of accession.

Progress in accession

Progress to date

In spring 2001, 28 working parties formally existed to consider the accession applications of prospective WTO Members (Table 9.1). Most of these had been established for some time, and apart from few exceptions (for example those on Algeria and Laos) most of them remain active. The oldest are those on Algeria and China, which were established in 1987 (see WTO, 1999j). On average the working parties have been in place for

Table 9.1   Timetable of accessions to the WTO as of 1 May 2001

	Establishment of working party	Memorandum	Tariff offers	Service offers	Draft working party report
Algeria	6/87	7/96	–	–	–
Andorra	10/97	2/99	9/99	9/99	–
Armenia	12/93	4/95	1/99	10/98, 7/99	8/99
Azerbaijan	7/97	4/99	–	–	–
Belarus	10/93	1/96	3/98	5/99	–
Bhutan	10/99	–	–	–	–
Bosnia–Herzegovia	4/00	–	–	–	–
Cambodia	12/94	6/99	–	–	–
Cape Verde	7/00	–	–	–	–
China	3/87	2/87, 9/93	4/94	9/94, 11/97	12/94, 5/97
Chinese Taipei	9/92	10/92	2/96, 8/99	9/94, 8/99	8/98
FR Yugoslavia	1/01	–	–	–	–
FYR Macedonia	12/94	4/99	–	–	–
Kazakhstan	2/96	9/96	6/97	9/97	–
Laos	2/98	–	–	–	–
Lebanon	4/99	6/01	–	–	–
Nepal	6/89	2/90, 9/98	–	–	–
Russian Federation	6/93	3/94	2/98	10/99	–
Samoa	7/98	2/00	–	–	–
Saudi Arabia	7/93	7/94	9/97, 6/99	9/97, 6/99	
Seychelles	7/95	8/96	6/97	5/97	–
Sudan	10/94	1/99	–	–	–
Tonga	11/95	5/98	–	–	–
Ukraine	12/93	7/94	5/96	2/98, 6/98	–
Uzbekistan	12/94	9/98	–	–	–
Vanuatu	7/95	11/95	11/97, 5/98	11/97, 11/99	11/99
Vietnam	1/95	9/96	–	–	–
Yemen	7/00	–	–	–	–

Source: WTO.

67 months. If one excludes from the calculation the outliers (that is, the two oldest), those on China and Algeria, which can be considered special cases, and the three newest, which have not really started their work, the average life of the existing working parties is also 67 months.

On average it takes a little more than five years from the time the working party is established to the time that WTO membership enters into force. The eight most recent cases of WTO accession (Albania, Croatia, Estonia, Georgia, Jordan, the Kyrgyz Republic, Latvia and Mongolia) on average took more than five years, with Georgia and the Kyrgyz Republic being the fastest at a little over three years.

A number of countries are at an early stage in the negotiating process, including Azerbaijan, Bosnia-Herzegovina, Cape Verde, the Federal Republic of Yugoslavia, the Former Yugoslav Republic of Macedonia, and Yemen. Several others – such as Armenia, Belarus, Kazakhstan, Russia and Ukraine – have been involved in the accession process for a long time, but for various reasons are not yet close to completing it. A number of others are at a more advanced stage, with initial or revised offers on goods and services having been made, or the drafting of the working party report being under discussion (China, Chinese Taipei and Vanuatu). For most of these countries accession to the WTO is imminent, provided agreement can be reached with WTO members on the remaining points of contention.

Why does it take so long?

To understand why it takes so long to accede to the WTO, one has to look more closely at the various phases of the accession process and investigate the reasons why delays may occur.

Weak follow-up

There have been several cases where a government has applied for accession and a working party has been set up, but then the applicant has not prepared a memorandum on its policies, or has done so only after a long delay. The reasons for this may include uncertainty about following through the decision to join (Nepal and Uzbekistan), or internal political conflict delaying the process (Algeria and Sudan).

In the case of Algeria, the working party was set up in 1987 but the Algerian government did not produce a memorandum until 1996. Similarly the working parties for Uzbekistan and Sudan were set up in 1994, but their memoranda of foreign trade policy were only submitted in September 1998 and January 1999 respectively.

Political issues

There are a few cases where political differences between an applicant and one or more influential WTO members have caused delays in the process. Arguably, this has to some extent been the case with China (and Chinese Taipei, which is linked to it) and the Former Yugoslav Republic of Macedonia.

Inherently time-consuming processes

Even in the absence of the above problems, the process of accession is inherently time consuming. The preparation of the memorandum presents serious difficulties to governments that lack the necessary human or material resources to address the relevant issues, which have to be analyzed in detail. In some cases there is a lack of familiarity with the concepts and legal and economic issues involved. This has been true of countries in transition and many developing countries, most of which had to seek assistance from outside experts (funded by bilateral aid agencies), the WTO itself and the World Bank. Despite this assistance, on average it took about ten months to prepare the initial memorandum (even excluding the extreme case of Algeria).

The question and answer process is also time consuming because institutional weaknesses in applicant countries can mean that it takes a long time to ascertain the consistency between the existing legislation and regulations and the WTO requirements, as well as to design and put in place the required amendments, legislation or regulations. This is compounded by the range and extent of the legislation needed, and by the fact that legislative processes are themselves time consuming. At the same time, the discussions between the applicant and the working party on points of detail can be protracted: on average it takes nine months from the time of circulation of the memorandum for the first questions and answers on it to be distributed.

The subsequent fact-finding process can also stretch over several years. In part, this can again be due to weaknesses in the institutional capacity of the applicant. The WTO secretariat can assist only in a very limited way in the accession process: the WTO budget allocation for the accession of new members is very limited and the WTO members do not devote large resources to support the accession process.[4] The five staff in the WTO Accession Division (established in 1995 – GATT had no explicit secretariat resources for the processing of new members) are hard pushed to service even the procedural needs and paperwork generated by the 25 or more active working parties. Finally, delays occur because fact finding about policies merges into negotiations about how existing policies need to be changed to ensure conformity with the WTO requirements.

Negotiations

The negotiating phase can be, and frequently has been, the most time-consuming phase in the accession process. The negotiations are partly about whether the applicant's policies and institutions are consistent with various aspects of the WTO agreements and partly about specific tariff bindings and commitments in agriculture and services. Delays can be caused by both sides. The applicant may be unwilling to make the necessary liberalization commitments and slow the process by, for example, not offering to liberalize its non-tariff barriers or proposing to bind tariffs at levels much higher than the current applied ones; and WTO Members may be unsatisfied with the level of liberalization proposed or unwilling to accept delays in bringing the applicant's laws and institutions into line with the WTO provisions.

Applicants' strategies and tactics.   Within the rules and disciplines of the WTO, each applicant has considerable scope in respect of how restrictive or liberal its trade regime will be. There are no specific rules on the maximum level at which an applicant has to bind its tariffs, how many services it will liberalize, whether or not it will establish antidumping legislation, or how fast it will liberalize its agricultural trade. Applicants thus have a strategic choice to make during the negotiating phase: how liberal their trade regime will be, subject to the overall WTO disciplines.

One strategy that some countries have pursued in their accession negotiations is to offer the minimum degree of liberalization necessary to ensure accession. The logic of this strategy is that, for the most part, improvements in market access cannot be negotiated during accession, so it is desirable to try to maintain significant levels of protection to use as bargaining chips to obtain improved access in future negotiating rounds. Some of the countries that have used this strategy, for example China and Russia,[5] also feel that significant levels of protection are necessary during the transition period in which the restructuring of inefficient state enterprises is undertaken. In a somewhat different vein, a number of transition economies that already have relatively low tariffs and liberal trade regimes – partly because strong devaluation of the exchange rate in the early stages of transition provided protection to domestic industry – have presented initial offers that involve binding their tariffs at rates much higher than those currently applied.

Similar issues arise in services. Many transition and developing economies feel that their service sector is underdeveloped and would like to limit the commitments they make to open it up to foreign competition. This is a particular issue in areas such as financial services and telecommunications, sectors in which they frequently face requests from WTO members to establish liberal policies on commercial presence. The latter would permit foreign service suppliers to establish subsidiaries or joint ventures based on the principle of national treatment, which prohibits discrimination against foreign service providers and thus has a direct bearing on foreign direct investment.

However the minimum liberalization accession strategy can have negative effects. Individual countries, especially small developing economies, have little leverage in market access negotiations; hence any benefits they might obtain through such a strategy may be very small. At the same time, maintaining protection through relatively high tariffs and protected agriculture and services, simply means that they impose a cost on their own economies by foregoing the benefits of a more liberal trade regime, which in the first instance accrue to the country itself.

On the other hand, if countries bind their tariffs at levels higher than those currently applied and assume few commitments on agriculture and services, both of which are possible under the WTO rules, they are subject to another risk: they create an opening for domestic interests to exert political pressure for additional protection in the future.

A different strategy has been pursued by many of the transition countries that have recently become or are about to become WTO members, including Albania, Estonia, Georgia, the Kyrgyz Republic, Latvia and Mongolia.[6] In most of these cases the governments in question have adopted a liberal trade strategy as part of the accession process, including binding tariffs at the (usually low) prevailing levels agreeing to reduce and bind tariffs at low levels as part of the negotiations; agreeing to a liberal trade regime in agriculture and services; and at an early date after accession, participating in such agreements as the government procurement code, which serves to increase competition and transparency in the operation of their markets.

The fundamental benefits of such a strategy, are economic: it provides countries with the benefits of liberal trade and investment. But it has a number of other advantages: it tends to facilitate the negotiating part of the accession process; it provides governments with political cover against domestic protectionist interests that may otherwise succeed in subverting the existing liberal trade regime; and the legally binding WTO commitments make it more difficult for future governments to reverse the liberalization. Increased protection to safeguard against serious damage to domestic industry is permitted under the WTO rules, but it is supposed to be decided on the basis of a detailed and transparent investigation to demonstrate such damage, which is then notified to the WTO and subjected to the scrutiny of other members. This is far more difficult to do than for a powerful domestic industry to seek government support to raise tariffs beyond the applied level but below the higher bound level, which a government can do almost without constraint. The point about the WTO is not that it prohibits protection, but rather that it permits it only according to certain rules, and that obeying these rules makes protection more transparent as well as more difficult to initiate and spread.

The Chinese accession process, on which the bilateral negotiations have almost concluded, has combined elements of both strategies and has raised a number of additional issues that may have a spillover effect on the accession negotiations of other developing countries. First, China has used the process to stimulate and make irreversible substantial trade liberalization and more broad-based reform. Second, China, which in many ways is an economy in transition, considers itself a developing country and has been seeking to obtain the transition period and other special and differential treatment that WTO agreements extend to developing countries. The latter (as noted in Chapter 3) includes non-reciprocity, preferential market access, and different commitments and time limits for the implementation of the provisions of various aspects of the agreements, ranging from agriculture to subsidies and TRIPS. China, because of its status as a large market, has also bargained over certain aspects of its market access, such as on textiles and on issues related to its designation as a non-market economy (Michalopoulos, 2000b).

WTO Member attitudes and policies. The demands made on newly acceding countries are greater, in a variety of ways, than the disciplines on existing members. Based on recent accession experiences, the following areas are ones in which Members typically request that acceding countries make commitments in excess of what many existing Members at similar levels of development have agreed to:

- *Tariffs.* Acceding countries are requested to bind all tariffs, but a large portion of the tariff schedule of many developing countries is still unbound. Ceiling bindings have been accepted, but there is pressure for the bindings to be close to the applied rates.

- *Agriculture.* In addition to binding their tariff schedule, commitments are expected on aggregate measures of support and export subsidies. As many acceding countries have not provided substantial support to agriculture, but rather penalized it, the requests they face for reductions in aggregate measures of support may not be warranted, and in any case meaningful calculation of commitments in this area is subject to serious statistical difficulties, especially for economies in transition.[7]
- *Rules and disciplines.* Acceding countries are typically required to meet all commitments at entry (for example with regard to TRIPS, customs valuation, standards and sanitary and phytosanitary regulations), without time limits such as those available to existing members at similar levels of development, and regardless of whether institutional weakness makes it difficult for them to fulfil such commitments. Such weakness relates broadly to aspects of the operations of a market economy where it will take time to establish the proper institutional infrastructure to enable them to discharge their responsibilities properly under the WTO agreements (see Chapter 4). When such weaknesses are brought out in the negotiations, applicants are advised to seek technical assistance (available from a variety of bilateral and multilateral donors), and are asked to present details of the particular aspects of the relevant WTO provisions in which weaknesses exist, as well as how and over what time period it proposes to remedy them.
- *Plurilateral agreements.* There is pressure on countries to examine the provisions of the plurilateral agreements on, for example, government procurement and civil aviation at the time of accession and to sign up to the agreement soon after accession.
- *Market economy issues.* The WTO agreements have no explicit requirement for member states to be market economies.[8] On the other hand the requirement for new Members to have a fundamentally market economy is pushed *de facto* by existing members as part of the leverage they have in the accession process. Pressure has been exerted on all acceding countries, including China, where an explicit understanding has been reached with regard to the existence of state trading in specific sectors.

At the same time the Quad countries have been unwilling to modify their own antidumping procedures in respect of applying the designation of 'non-market economy' to transition economies that have become WTO Members. This designation is used to apply different, less transparent and potentially discriminatory practices in the determination of antidumping and, in the case of the EU, safeguard actions against imports from a number of these countries, including many former Soviet countries and China (Michalopoulos and Winters, 1997). It has been a major cause of trade friction between many transition economies and the US and EU.

The only plausible legal justification for such practices can be found in Article 2.7 of the WTO Antidumping Agreement, which refers to the second supplementary provision in paragraph 1, Article 6, Annex 1 of GATT 1994, which appears to permit different treatment 'in the case of imports from a country which has complete or substantially complete monopoly of its trade and where all domestic prices are fixed by the State' (Palmeter, 1998, p. 116). Such practices were perhaps fully justified when practically all trade was controlled by state trading enterprises or ministries, and prices were fixed by the state and hence could not be taken to reflect 'normal' value. Countries in transition, however, have made great progress in introducing market forces and eliminating state trading in recent years. It would very difficult to argue that, for example, China or Russia currently have 'a substantially complete monopoly on trade' or that all domestic prices are fixed by the state. Hence the continuation of traditional EU and US antidumping practices in the new setting appears not to be justified.[9] However, because the antidumping provisions of GATT accept national legislation and practices as decisive, it is possible to have the odd situation where a country acceding to the WTO is still designated as a non-market economy for antidumping purposes.

Lessons from experience and issues for the future

The most important lesson gained from the accession experience is that the negotiations and their dynamics vary from case to case. Thus it is difficult to generalize. Nevertheless the cases of a number of small countries that have concluded the accession process recently suggest that the smaller the country and the more liberal its regime, the faster the accession process. This is because smaller countries realize that the costs of protection are high in small economies, and because the small size of their economies raises fewer market access problems for the major WTO members.

It is politically difficult to adopt a liberal trade strategy at accession, especially when major WTO trading partners take advantage of opportunities to limit market access that are perfectly legal under the WTO, for example maintaining high levels of protection in agriculture. While recognizing the political difficulties involved, there are strong indications that if the developing and transition economies that are currently applying for WTO membership adopt a liberal trade strategy at entry, they will maximize the benefits and opportunities for integration into the international community that WTO membership offers.

It is fair to ask whether countries should not maintain some flexibility when making their initial offers, as they are bound to face some liberalization demands by existing Members, almost irrespective of the level of protection they initially propose. However, while there is some merit to this point it should not be pushed too far. Recent experience suggests that countries that make an initial offer to bind their tariffs at levels that differ significantly from the applied levels encounter serious difficulties upon accession, although the practice is quite widespread among existing developing-country Members, many of which have failed to bind a large portion of their tariff schedule. When such an initial offer is put on the table, working party Members may refuse to consider it or to enter into negotiations on that basis, as happened with several FSU countries and other applicants for accession. Rather they inform the country that it must submit a revised offer with bound rates that are closer to the applied ones before serious negotiations can begin.

China's accession is very unique for political and economic reasons, and lessons from it have to be drawn with extreme care. Undoubtedly China has used WTO accession to promote and lock in wide-ranging reforms. It has also been able to secure a number of transition periods (with regard to, for example, eliminating quantitative restrictions, licensing and state trading) and to maintain tariff quotas in agriculture. At the same time it has had to accept limitations on market access that other developing countries have not; for example in agreeing to be subject to product-specific selective safeguards, in accepting three more years of restrictions in the implementation of the ATC (from which it had been completely excluded) and in agreeing to be designated a non-market economy for 15 years.

Among the recently acceding countries, only China has succeeded in negotiating such transition periods, but probably has much more bargaining power than all these other countries put together. It is a moot point whether the time limits and extensions obtained by China (which were much less than it requested) are compatible with its economic interests, or whether more rapid liberalization of its trade regime would be more conducive to its long-term development. On the other hand, to the WTO Members negotiating China's accession, it is almost irrelevant what Chinese protection does to the Chinese economy. They are more concerned about the impact of such protection on their exports to the potentially large Chinese market. Hence the more exceptions a large country such as China seeks to obtain, the more WTO Members will seek to maintain provisions that inhibit full access by the acceding country's products to their markets (Michalopoulos, 2000b).

While the WTO Members' insistence on the existence of a liberal commercial policy at entry is likely to serve both acceding countries long-term development interests and WTO Members' commercial objectives, their insistence on adherence to all the WTO commitments at entry and without transition periods in areas such as customs valuation, TRIPS, standards and sanitary and phytosanitary measures – where obvious institutional weaknesses are present in LDCs and transition economies, raises serious problems. Applicant countries, because of their strong desire for membership, may end up agreeing to obligations that their weak institutional capacity will make difficult to implement, leaving them open to subsequent complaints. Alternatively, providing generous transition periods, while the transition periods for countries that are already Members are expiring, will create inequities between the existing and new Members. One solution to this problem may be substantially to extend some of these periods for both existing WTO low-income Members and acceding LDCs and transition economies, as the transition periods were set arbitrarily in the first place (see Chapters 3 and 11).

Sometimes, as in the case of some of the Baltic countries, accession delays have been caused not so much by problems encountered during the process *per se*, but by the link between WTO commitments, for example in the area of agriculture or services, and the possible future association of the applicant with the EU. For example Estonia, which has a very liberal trade regime in agriculture, had to review its WTO policy commitments in that sector in light of its interest in joining the EU and phasing in the latter's more interventionist agricultural policy. The accessions of Albania, Croatia, Estonia and Latvia were all delayed on account of EU–US disagreements over their commitments on audiovisual services.

Finally, WTO membership undoubtedly tends to create pressure to terminate non-market designation in national practices of antidumping and to permit all WTO Members to be treated the same in major markets. The experience with China, however, together with the inclusion by the EU of the Kyrgyz Republic and Mongolia in its list of non-market economies after both had become WTO Members, suggest that this anomaly is likely to continue.

It might be useful in concluding this analysis to compare briefly the WTO accession process for former Soviet countries (or any other countries for that matter) with that of membership of the Bretton Woods institutions. The speed of the former Soviet countries' accession to the Bretton Woods institutions can be explained by factors that are inherent to differences between the institutions, but it is also related to the policies and attitudes of the major developed countries, which are the largest shareholders of the Bretton Woods institutions and major actors in the WTO.

Compared with membership of the WTO, there are fewer issues on which proper legislation and regulations have to be in place before membership of the Bretton Woods institutions can be achieved. As the enactment of new legislation is a time-consuming process, this by itself can explain why membership of the WTO takes longer to achieve than membership of the Bretton Woods institutions. There is also much less negotiation on policies in the case of the Bretton Woods institutions, and certainly nothing comparable to the negotiations that take place over specific tariff bindings and commitments in services in the WTO.

An equally important factor in delays in the WTO negotiations is that the political economy of international trade policy is dominated by particular commercial interests in all countries. Thus while at the general policy level WTO Members might agree that accession of a country to the WTO is of paramount importance to their national interest – and for some large countries such as China to the very operation of the international trading system – accession cannot occur until the particular commercial interests in all countries are satisfied; and that takes time.

Moreover the developed countries, whose governments play a decisive role in determining the budgets of both the Bretton Woods institutions and the WTO, ensured that large incremental resources were made available to the Bretton Woods institutions to expedite membership by the countries emerging from the ruins of the Soviet Union.[10] In contrast, while the WTO budget for accession has been increased, the burden of preparing for accession still falls primarily on the acceding countries, supported by a number of usually uncoordinated multilateral and bilateral assistance efforts funded by aid agencies, as all countries' Trade Ministries are not mandated to help with the integration of other countries into international trade system, rather their job is to protect national commercial interests.

UNCTAD, the World Bank, the EU, Switzerland, the US and the WTO all have technical assistance programmes for various aspects of the accession process, especially the preparation of the initial memorandum. Anecdotal reports on these programmes suggest a somewhat uneven performance. Most countries have reported very helpful contributions by foreign consultants and advisors in the preparation of the memorandum. In some cases, however, the advice provided by outside experts has actually slowed the accession process, because the consultants have suggested and the countries have agreed to a bargaining strategy involving binding tariffs at high levels and limiting offers on services. At the same time, as with assistance for other purposes, there have been coordination problems among the various donors, as well as between the bilateral aid agencies providing assistance and their colleagues in the Trade Ministries negotiating the accession.[11]

Notes

1. Belarus (and until recently China) is subject to annual waivers; the rest have been found to be in full compliance and have received 'permanent' but conditional MFN status. However when Georgia, Mongolia and the Kyrgyz Republic became WTO Members the US exercised its right of non-application under WTO Article 13 which means that it did not provide these countries with unconditional MFN status (or for that matter with any other WTO rights) and thus *de facto* did not accept their accession. Subsequently legislation was enacted permitting the US to notify the WTO that it had accepted membership of these countries. In the case of the China, the US had to address this important issue through amended legislation *before* the membership negotiations were concluded.
2. Usually an ambassador permanently attached to the WTO. Countries often request and obtain observer status at the WTO to familiarize themselves with the institution, prior to a formal request for accession.
3. All service commitments are typically more general and open ended than is the case with goods. For a discussion see Hoekman (1996).
4. The EC, for example, has assigned six staff to support the accession process in Brussels; the US has a similar number in Washington to deal with the accession issues that arise in the more than 20 active working parties. Many WTO members however, notably the EC, the US, and Switzerland, support the accession process through technical assistance from their aid programmes.
5. See G. Gabunia, 'Reasonable Protectionism', *Expert*, 7 September 1998, p. 33.
6. The trade regimes of Croatia and Jordan, which acceded recently, are somewhat less liberal.
7. Requests to reduce the aggregate measures of support relative to a 'representative' period, usually the three years prior to the application for accession, can involve serious statistical and economic pitfalls. For example the three years prior to the accession application frequently coincide with the early 1990s, when transition economies were in the midst of hyperinflation and their exchange rates were unstable, and could hardly be viewed as representing 'equilibrium'. Similar problems arise if the late 1980s are used as 'representative'. Thus measures of support for such reference base periods, calculated in either national currencies or foreign exchange, are not especially meaningful.
8. GATT Article XVII calls for notification of enterprises engaging in state trading practices. However this article was never intended to address problems that

come up when the bulk of external trade is controlled by the state. Indeed the old GATT accommodated several countries that at the time had centrally planned economies, for example Romania and Czechoslovakia.

9. Michalopoulos and Winters (1997). In late 1997 the European Commission proposed the liberalization of EU policy on this issue *vis-à-vis* Russia and China. This involved terminating their designation as non-market economies at the country level and permitting determinations to be made on a case-by-case basis, taking into account the market conditions prevailing in each commodity in which dumping had been alleged (Croft 1997). This was similar to the practice of the US.

10. See World Bank (1995). During the periods 1989–90 and 1991–93 the author was part of the World Bank management team directing the implementation of premembership activities, first in Eastern Europe and later in the former Soviet Union, and headed the preparation of the World Bank economic reports in three countries: Bulgaria, Moldova and Ukraine. These reports are analogous to the 'Memorandum on the Foreign Trade Regime', but they are broader in scope and coverage, and are prepared by World Bank staff rather than the government in question.

11. Based on the author's personal observations during World Bank missions to several countries applying for accession, including China, Kazakhstan, Russia, the Kyrgyz Republic, the Former Yugoslav Republic of Macedonia and Yemen.

10
Towards a Development Round

Introduction

The failure of the WTO ministerial meeting in Seattle, which was to have launched a new Round of multilateral trade negotiations, was a setback for the development of a liberal international trading system governed by multilaterally agreed rules. This failure should be a cause of concern to developing countries as they would benefit greatly from a rules-based trading system. The lack of agreement in Seattle to review existing rules that are unhelpful to development will not make the problems of developing countries disappear. Furthermore their reasonable concern about the implementation of the Uruguay Round agreements and their need for additional assistance will not be addressed. Of course no deal is better than a bad deal, and it is doubtful whether the deal the Quad was proposing at the time was, broadly speaking, in the developing countries' interests.

The Seattle meeting left a number of loose ends, for example with regard to transition periods that have expired and a number of smaller issues on which agreement was needed for the ongoing operation of certain agreements, such as that on TRIPS (see Chapter 7). At the same time the WTO negotiations on agriculture and services, already mandated under the Uruguay Round have started, as has a review of the TRIPS agreement. And the possibility of a new Round is being kept alive by the developed countries. Thus in the months and years ahead, developing countries will need to develop strategies for the ongoing negotiations, identify topics that they themselves want to bring to the WTO as well as their position on issues that others propose for a new Round of negotiations. No single strategy will suit them all. Their varying trading interests require them to develop different strategies and pursue these in coalitions with other WTO Members.

Nevertheless there are a number of issues on which most developing countries would agree. These include concern that the way the Uruguay Round agreements have been implemented has not been beneficial to their interests, and broad opposition to a number of proposals developed countries have put forward for inclusion in a new Round. This chapter discusses various aspects of implementation, based on the analysis in Chapters 4 and 6 of developed- and developing-country policies and practices. It then reviews the ongoing discussions on agriculture and services, as well as the new issues that have been proposed as subjects for negotiation in a new multilateral Round. The concluding section makes recommendations for the scope and modalities of a new Round that would help promote sustainable development in developing countries.

Implementation

Developing-country concerns about implementation stem from a general unease that the Uruguay Round agreements did not bring tangible benefits to them. This is in some ways part of their overall concern about their economic prospects and the issues they face in the process of globalization. In the WTO context, these concerns have focused on the failure by developed countries to live up to the letter or spirit of their Uruguay Round commitments. Concern has been expressed about two kinds of developed-country commitment: those involving action by developed countries to implement the special and differential provisions of the agreements (Chapter 3); and other actions – for example in implementing the agreement on textiles and clothing and the Agreement on Agriculture – that have an important bearing on developing-country interests. Many developing countries argue that weaknesses in their own institutions, combined with failure by the developed countries to live up to their part of the bargain, for example with regard to the provision of technical assistance, has made it difficult for them to meet their own Uruguay Round commitments. In addition some countries feel that particular provisions, for example those to do with export subsidies or TRIPS, unduly restrict their flexibility and are inimical to their development. This has led many low-income countries and LDCs to oppose the launching of a new Round before steps are taken by WTO Members to address the implementation issues.

Egypt, India and Pakistan and the 'Like-Minded group'[1] have been providing leadership on this position for countries that, on the whole, have less liberal trade regimes and too weak an institutional infrastructure to support international trade. These are the same countries that have tended to emphasize the special and differential aspects of their participation in the WTO (see below). In a way the arguments put forward by these countries are eerily reminiscent of the arguments raised by some of the same countries in the years before the Uruguay Round was launched. At that time India and Egypt (with Brazil and Yugoslavia) led the developing-country opposition to the launching of what eventually became the Uruguay Round on the ground that neither the Framework Agreement of the Tokyo Round – which contained the special and differential provisions for developing countries under GATT – nor the decisions of the 1982 GATT ministerial meeting and the GATT work programme had been fully implemented (Michalopoulos, 1985, pp. 18–19, 57).

Concerns about implementation also involve the developing countries establishing a bargaining position to fend off developed-country demands for liberalization commitments in a number of new areas that many do not wish to pursue. In the 1980s these involved trade in services, whose inclusion in the Uruguay Round many developing countries vehemently opposed. At present they involve such topics as investment, labour standards and the environment.

Different groups of developing countries have identified different inadequacies in the implementation of the Uruguay Round agreements. Some groups – ASEAN, textile exporters and the Cairns group – insist that flaws in the way the WTO agreements have been implemented are damaging their trading interests. Other countries, especially but not exclusively the lower-income ones in Africa and elsewhere, focus on the special and differential aspects of the agreements and the developed countries' failure to implement the 'best efforts' commitments they have made in practically all WTO agreements, together with the insufficiency of the technical assistance provided and the inadequacy of the transition periods.[2]

General commitments

When considering the implementation of the Uruguay Round commitments it is necessary to look first at what has taken place in the main areas in which agreements were reached. First, on the question of tariff reductions in manufactures and the liberalization of services, undeniably important achievements of the Round, no accusations have been made that developed countries have failed to honour their commitments. The same appears to be true of developed countries' commitment to eliminate voluntary export restraints, which had been a big problem in the 1980s. Reductions and other liberalizing steps seem to have occurred on schedule. This liberalization can be expected to benefit developing countries through the improved market access they entail; but the greatest benefits will come from the gains individual countries will obtain as a result of their own liberalization. And the countries that have liberalized the least for example in Africa, can expect the smallest gains (Harrison *et al.*, 1996).

Second, there is considerable evidence that the Agreement on Agriculture has not significantly reduced protection, but it has made it more transparent (see Chapter 6). Aggregate support to the agricultural sector and export subsidies may have been reduced, but they are still so large as to inflict a considerable burden on developing countries (World Bank, 2000d). Hence a clear case can be made that while the letter of the agreement has been followed, it has generated few benefits in practice. Additional liberalization is urgently needed and should be sought during negotiations on agriculture now in progress.

Third, a similar conclusion can be reached on the implementation of the agreement on textiles and clothing. Developing countries are decrying the fact that the benefits under the agreement are backloaded. But it was quite obvious at the time the agreement was signed that the benefits were to be backloaded, and that the developed countries could stay within the letter of the agreement without liberalizing meaningfully in the first few years. What is also forgotten in discussions about the agreement is that the net benefits developing countries as a group will obtain from the liberalization of trade in textiles and clothing trade will be very small, if any. This is because liberalization will result in a significant reduction in the rents obtained by the main developing-country exporters, whose quotas are currently constrained under the system. Liberalization of the system will benefit the low-cost developing countries (some of which may not be the main exporters of today) plus the consumers in all countries, especially in the developed countries (Harrison *et al.*, 1996).

Fourth, with regard to the agreements on trade remedies (antidumping and safeguards), the analysis in Chapter 6 suggests that the agreements did little if anything to change developed-country practices that result in disproportionate use of these instruments against developing countries. At the same time there is evidence that after the Uruguay Round developing countries continued their earlier practice of rapidly increasing their own use of antidumping measures and, more recently, safeguards. Again, there is little that can be said about implementation in this area, except that the developed countries have failed to live up to the spirit of the agreement in respect of treating developing countries more favourably.[3] The key concern about this agreement is that it allows protection measures that may be damaging to the interests of all countries, not just developing ones.

Finally, there is a number of other agreements, including those on TRIPS and TRIMS, in which it was the developing countries that committed themselves to implementing certain policies, in most cases after 2000. Here no implementation issues by developed countries as such arise, although there are some important questions about the adverse effect of the provisions of some of these agreements on developing countries.

In sum, with regard to these general Uruguay Round agreements it is difficult to see what the developed countries have failed to implement, or what steps they need to take in advance of a new round. However there is concern that the developed countries' liberalization efforts are not in keeping with the spirit of the agreement, especially in the case of agriculture. The same is true of antidumping and textiles. But in these cases it is unclear whether developing countries in general would have been the main beneficiaries of better enforcement of the spirit of the agreements.

Commitments for special and differential treatment

A large number of developing-country concerns have to do with the commitment by developed countries to implement provisions involving special and differential treatment. Recall in this respect (Chapter 3) that developed countries are supposed to provide developing countries with three types of special treatment: (1) preferential market access; (2) more favourable treatment in the implementation of Uruguay Round provisions; (3) technical assistance to help them implement their Uruguay Round commitments. The LDCs are supposed to receive even more preferential treatment in these areas.

The practice of special treatment continues to suffer from similar shortcomings to those in evidence at the beginning of the Uruguay Round. Three main problem areas have emerged: (1) the developed countries' commitments on preferential market access and other treatment are in practice much less important than they appear to be on paper; (2) the commitments aimed at addressing developing countries' institutional constraints were made without serious thought being given to how they would be implemented; and (3) there is increasing questioning of the verity of one of the fundamental premises of special and differential treatment, namely that less liberal trade policies are optimal for developing countries.

Market access and other more favourable treatment by developed countries

With regard to preferential market access, as noted in Chapter 6 the preferences provided under the generalized system of preferences (GSP) have been further eroded by two developments. Preference margins have been reduced as a consequence of the MFN tariff reductions under the Uruguay Round. Moreover additional regional arrangements that provide deeper and more secure preferences have been put in place, in some cases, involving arrangements between developed and developing economies – such as NAFTA and the Mediterranean agreements with the EU, and others among developing countries themselves (for example MERCOSUR) – that make the preferences provided under the GSP less important. Indeed in the EU, which has put in place the largest number of regional preferential arrangements, to be awarded GSP preferences is tantamount to being on the lowest rung of the EU preference ladder for practically all countries, except those to which MFN tariffs are extended, such as the US, Japan, Australia and a few other developed countries.[4]

Other developed-country commitments under the WTO agreements also suffer from shortcomings: either they are too broad and general in nature to be of any practical significance – such as those included in the many preambular statements; or they are of the 'best efforts' variety, for example those regarding the implementation of the antidumping agreement or in connection with the agreement in textiles and clothing. In either case they are not legally enforceable and developed countries cannot be held strictly accountable for not implementing them. Indeed, as discussed earlier in the context of antidumping, there is no evidence that developed countries have used constructive remedies before applying measures that adversely affect developing-country exports, and developed countries have continued to take proportionally more antidumping actions against developing countries than their share of international trade.

There are two fundamental issues that unless addressed will undermine any future efforts to provide developing countries with meaningful differential treatment in respect of market access, more favourable treatment or the provision of technical and other assistance. The first is that developing countries' capacity to export and compete in international markets differs vastly between countries, as their recent trade performance demonstrates (see Chapter 2). Hence the degree of assistance they need to break into foreign markets is also very different. Yet the WTO rules on the treatment of developing countries by developed countries in most cases do not reflect these differences.[5] Singapore and Korea are supposed to be treated the same way as Ghana and Saint Lucia; Argentina and Brazil the same as the Maldives and Senegal.

The 'Enabling Clause' provisions incorporate the principle of graduation as well as refering to developing countries contributing to liberalization according to their level of development. Developing countries have been treated differently by developed countries in the latter's unilateral implementation of the GSP. There is very little economic reason to suggest that some of the more developed of the developing countries cannot compete with the developed countries in the products in which they have comparative advantage, and there is very little political support for extending preferences to them. Indeed protectionist interests in developed countries frequently succeed in discriminating against them on products in which they enjoy comparative advantage. But there is no formal differentiation embedded in the WTO agreements. Leaving this up to the individual developed countries invites the introduction of extraneous political considerations into the determination of which countries should receive which preferences and how much.

There is one precedent for differentiation on a per capita income basis, and this is incorporated into the export subsidies agreement. During the Seattle meeting developing countries attempted to have this definition expanded to include all lower-middle-income countries. From a development standpoint there is little justification for providing lower-income developing countries or LDCs with greater flexibility in subsidizing exports: given the budgetary constraints these countries face, it could be argued that export subsidies might result in a very bad allocation of scarce revenues. But the principle of using a per capita income cut-off point is of importance and could be pursued in other, more appropriate, aspects of special and differential treatment.

From the development standpoint, the developed countries' response to proposals that involve improved market access for developing countries is very worrisome: their response has not been determined primarily by whether a particular proposal has developmental merit, but on the basis of the potential cost they will have to face in terms additional imports from developing countries. Hence they are prepared to accept export subsidies from LDCs almost indefinitely because these subsidies may not cause serious problems for their own domestic industries, not because it makes sense for LDCs to promote their exports through budget subsidies.

The analysis in Chapter 5 suggested that low-income countries and LDCs have a great need for technical and other assistance to deal with trade-related capacity weaknesses, and that the efforts of the international community should be strengthened in this respect. But developed countries cannot be reasonably expected to provide trade-related assistance to developing countries that do not truly need it. The problem is compounded by the fact that preferential market access or other preferential treatment is supposed to be extended indiscriminately and include even advanced developing economies whose capacity to compete in international markets is not in doubt. Both of these problems are linked to problems with the overall coherence of development policy, a topic discussed in Chapter 11.

Flexibility and reciprocity

On the matter of flexibility in the implementation of WTO commitments, a growing body of analytical and empirical work suggests that the very exercise by the developing countries of their rights under the various provisions that exempt them from WTO disciplines has had a negative effect on their trade and development prospects.[6] Two distinct lines of inquiry have been followed to reach this conclusion. The first suggests that developing countries, by not participating in the exchange of reciprocal reductions in trade barriers, have missed the opportunity to gain reductions in developed-country trade barriers on products of specific export interest to them – as evidenced by the fact that developed-country tariffs on manufactures of special interest to the developing countries are higher than average (Martin and Winters, 1996; Hertel and Martin, 1999).

The second line of thinking, which has gained increasing acceptance, attacks the very premise on which exception from WTO disciplines is based, namely that higher levels of protection and the subsidization of exports are conducive to development. According to this line of thinking, the permissiveness of the WTO provisions has enabled developing countries to maintain higher levels of domestic protection. But this protection has created distortions in domestic resource allocation, encouraged rent seeking and waste, and adversely affected growth in productivity and sustainable development. Likewise balance of payments problems are best addressed through macroeconomic policy measures, including exchange rate adjustments, that do not have such adverse effects on resource allocation and productivity. And export subsidies – often used to offset the disincentives of protection – are a drain on the budget and therefore unaffordable, and cannot be relied upon to provide sustainable export growth.[7]

There is one aspect of special and differential treatment, involving greater flexibility in the implementation of the WTO provisions by developing countries, that currently deserves serious attention. This relates to the transition periods in which certain obligations under the agreements are to be implemented by developing countries and LDCs. As noted in Chapter 3, time extensions have been provided for a variety of obligations under the TRIPS and agriculture agreements, and in the case of subsidies and countervailing duties. The transition periods negotiated at the conclusion of the Uruguay Round were arbitrarily set and bore little relation to the time it would take to build appropriate institutions to implement the commitments.

Developing countries have found it impossible to implement many of their commitments in the time allowed. The reasons for this relate to the inadequacy of their institutional capacity at the beginning of the implementation period, the high cost of implementing the changes needed, the insufficient assistance provided by the developed countries for this purpose, and insufficient appreciation of the time needed to make the necessary institutional changes. The result has been slippage in the implementation of the various agreements, and requests by many developing countries for extensions to the transition periods – which have not yet been agreed to by the developed countries. There is little reason to believe that many of those that failed to notify or request an extension were aware of the options they had and chose not to avail themselves of the latitude provided. At the same time the developed countries, with few exceptions,[8] have not challenged the failure of the developing countries to meet their WTO commitments on a timely basis by lodging complaints under the dispute settlement mechanism.

Least developed countries

There are two questions on the nature and scope of special and differential treatment for LDCs: (1) what, if anything, needs to be implemented in advance of a new Round; and (2) what principles of special treatment should be included in the negotiations during that Round?

As noted earlier there is already some indication that developed countries may be prepared to go further in extending voluntary preferences to these countries, perhaps even offering duty-free access to all LDC exports in advance of a new Round – as proposed by the EU. Such commitments are easier to make in political economy terms, as LDCs account for a very small fraction of developed-country imports in most product categories. As a consequence LDCs may not have to offer any new liberalizing commitments in order to obtain improved market access. On the other hand, most analyses suggest that the main constraints to LDC export expansion derive from weaknesses in institutional capacity as well as from supply-side factors (UNCTAD, 1998; WTO, 1998c).

Thus the key implementation issues in advance of a new Round is to come up with coherent and effective technical assistance in the context of the Integrated Framework. It may well also be that a development-country commitment to total duty- and quota-free access for LDCs will prove important in improving the general atmosphere in advance of a new round.

For the negotiations during a new Round, the key factor is ensuring concrete and effective support for trade-related capacity-building measures in such areas as agriculture, services and TRIPS. At the same time it is important for LDCs to recognize some of the implications and pitfalls of developing-country flexibility in the application of WTO rules and disciplines, as shown by past experience. It could be argued, for example, that the existing special and differential provisions permit LDCs the greatest freedom of policy choice in areas that they can least afford, such as subsidies. Tighter WTO discipline in some policy areas may be helpful to LDCs governments that wish to introduce and gain domestic support for trade policy reform.

Implementation priorities

The above analysis of the special and differential provisions in the WTO agreements suggests the need for a fundamental reorientation of priorities by both developed- and developing-country members of the WTO. Three major conclusions have emerged. First, active participation in the exchange of liberalizing concessions is the only way to maximize the benefits that developing countries may obtain from the forthcoming negotiations. The more developing countries rely on non-reciprocal concessions, the fewer benefits they are likely to derive. This is an important matter for the many countries – especially in Africa, but also in Asia – that did not actively participate in the Uruguay Round and have bound tariffs in only a few industrial products and high ceiling bindings in many others. They can use these as leverage to obtain concessions in other areas of importance to them.

Second, there is increasing recognition that the institutions in many developing countries, including those that are supposed to implement trade policies and bear the costs of adjustment to globalization, are too weak and inadequate to cope with the WTO obligations. In addition, supply-side constraints are a strong impediment to many developing countries' effective integration into international trade. The most extensive evidence of trade-related institutional inadequacies and constraints comes from the LDCs, but other low-income developing countries suffer from similar inadequacies. And this conclusion highlights the need to maintain and emphasize certain dimensions of special treatment. But there is much less analytical and empirical evidence that trade policies in developed and developing countries should differ in principle.

The third major conclusion is that the GATT/WTO agreements have fostered a 'pretend' culture with regard to special treatment. Developing countries find it politically easier to pretend that they all should be treated the same, with the exception of the LDCs; and developed countries pretend to provide meaningful special treatment but in practice their commitments are not legally enforceable in respect of market access, preferential treatment and technical assistance. The capacity of developing countries to export and compete in international markets differs vastly between countries, as their recent record of export expansion in developed-country markets demonstrates. Hence their need for preferential treatment or assistance in breaking into foreign markets also differs vastly. Yet with the exception of LDCs the treatment of developing countries by developed countries under the WTO is not systematically differentiated and there is no general and effective graduation policy.

However developing countries have been treated differently by developed countries when it comes to the generalized system of preferences. Leaving this choice to the developed countries invites the inclusion of extraneous considerations in the determination of which countries obtain which preferences and how much. Unless developing countries accept some degree of differentiation in their treatment beyond that applied to the LDCs, as well as some type of graduation, there is very little prospect of meaningful, legally enforceable commitments that generally favour all developing countries being implemented in the WTO context.

The overall objective of the international community should be the provision of more meaningful and real special treatment – by means of appropriate instruments – to the countries that truly need it. The conceptual underpinnings of this reorientation require a full understanding of the links between trade and development and the constraints faced by different developing countries in their integration into the international trading system. This has been attempted in the past in both GATT and the WTO, and needs to continue in the future.

The above analysis suggests that three actions need to be taken in advance of a new Round:

- Reexamination of all the transition periods agreed in the Uruguay Round that are affected by developing-country institutional weaknesses (as discussed in Chapter 5), but not necessarily the transition periods for policy reforms, such as subsidies.

- Agreement on an effective programme of assistance for LDCs under the Integrated Framework.
- Implementation of a scheme for duty- and quota-free market access for the LDCs by all developed countries based on the EU proposals, and perhaps similar commitments for access to high-income developing countries.

These are the kinds of steps needed to strengthen developing countries' confidence in the international trading system and permit agreement on the launch of a new development Round. But perhaps even more important to the longer-term integration of developing countries to international trade is the reorientation of development priorities. The main elements of the latter are as follows.

Greater emphasis on instruments to strengthen developing countries' institutional capacity

The main differences between the developed and developing countries lie not in the trade policies they pursue but in the capacity of their institutions to pursue them. This means that special provisions for technical and financial assistance as well as longer transition periods (which are linked to institutional reform and capacity building) should be emphasized. Less emphasis should be placed on special provisions that give developing countries greater opportunity to protect their domestic markets or subsidize their exports of goods and services. This does not mean that markets in developing countries are assumed to work better or that more liberal trade policies have no costs; rather that government intervention, other than through border trade measures, is usually more suitable and should be strengthened where it is not available; and that 'flexibility' in trade policy has both costs and benefits.

A sharper differentiation between developing countries

There are many problems with institutional capacity that are common among LDCs and other low-income developing countries with limited participation in international trade, but are not faced by the more advanced developing countries. Per capita income and/or share of world trade indicators need to be introduced to extend the focus of assistance to capacity building, as well as more favourable treatment and market access by developed countries to these developing countries, excluding the more advanced developing countries. In the absence of a graduation policy, which would permit a narrower definition of which countries should be eligible for special treatment, developed countries will continue to make commitments to developing countries that are not concrete; make concrete commitments only to LDCs that have a very small share of world trade; and rely on their own criteria – frequently non-transparent and politically motivated – to determine which countries should receive more favourable treatment or market access.

Differentiation and graduation will be difficult for developing countries to accept. Substantial differentiation, however, already exists in the case of financial flows from all the international financial institutions and the UNDP. In the case of the World Bank, some developing countries receive no assistance at all, others are only eligible for loans on hard terms, others for soft loans, and still others for a mix.[9] Why should the principle of differentiation be acceptable in the case of finance but not for trade? Remedying this may be difficult, but an effort has to be made.

Avoidance of efforts aimed on permanently binding preferential margins or similar arrangements

Preferential margins – including in agriculture, where protection is currently very high – can be expected to decline over time as tariffs are liberalized on an MFN basis, and no special provisions should inhibit this liberalization. One way of helping developing countries that truly need assistance to break into foreign markets is to cease giving preferences to developing countries that do not need them; another is to help them to strengthen their institutional capacity and reduce supply-side constraints.

Promotion of transparency in the provision of special treatment by mandating a regular review of its implementation

This could be done through a systematic annual review (Whalley, 1999) of donor assistance commitments and other measures taken in favour of developing countries. Alternatively a systematic review could be undertaken on a country-by-country basis in the context of the trade policy review mechanism.

The built-in agenda for negotiations

There are two areas where negotiations are ongoing: agriculture and services. There are also ongoing discussions on topics such as TRIPS, non-preferential rules of origin and others that may be included in a new Round (Croome, 1998).

Agriculture

The agriculture negotiations, which started in 2000, have made some progress in identifying the issues to be dealt with and the modalities of the negotiations. But countries have not gone very far towards engaging in actual negotiations.

As noted in earlier chapters, the developing countries' interest in agricultural trade varies considerably. First, the position of the Cairns group of major agricultural exporters (including Argentina and Thailand) is already clear. They will be looking for the following:

- The early elimination and prohibition of export subsidies that undermine the competitive position of efficient developing-country producers; and in the same connection, regulation of the provision of export credits.
- Deep cuts in tariffs, the removal of non-tariff barriers, and increases in the trade volume under tariff quotas so as to enhance market access prospects.
- The elimination of trade-distorting domestic support measures (WTO, 1998a).

Second, there is a large group of countries (the net-food-importing developing countries and others) that have a significant agricultural sector and export various agricultural products but also import food. The past policies of many of these countries tended to penalize rather than support the agricultural sector. Third, there is a group of countries with small, non-diversified agricultural sectors that are not (because of climatic conditions or land constraints, for example small island economies) very competitive in agriculture and tend to have protectionist policies.

Several concerns have been raised by the latter two groups of countries. While supporting reductions in export subsidies and trade-distorting domestic supports in developed countries, these countries have argued that the limits imposed on aggregate support and export subsidies (and their possible further tightening in the new negotiations) will impair their capacity to increase support to the agricultural sector should they need to do so in the future. Second, although the reduction in export subsidies by developed countries will be beneficial to their own domestic agricultural production, the resulting increase in the prices of foodstuffs will increase the foreign exchange outlays of poor, net-food-importing countries, which can ill afford them.

While the Uruguay Round agreement on agriculture focuses on distortions to agricultural trade that were primarily due to developed-country practices, it contains provisions that permit developing countries to increase their support to agriculture (and to poor consumers) by means not available to developed countries. Moreover there is a considerable difference between the applied and bound tariff rates in agriculture for these countries. Simple (unweighted) applied tariffs in agriculture averaged 25 per cent compared with 66 per cent for the bound rates for 31 developing countries (excluding Cairns group members), which suggests that there is considerable scope for increased protection of their agriculture should they wish to do so.

As noted in Chapter 4 however, investment and input subsidies provided to poor rural households are exempted from the calculation of the AMS but are subject to the 'peace clause' (Article 13 of the agreement on agriculture). Termination of this exemption will impose a constraint on low-income developing countries that wish over time to increase their support for the rural poor. To eliminate this problem, such subsidies could be included in the 'green box' of measures that are permitted under all circumstances.

It is in recognition of these issues that a number of developing countries have proposed the establishment of a 'development box', which would include provisions to support agriculture and food security that would be exempt from WTO disciplines (see Chapter 4, where the US support for these ideas was also noted).

The large number of developing countries for which agriculture is an important source of income and employment, especially for the poor, would benefit from further liberalization of the sector, subject to some conditions discussed below. To this end they should join the Cairns group in their effort to secure a very substantial reduction in export subsidies (these subsidies, which are primarily extended by developed countries, tend to undermine developing countries' efforts to stimulate an increase in their own agricultural output), and to improve market access for their potential agricultural exports by pressing for significant reductions in tariffs and the opening up of tariff quotas.

At the same time they need to safeguard those aspects of the agreement (as well as add new ones, as appropriate) that permit them to provide assistance of various types to poor farmers as well as to maintain their assistance to and food security programmes for the poor in general. But these measures should not create distortions between sales to the domestic market and abroad, or between sectors. Finally, as noted earlier the matter of increased costs to net-food-importing countries is better addressed in the context of concessional finance to these countries, rather in the context of food aid.

It is unclear at this juncture what direction the negotiations on improving market access in agriculture will take; that is, whether a formula for cuts in tariffs will be agreed upon or not. The variation in tariffs on agricultural products tends to be higher than that for tariffs on manufactures in both developed and developing countries. In such circumstances, a formula that results in proportionally greater reductions in peak tariffs is more likely to result in trade increases. For the developing countries, given the escalation in many developed countries' tariffs, it may well be advantageous to push for a formula that will lead to a greater reduction in the tariffs on processed food products.

Reciprocity in tariff cuts and other aspects of liberalization are discussed more systematically below. At this point it suffices to say that in seeking to open up other markets, developing countries need to consider not only how much they have to 'pay' in the traditional WTO/ GATT sense, but also how the further opening up of their own markets will result in improvements in their long-term efficiency and the incomes of their poor.

Services

Despite the strong confrontation between developed and developing countries over the inclusion of services in the Uruguay Round, the implementation of the agreement has provoked comparatively little controversy. This is partly because the services agreement involves, on the whole, voluntary liberalization through a combination of positive and negative lists that exclude modes of supply or sectors in which countries wish to avoid foreign competition. It also reflects the recognition by developing countries of the adverse effects that the protection of inefficient service sectors can have on the rest of the economy, for example through the high cost of service inputs on the competitiveness of the export sector. And it is precisely for this reason that many participated actively in the successful conclusion of two sectoral negotiations that took place after the Uruguay Round: those on financial services and telecommunications.

Nonetheless it is clear that developing countries have made far fewer commitments on service liberalization than developed countries, and will find themselves under pressure to make more. Also, some countries have liberalized certain aspects of their service provisions but have not bound these commitments in the WTO; which raises an issue analogous to that of how to give credit to such autonomous liberalization in the context of negotiations, an issue which had been raised in the Uruguay Round with respect to goods. Finally, one factor that is preventing some countries from liberalizing further is the absence of a suitable safeguard clause in GATS. While Article 10 of GATS requires negotiations whose consequent agreements should take effect no later than three years after the entry into force of the WTO agreement (that is, by 1998), this has not happened.

What is the appropriate strategy for developing countries in this setting? In this respect there are no obvious developing-country groupings as there are with agriculture. Rather there are LDCs with scarcely any modern domestic service providers; there are middle-income countries with some very advanced service sectors and an eye to market access to developed countries; and there are many countries in between. There are also some countries that have a comparative advantage in certain kinds of service and are concerned about market access issues in developed countries for these sectors. However, as noted in Chapter 6, there is one mode of supply and two sectors of special interest to many developing countries: the movement of persons; and construction and maritime services. Developing countries may wish to press for the liberalization of 'mode four' supplies in more professional categories by limiting the use of the employment needs test in specific sectors and making the test criteria transparent and consistent. Progress is desirable in this area, although it should be recognized that developing countries also have restrictions on this mode of supply that should be lifted as part of the negotiations.

In addition to these specific areas of interest, developing countries need to press for the establishment of a suitably transparent and non-discriminatory safeguard mechanism. While further liberalization of their service sectors will in many cases be in their own interest, the political economy of trade reform requires that a suitable safeguard mechanism be put in place for trade in services, just as it has been for trade in goods.

In sum, the service negotiations offer opportunities for developing countries to open up their own service sectors (and many may wish to do so) in order to reap the benefits of increased efficiency. In exchange they should seek liberalization in certain sectors and modes of supply of interest to them, but condition any offer for further liberalization on agreement on a suitable safeguard mechanism on services.

Rules of origin

Negotiations on the establishment of harmonized rules of origin have been under way for some time, and an effort should be made to reach agreement before a new set of negotiations start. If this does not happen the topic may end up becoming part of future negotiations. The key interest of the developing countries is to avoid the setting up of rules that could be used as substitutes for, or to reinforce, the quantitative restrictions being phased out under the agreement on textiles and clothing (Croome, 1998).

Potential subjects of new negotiations

Beyond the ongoing issues outlined above, a variety of other subjects have been suggested for inclusion in a possible new Round of multilateral negotiations. For some of these, for example the environment, competition and investment, preparatory work is under way based on previous WTO ministerial decisions or, as in the case of government procurement, under GATS. For others, for example trade facilitation and electronic commerce, work has started only recently and there has been no agreement on whether they should be included in a new Round. Some subjects involve general reviews mandated under the provisions of the existing WTO agreements. These have already started and could be folded into a new Round, for example those on TRIPS. Finally, there are subjects that have not been generally agreed for consideration, but which various WTO members propose be included, for example industrial tariffs and labour standards.

This is a vast array of subjects from which to choose. In the case of TRIPs, developing countries need to develop their position for the ongoing review, and the question is whether to include this in a wider array of negotiations or not. But in practically all other cases the developing countries have a choice of whether to support multilateral negotiations on the subject, and whether to do so in separate negotiations or combine the negotiations in a single undertaking.

The criteria countries use in reaching a decision should include: (1) the net benefits they can expect to obtain for their economies through their own liberalization and through improved access to the markets of others; (2) the net benefits that will result from setting new rules and/or changing existing ones; and (3) the institutional capacity needed to implement whatever new agreements are reached. The last criterion is very important because of the problems many developing countries have encountered in implementing the existing agreements.

Based on these criteria, different developing countries may well reach different conclusions on which if any of the topics to include in the proposed negotiations. An attempt is made in the discussion that follows to reach some broad conclusions on the general desirability of negotiations in each of the above areas from the standpoint of developing countries as a whole, recognizing that such generalizations need to be carefully scrutinized in the case of individual countries or groups of countries.

A potential developing-country agenda

Industrial tariffs[10]

Both developed and developing countries have called for new negotiations to be held during the preparations for the next WTO ministerial meeting. The average trade-weighted MFN applied tariffs facing developing countries' exports of manufactures in OECD markets, though small in absolute terms (3.4 per cent), are almost four times as high as those faced by other OECD countries. Industrial products make up more than 70 per cent of the exports of developing countries and are of importance practically everywhere except Sub-Saharan Africa (Hertel and Martin, 1999). Such negotiations will also offer an opportunity to address the continuing problem of tariff peaks, which are still present in developed-country markets for products of interest to developing-country exporters.

In order to obtain such reductions, however, developing countries will need to allow increased access to their own markets for such products. Their applied industrial tariffs are typically higher than in industrial countries and have a greater degree of dispersion – that is, there are tariff peaks in developing countries also. Moreover developing-country exports of manufactures are increasingly going to other developing countries rather than developed-country markets. But apart from Latin America, a large number of developing countries have not bound significant portions of their industrial tariffs. Even those that have, often use 'ceiling bindings', with the bound rates being much higher than the applied rates.

To achieve reductions in tariff peaks a formula approach could be used that will result in greater proportional reductions in the high bound tariff rates in both developed and developing countries (Laird, 1999). Other approaches may also be feasible, but in such cases developing countries may be at a disadvantage because few of their markets are large enough to be of interest to the developed countries participating in the negotiations. Furthermore the difficulty of reducing tariff peaks should be recognized. Tariff peaks in developed countries (as discussed in Chapter 6) exist for the following products and product groups:

- Major staple foods such as meat, sugar, milk and cereals.
- Cotton and tobacco.
- Fruit and vegetables.
- Processed food products - tinned meat, fruit juices and so on.
- Textiles and clothing.

- Footwear and leather products.
- Selected automotive and transport equipment products.

The first four of these product groups are agricultural commodities and will be the subject of the negotiations on agriculture.

Leather and footwear and transport equipment are important to a number of developing countries, but obviously a smaller number than those also affected by tariff peaks in agriculture and textiles. It will be difficult to persuade developed countries, especially the US, to reconsider their tariff rates on textiles and clothing, which under the ATC will be the only protective mechanism available in this sector (for WTO members) after 2005. But clearly an effort should be made. After all, the developed countries will be asking developing countries to make commitments in a number of sensitive sectors as well.

Despite the difficulties it would be mutually beneficial for developing countries to reduce their ceiling bindings - and perhaps their applied rates as well - in exchange for developed countries further reducing their industrial tariffs. This would yield a number of benefits for the developing countries. They would benefit from their own liberalization – which typically accounts for the bulk of the estimated welfare gains – and stabilize their trade regimes by binding more products, and doing so closer to the applied rates. And they would benefit from increased market access to other developing- and developed-country markets.

TRIPS

Perhaps no other Uruguay Round agreement has generated more concern in the developing world than that on TRIPS. This is an area where changes to the existing rules would benefit development, but may be resisted by entrenched interests in developed countries.

As discussed in Duran and Michalopoulos (1999) and Chapter 7, the agreement poses several problems. At the general level there is a concern that the efficiency losses resulting, for example, from a significant increase in the price of pharmaceuticals would exceed any dynamic gains resulting from increased research and development or larger flows of foreign direct investment; and that the duration of patent protection is excessive. There is also general concern that the agreement does not provide for a reasonable balance between the rights of producers and those of the users of knowledge and technology; and that it is based on an outdated concept of 'knowledge' that does not take account of the externalities of knowledge dissemination. But there is little agreement on how these broad issues should be addressed.

The patent system poses a variety of problems for a number of poorer developing countries with an agriculture-based economy. First, the patent system is unlikely to encourage local innovations, except in countries with a significant private scientific and technological infrastructure. At the same time the agreement, by not recognizing community proprietary rights to traditional knowledge, has led commercial firms in developed countries to seek proprietary rights on traditional medicines and product varieties (basmati rice and the bark of the neem tree are the best known examples). The agreement may also constrain farmers from using their own seeds, saved from the harvest for replanting; and it has already encouraged the patenting of biotechnological processes aimed at providing substitutes for existing developing-country exports. Last but not least, developing countries have found it difficult to implement the procedural and legal commitments required by the agreement.

Several of these issues have been raised by developing countries in the context of the TRIPS review. But it appears that not much progress has been made in addressing their concerns. Changing a number of these provisions to make the agreement more development friendly through the WTO review process is unlikely. The strength of the commercial interests in developed countries that TRIPS supports will make it difficult to introduce changes. Perhaps the only way for developing countries to obtain the rule changes they want is to make this topic part of a larger package. It will not be easy, but it will certainly be worth the effort for developing countries to make changes to the most detrimental aspects of the agreement a fundamental condition of participation in future trade negotiations.

Good ideas, but can they be implemented?

There are three issues – government procurement, electronic commerce and trade facilitation – in which new agreements could result in welfare improvements for developing countries but whose institutional requirements may impose a serious burden on many WTO Members.

Government procurement

Few developing countries have conformed to the plurilateral agreement already in place. Some (for example, Chile, Hong Kong, China) agree with the objectives of the agreement but find its implementation provisions quite cumbersome, partly because the agreement is based on the principle of bilateral reciprocity. On the other hand adherence to the agreement has become almost mandatory for newly acceding Members, with the US insisting on all acceding countries making a commitment in this regard (see above Chapter 9).

There is little doubt that developing countries could benefit signifi-cantly from liberalizing their government procurement procedures – not so much because of their capacity to gain international contracts, but in terms of improved resource utilization through more transparent and competitive procurement practices. As most government purchases relate to services rather than merchandise, the issues are essentially to do with liberalization and national treatment of foreign service providers. Indeed Evenett and Hoekman (1999) suggest that it is important to eliminate preferences in government procurement before improved competitive practices are put in place. This is because, if the opposite procedure is followed, under certain circumstances preferences on government procurement could lead to increased resource misallocation.

The issues have to do with implementation: can it be said that this is an important enough area for developing-country WTO members to adopt new multilateral rules? What should these rules be? Is it desirable to keep the government procurement agreement as it is, or should it be made a truly multilateral arrangement? Can developing countries be sure that any technical assistance they need to implement the new provisions and probably the required new legislation will be forthcoming? And why should the agreement *a priori* exclude procurement under assistance programmes, such as tied aid, provided by developed countries?

Trade facilitation

In recent years this topic has generated considerable interest in the private sector of developed countries and is seen as one of the areas in which new rule-making efforts may be desirable. As formal trade barriers go down, procedural requirements of various kinds are impeding the flow of goods and services. Innumerable non-standardized documentation require-ments exist for exports and imports. On average about 60 documents are used in an international trade transaction, and they often differ from country to country. This is compounded by antiquated official clearance procedures. Lack of transparency and predictability is a major source of uncertainty in terms of the costs and time incurred in commercial transactions. The problems are typically much greater in those developing countries where automated procedures in customs administration do not exist.

Proposals have been made for improvements and revisions aimed at simplifying and standardizing procedures in the following areas: govern-ment-mandated information requirements; procedures for customs clearance; transparency and review; and transport and transit. There are at least eight international conventions and agreements guiding these areas, of which the most important is the 1973 International Convention for the Simplification and Customization of Customs Procedures (the Kyoto Convention of 1973), in which no more than half of the WTO Members participate.

There is little doubt that developing countries' trade would benefit significantly from such trade facilitation measures. There is also little doubt that few have the technical capacity to adhere meaningfully to multilateral rules on such procedures without significantly strengthening of their institutions. While technical assistance would obviously be needed, such assistance might not be sufficient to modernize their institutions in a reasonable period of time. As a consequence, meaningful progress in this area might best be made by first establishing an agreement that countries would have the option of joining at a suitable time in the future, rather than a multilateral agreement that would be part of a single undertaking with rules that developing countries might have serious difficulty implementing.

Electronic commerce

Electronic commerce accounts for a small but rapidly growing proportion of world trade in goods and services (World Bank, 2000d, ch. 4). This growth has occurred in a legal vacuum with few accepted rules and disciplines. Moreover the cross-border nature of the transaction has made the issue of legal jurisdiction unclear. There is little doubt that over time a framework of global rules for transactions through the Internet will have to be established. The key issue is whether there is enough understanding of the issues and enough international consensus to attempt to reach an agreement in a new Round of WTO negotiations.

The topic was first raised by the WTO during the Geneva ministerial meeting of 1998. At that time a standstill was agreed provided the WTO members 'continue their current practice of not imposing customs duties on electronic transmissions' and produced a report containing recommendations for action (WTO, 1998b). The original US proposal was to establish a multilateral agreement that would permanently exempt electronic transmissions from customs duties. Many developing countries dismissed the proposal at the time as it was felt that it had not been sufficiently explored and discussed. Some observers thought that consideration of the proposal was the 'price' of getting US President Clinton to participate in the ministerial meeting. In subsequent discussions developing countries voiced a variety of concerns. Some thought that such a commitment would result in countries foregoing future opportunities to collect customs revenues; others were concerned about whether electronic service supply should be given preferential status relative to other modes that were being regulated. Most were unwilling to commit themselves because they felt they did not have enough understanding of the issue involved, and because of their uncertainty about the policy implications of future technological change.

The involvement of developing countries in electronic commerce is, as with other aspects of their integration into international trade, very uneven. And while the Internet carries the potential of increased productivity and decreased costs, it also has the potential to increase inequalities within and among countries (World Bank, 2000d).

The developing countries' concern about foregone tariff revenue is exaggerated. It is clear that tax authorities would find it more difficult to tax certain transactions, but the impact of the standstill on developing-country revenue is expected to be miniscule – less than 0.2 per cent for major developing-country importers (World Bank, 2000d), many of which already provide large exemptions to their existing tariff schedules.

In further WTO discussions consensus was reached on a few points, for example that the electronic delivery of services falls within the scope of GATS and all GATS provisions are applicable to it; and that the 'technological neutrality' of GATS means that the electronic supply of services is permitted unless specifically excluded. However many uncertainties remain:

- How should Internet access and services be classified?
- Should certain electronically transmitted products be classified as goods?
- What are the proper links to the telecommunications agreement?
- How can the privacy of transactions be ensured, and how should encrypted data be valued?
- What are the links to TRIPS, for example copyright protection for electronic and database material?
- How can it be ensured that policies aimed at regulating services provided electronically do not discriminate against service delivery by traditional means?

In addition, many standard-related issues involving the interconnection and interoperability of systems need to be addressed to ensure that standard-setting by governments does not impede electronic commerce (WTO, 1999h).

The major problem that many if not most developing countries have in the area of electronic commerce is that they simply do not have the technical capacity to negotiate and implement a multilateral agreement at this time. Thus it may well be that developing countries should agree to continue the standstill on protection, and defer multilateral negotiations on this issue until a later date. Of course if a significant number of WTO members feel the need for such an agreement, it could be put in place but should not be part of a single undertaking.

Some difficult issues

The environment

The various links between trade and the environment have been discussed extensively in the WTO for many years.[11] The issues involved are thorny, complex and driven by two concerns: the developed countries' desire to be responsive to the strong pressure exerted by domestic environmental groups to preserve global biodiversity and prevent environmental damage by all possible means, including trade restrictions; and the developing countries' concern that developed countries are violating WTO rules when they restrict access to their markets on environmental grounds (these are sometimes unilaterally determined), and especially when the alleged environmental damage has occurred beyond the developed countries' borders and extends to the processing or production methods of the merchandise in question.

Several interrelated issues have formed the basis of the debate so far, and the positions on these issues vary among and between the developed and developing countries. Only an outline of the issues will be provided here, rather than a full discussion of the positions taken by different countries.

Issue 1: the relationship between the trade provisions in the multilateral environmental agreements and the WTO. This includes questions such as which agreement to include, what to do if the measures are incompatible with the WTO provisions, what to do about countries that are not party to a particular agreement, and which dispute settlement mechanisms to use.

Issue 2: when framing trade rules, whether and how to take into account processes and production methods with environmental consequences; what weight to put on multilateral agreements (for example on ozone-depleting substances) or unilateral decisions, such as that in the US following the tuna–dolphin case and the precautionary principle adopted by the EU; what to do about ecolabelling schemes, which could adversely affect imports from specific developing countries, and how to bring them in conformity with the broader WTO rules on standards.

Issue 3: the general relationship between trade, the environment and development. This has many facets, including the following: formal recognition that poverty is a major cause of environmental degradation;

providing assistance to developing countries to promote sustainable development; issues related to the impact of the developed countries' new environmentally motivated standards on the competitiveness of developing-country exports; and the broad relationship between trade liberalization measures and the environment (see Bhagwati and Srinivasan, 1996).

Developing countries face the following dilemma: should they negotiate an agreement on the varied and complex trade and environmental issues, which would involve legitimizing, through explicit and detailed understandings, various market access restraints on environmental grounds, and would limit the more blatant unilateral abuses by developed countries; or should they leave the system as it is (with developed countries being able to use the broad language of GATT Article XXb to restrain trade on environmental grounds – as recently interpreted very broadly by the Appellate Body in the shrimp-turtle case) and rely on the DSM to curb developed-country abuses? Different developing countries will respond to this dilemma in different ways. But on balance, given the strong pressure that the EU and the US will bring to bear on the inclusion of this issue and the difficulties developing countries have faced when using the DSM, they may agree to the environment being included in the agenda in exchange for negotiation on, for example, the restriction of developed-country subsidies on energy, fisheries and agriculture, which may have adverse effects on the environment, and/or the provision of assistance to developing countries to help them address poverty-related activities that contribute to environmental degradation.

Competition

This issue was originally placed on the WTO agenda by the US as a means of promoting greater market access, especially to the Japanese market, where it felt that poorly enforced competition laws were disadvantaging US exporters. After the WTO ministerial meeting in Singapore a working group was established to analyse the issues involved. The EU is currently promoting competition policy as an issue for plurilateral agreement, but the US has dampened down its advocacy of any WTO agreement.

There is no agreement on how to proceed in the WTO. The alternative approaches being considered include the following:

- The establishment of minimum antitrust standards that would prohibit certain practices while applying notification requirements on others. These would be administered by national authorities.
- Linking competition policy to limitations on the use of other WTO practices, for example antidumping.

- Extending the coverage of WTO rules under Article XXIII of GATT, which allows WTO members to challenge practices that, while not illegal under the WTO rules, result in nullification of the benefits negotiated in trade agreements.

For small developing economies, an open trade regime and liberal policies towards foreign investment may be sufficient to cope with most problems arising from domestically generated restrictive business practices. For those with competition laws, implementation capacity is often limited. The highest priority for many is to establish and implement proper national competition policies that focus on facilitating new entry, eliminating administrative obstacles to the establishment of new firms (including foreign ones), reducing transport costs in order to eliminate local monopolies, and so on, rather than establishing and implementing an antitrust machinery. Moreover for small developing countries the key issue in restrictive business practices may be the activities of transnational corporations (Low and Subramanian, 1996; Hoekman and Holmes, 1999). These corporations have the potential to dominate small economies or reduce the benefits that accrue to host countries, for example through transfer pricing and related actions that stem from the large proportion of intrafirm transactions in international trade. Unless such activities are brought under the proposed competition rules, which has not been the case so far, there is little reason to focus on multilateral rule making for developing countries in this area.

Neither the US nor the EU is interested in introducing competition mechanisms to deal with issues covered by antidumping. And the recent upsurge of antidumping actions by many developing countries suggests that many of them hold the same view. Finally, there is little to be gained by developing countries – in respect of improved market access to developed-country markets – by the establishment of multilateral antitrust rules. Most of these markets already have reasonably well-functioning antitrust systems that could be used by developing countries.

For all these reasons, developing countries should probably resist the inclusion of competition policy in a new Round. There is little that a multilateral agreement focusing on antitrust rules, as the EU is suggesting, would do to help them. And should an agreement be reached, its implementation would require the building of institutional capacity in an area that is not of high priority to most developing countries.

Foreign investment

Foreign investment *is* of great importance to developing countries. But the key questions relate not to its importance to development but to whether a balanced agreement – one which reflects the interests of developing countries and those of Transnational corporations (TNCs) and foreign investors – can be reached on the issue, and whether the WTO is the right institution through which to pursue it. The recent history of international negotiations suggests a negative answer to both questions.

The issue was raised in the Uruguay Round, only to be limited to the trade-related aspects of investment measures because of developing-country opposition. A WTO working group on investment was established after the Singapore ministerial meeting. At the same time there was an effort to conclude an agreement within the OECD, the so-called Multilateral Agreement on Investment (MAI). When that failed the EU proposed that the issue be pursued in the WTO, but the US maintained that there was no need for this.[12] It should also be recalled that in the 1970s, long before the MAI, several efforts were initiated by UNCTAD and backed by many developing countries to reach an international understanding on the restrictive business practices of TNCs – these too failed because of opposition by the developed countries.

The attempt to pursue an agreement within the OECD – which excluded most developing countries – was ill-advised. In addition, developing countries and many NGOs argued that the draft MAI did not contain a proper balance between the rights and responsibilities of TNCs, nor between the rights and responsibilities of TNCs on the one hand and the governments receiving foreign investment on the other.

Since the early 1980s there has been a great deal of analysis of the enormous potential that foreign private investment offers for development, and also of the potential problems and pitfalls of a totally unregulated foreign private investment regime in developing countries with weak supervisory institutions. During this period developing countries have liberalized their capital markets and their regulations on foreign private investment, both direct and portfolio, which has led to spectacular increases in the volume of private capital flows to developing countries, all without a multilateral agreement. Private capital flows have been concentrated among certain countries, and many countries – for example those in Sub-Saharan Africa – have been unable to attract foreign investment. It is doubtful, however, that such countries need a multilateral agreement to increase their future inflow of foreign investment.

Given the history of international negotiations on this topic, there should be little optimism about achieving a formal agreement that balances the interests of foreign private investors and those of developing countries. Despite developing countries' generally more favourable attitude towards foreign private investment, the recent volatility of private capital has, if anything, made such an agreement even more unlikely. And it is not clear whether such an agreement, while potentially helpful, is actually necessary to developing countries that wish to attract foreign investment.

Various aspects of foreign investment are already addressed in GATS, which offers the opportunity for voluntary commitments. As Hoekman and Saggi (1999) argue, the potential exists for developing countries to increase their commitments in this area and a more general agreement is neither needed nor feasible. Developing countries consider that the only interest developed countries have in going beyond voluntary commitments is that they think the WTO would permit trade retaliation for any violations of an agreement on investment. However the WTO already has enough problems on its plate, and the last thing it needs is to be additionally burdened by the multitude of disputes that are bound to arise from any agreement that sets general rules on foreign private investment.

Labour standards

Despite being repeatedly rebuffed – most recently at the Seattle ministerial meeting – the US continues to bring up labour standards as a topic for possible WTO negotiations. In this it has enjoyed the support of a few developed countries, especially in the EU which however has backed off from the inclusion of labour standards in the WTO negotiations. But the international community as a whole has always been of the view that the issue belongs to and should be addressed by the International Labour Organization (ILO).

The proposal to include labour standards in a new Round is intended to placate the protectionists in US and to some extent EU trade unions. It is also supported by a number of well-meaning developed-country NGOs, whose legitimate concern in this area, including child labour, indirectly provide cover and support to protectionists. It can bring no plausible benefits to developing-country trade, nor is the WTO the proper body to consider regulations on labour standards. Therefore it should be strongly resisted by developing countries as a topic for inclusion in a new Round of negotiations.

Antidumping

The governments of many developing countries (and other countries as well, for example Japan) have complained about the increasing use of antidumping measures by developed countries to limit market access in products of interest to developing countries. They have also expressed concern that developed countries have done little to provide developing countries with favourable treatment in the implementation of the antidumping agreement. At the same time, developing countries themselves have been using antidumping measures with increasing frequency. Many academic economists, noting this trend and the potential that antidumping measures have for abuse and non-transparency, have called for a tightening of the existing WTO disciplines in this area and for the inclusion of this topic in a new round of negotiations.

Undoubtedly such a tightening would help improve market access conditions in both developed and developing countries, and in principle it would be desirable to discuss the setting up of such rules in a new Round of negotiations. But these rules should cover all antidumping actions against developing countries, whether initiated by developed or other developing countries. It would be wrong, for example, to insist that the US limit its use of antidumping measures against developing countries while giving Brazil or India greater latitude to do so. Politically, however, it may not be a propitious time to discuss this topic. Many developing countries will find it difficult to agree to a tightening of the rules on an instrument they have just developed the capacity to use.

Strategic options

The above analysis of topics for inclusion in future WTO negotiations reached two broad conclusions. First, in addition to agriculture and services, two other topics – TRIPS and industrial tariffs – are of definite interest to developing countries; and one other – trade and the environment – is of potential interest to a number of developing countries' negotiations. Second, there are certain topics for which multilateral negotiations may be either premature (trade facilitation, electronic commerce, procurement) or counterproductive (labour standards, foreign investment) for most developing countries. Given these conclusions, the question arises as to whether it is in the interest of developing countries for these topics to be negotiated individually or as part of an overall round of WTO negotiations.

There are very strong political economy arguments in favour of an overall Round involving a single undertaking but a relatively small number of topics – four or five, as outlined above – so that it does not severely tax the negotiating or institutional capacity of countries and can be concluded within a reasonable time. The main reason why a single undertaking is needed is that it will permit trade-offs across topics. Developing countries have a strong interest in developed countries liberalizing their agriculture, reducing tariff peaks in industrial products, modifying TRIPS and liberalizing specific service sectors and modes of supply. On the other hand developed countries will be looking for additional developing-country commitments in the form of more bindings and reductions in the bound and applied rates of industrial products, as well as some additional commitments in the service sector. The only way that developing countries can overcome the entrenched protectionism in developed countries – for example in agriculture, maritime services and textiles – is to take advantage of the pressure that export interests in the developed countries will bring to bear on their own governments to negotiate in order to open up developing-country markets – this will also serve to open up developed-country markets in areas of interest to developing countries (Krueger, 1999).

Such pressure and linkages will be maximized if they cover a wider set of topics as topic-by-topic or sector-by-sector negotiations tend to focus primarily on areas of interest to developed-country exporters. Once the latter's demand for increased access to a particular sector, for example information technology, is satisfied, they will no longer need to exert pressure on their governments, which will then only have to deal with the ever-present protectionist lobbies that oppose improved market access.

However there is a danger for developing countries that a large set of negotiations will tax their institutional capacity to negotiate and implement new agreements. This is why developing countries should attempt to keep the negotiating package to a maximum of four or five topics. To use an old bicycle analogy: the momentum of a new Round is needed to push the bicycle forward, but the bicycle should not be loaded with so much baggage that it collapses from the excessive weight (Michalopoulos, 1999c).

The other question developing countries have to address is the desirability of launching a new Round when the Uruguay Round agreements have yet to be fully implemented. Some developing countries have stated that a new Round should not be held until implementation is complete. This is obviously a good tactical move, especially in respect of fending off developed-country demands for the inclusion of topics that are not in the interest of developing countries. But it is clear that in the case of the agreement on textiles and clothing, there are legitimate developing-country concerns about the manner in which the agreement has been implemented by some developed countries. Similarly a number of the developed countries' commitments for special and differential treatment to be provided to developing countries have been couched in such general terms (for example the provisions under Article 15 of the understanding on Article 6) that it is unclear what specific actions still need to be taken or guarantees given.

As noted above, there are some areas in which it may be worthwhile for developing countries to seek specific commitments before the launching of a new round. These concern the review and revision of the transition periods allowed to developing countries to implement the Uruguay Round agreements (URA); the technical assistance that has been offered to developing countries to help them implement their commitments under the agreements; and improved market access for LDCs, which has become of symbolic importance.

Notes

1. This group includes the Dominican Republic, Indonesia and Malaysia (see Chapter 8).
2. There are 145 individual references to special and differential treatment of the developing countries in the WTO agreements (WTO, 2000b).
3. This issue is discussed more extensively in the section on special and differential treatment below.
4. For a recent review see Onguglo (1999).
5. There are two exceptions: the LDCs are treated differently as a group; and in subsidies a special per capita income cut-off has been established.
6. See Finger and Winters (1998); Srinivasan (1998).
7. See Chapter 4. For a major review of this literature see Edwards (1993); see also Krueger (1995); Papageorgiou *et al.* (1991) summarize another set of studies of developing countries, conducted in the 1980s under the auspices of the World Bank, and come to similar conclusions.
8. The US and the EC challenged India's failure to meet its commitments under the TRIPs agreement in 1997–98 (see Chapter 7).
9. The principle has also been accepted by the Advisory Centre on WTO Law, an international institution established in Geneva, Switzerland, to help developing countries pursue cases through the WTO dispute settlement mechanism (see Chapter 8).
10. The term 'industrial' is a slight misnomer: it basically includes all tariff lines other than those classified as agricultural. The latter were defined in the Uruguay Round (UR) to include HS categories 1–24 and a few additional lines from a number of other HS categories (WTO, 1995).
11. There is an enormous body of literature on the subject. A useful summary of the main issues in the debate from a developing country perspective is presented in Shahin (1997); see also OECD (1999).
12. Recently the EC has introduced greater flexibility into its proposals by suggesting the possibility of a plurilateral agreement on investment.

11
Policy Coherence

Introduction

The coherence between trade and other international economic policies and initiatives that affect the development prospects of developing countries has received increased attention since the conclusion of the Uruguay Round agreements (URA). The WTO agreement explicitly calls for collaboration between the new institution and the Bretton Woods institution; that is, the IMF and the World Bank (see Article III of the Agreement Establishing the WTO). After the conclusion of the Agreement the WTO, the IMF and the World Bank engaged in a series of discussions that resulted in formal understandings among the three institutions aimed at ensuring better information flows and stronger collaboration between their management and staff.

But of course the question of policy coherence both antedates the WTO and goes beyond it. There have always been tensions between the trade policies of developed countries at the national level and their efforts to promote development, especially through technical and financial assistance. Their trade policies have been dominated by commercial objectives, frequently narrowly defined. Their assistance policies, on the other hand, have been motivated by a variety of political, developmental and humanitarian as well as commercial and economic objectives. A good example of the latter is the practice of tied aid, which has characterized a significant proportion of the bilateral aid programme of almost all donors.

Questions of coherence at the national level also arise in developing countries, where trade policy implementation, typically by weak Ministries of Trade, sometimes runs counter to overall policy directives formulated by Ministries of Planning or Finance, often in the context of agreements with the IMF and the World Bank. At the same time, at the international level developing countries have on several occasions attempted to forge coherence of a different kind: to use trade-related policies to obtain resource transfers from developed countries. The most important of these attempts occurred in the 1970s and was aimed at stabilizing commodity market prices at higher than equilibrium levels through the proposed Common Fund. Such efforts failed because of resistance by developed countries, especially the US, which wanted to avoid using market distortions as a means of resource transfer.[1] Developing countries were also at the forefront of promoting the coherence provisions of the WTO in order to open up the possibility of the World Bank and the IMF providing compensatory financing to food-importing developing countries adversely affected by increases in the price of foodstuffs as a result of the reduction of agricultural export subsidies under the agriculture agreement.

This chapter analyzes the coherence between trade policies and other policies aimed at promoting development in developing countries. The focus is on coherence between trade and aid policies. Other aspects of coherence, for example between trade rules and other features of the global architecture (the environment, human rights and so on) are not addressed. The chapter will address issues of coherence as reflected in the policies and activities of the WTO and the Bretton Woods institutions, (BWI) and will discuss proposals for the greater coordination of these institutions' international initiatives. But the main emphasis will be on coherence at the national level, because after all it is the national governments that make up the membership of all three institutions in question.[2]

National policy coherence

The developed countries' aid objectives have always been very complex. Political/security objectives and the pursuit of domestic economic and commercial interests, sometimes very narrowly defined, often combine and dominate the promotion of development or global humanitarian objectives. The mix of the various objectives tend to differ between the various donor aid programmes. Political/security objectives, for example, were explicitly paramount in certain bilateral US aid programmes until the collapse of the Soviet Union (Jay and Michalopoulos, 1989). Mixed credits – that is, a combination of export credits with official development assistance, which results in a small degree of concessionality – tend to be motivated by the export promotion objectives of the donor rather than development objectives of the recipient. Multilateral assistance, which is usually untied by source, tends to be less dominated by the narrow commercial considerations of the major donors. Some donors nevertheless include procurement staff among their representatives at the World Bank in order to ensure they get a 'fair share' of the procurement.[3]

In keeping with the complexity of donors' objectives, aid policy is usually formulated by three ministries/agencies: the Foreign Ministry, an aid agency (which may be independent, but usually has some links with the Foreign Ministry) and the Ministry of Finance. The relative importance of each of these agencies in policy determination and representation tends to differ between donors and programmes. With regard to the IMF, policy formulation/representation usually rests on a combination of Ministries of finance and central banks, with Ministers of Foreign Affairs typically playing a subsidiary role and aid agencies, with few exceptions, having a very small input, if any. With regard to the World Bank, policy formulation/representation varies, but it has traditionally been dominated by Ministries of Finance because of the Bank's involvement in borrowing in developed-country capital markets. Over time the importance of aid or development agencies (in some combination with Foreign Ministries) in policy formulation and implementation has increased in many countries.

The coordination mechanisms used by these agencies in major donor countries tend to vary in both nature and effectiveness. These mechanisms generally include agencies that are involved in the setting of trade policy, such as Ministries of Commerce or Trade. But the links with agencies or units dealing with WTO matters tend to be minimal.

Trade policy in all countries is dominated by commercial objectives, frequently narrowly defined to reflect the interest of particular producer groups and formulated and implemented by Ministries of Commerce or Trade (which sometimes are incorporated into Ministries of the Economy), with various arrangements made for policy formulation and representation at the WTO. The coordination of positions on trade policy is conducted in the first assistance by the Ministries of Trade, with some participation by Ministries of Finance and Foreign Affairs, but in most cases a very limited input by aid or development agencies. The establishment of the WTO has resulted in the need for far greater interagency coordination as the WTO agreements include many sectors/activities that were previously considered the sole domain of domestic agencies.

In the case of the EU, commercial policy and WTO representation rests with the European Commission, which has its own commissioner for trade, as well as separate aid programmes. But there is extensive consultation with the EU-member trade authorities in both Brussels and

Geneva. Thus aid or development agencies' attempts to influence trade formulation have become more complex: they can try to influence their own Trade Ministries, and through them the Commission; and people in the Commission who concern themselves with development try to influence their colleagues on the trade side. Agriculture has traditionally been a special case, with the commissioner for agriculture playing a very important role in EU trade policy formulation.

Mutatis mutandis the arrangements in developing countries parallel those in developed countries. The ministry dealing with a country's overall development or planning tends to be the counterpart to aid agencies for economic assistance, with the Ministry of Finance also playing a role, and either one of the two ministries usually representing the government at the World Bank. For many developing countries, however, the most senior officials in Geneva come from Foreign Ministries rather than Ministries of Trade. The coordination of economic policy at the national level tends to be directed by the Ministries of Development (Planning) in cooperation with the Ministries of Finance. Trade ministries are charged with the implementation of trade policy but are often not in charge of its design or coordination, especially in the context of the WTO commitments, which involve a variety of other agencies/ministries.

The complexity of policy objectives and multiplicity of actors is bound to create problems with policy coherence in any national setting. Some of these problems result from the lack of coordination in the event of conflicting objectives. It is reported, for example, that when the US Trade Representative started to negotiate financial liberalization during the Uruguay Round, the US Treasury refused to provide it with relevant information on the financial sector (Winters, 2000b). But by far the most serious problems in developed countries arise from the domination of narrowly defined commercial objectives, which involve private benefits to a specific sector or group of producers at the expense of domestic consumers and the development objective. The result is usually the waste of national resources, made available through the aid budget. The most egregious examples come from the conflict between aid objectives and protection in so-called 'sensitive' sectors, such as agriculture in the EU and textiles in the US. There have been many examples over the years:[4]

- In Tanzania the Dutch Development Co-operation invested roughly 200 000 euros per year for a number of years to support the Tanga Dairy Development Programme, but little progress was made in marketing locally produced dairy products because of the availability of dairy imports from the EU made artificially cheap by EU export subsidies (EUROSTEP, 1999).

- In Jamaica milk dairies mainly use European milk, which benefits from the same EU export subsidies, but in 1999 the Commission sent a delegation to discuss assistance for the marketing of Jamaican fresh milk (Herfkens, 2000).
- In Sri Lanka the US made a major increase in economic assistance following the establishment of a new reform-oriented government in 1978. One of the main focuses of the reforms, encouraged and supported by USAID, was the stimulation of non-traditional exports such as textiles through the reduction of trade barriers and a market-based exchange rate. The reforms succeeded and in 1979, as a 'reward', the US imposed quotas on Sri Lankan textile exports under the MFA, the predecessor to the WTO agreement on textiles and clothing (author's records).

Despite the liberalization of trade barriers by developed countries noted in Chapter 6, continued protection against developing-country imports and other practices such as the tying of assistance, especially at a time of declining official development assistance, is a major example of international policy incoherence. Indeed in recent years, as traditional forms of border protection have declined other forms, frequently disguised as efforts to pursue a variety of legitimate international objectives, have started to pose obstacles to the free flow of goods and services. The protection of labour standards and the environment are two such areas.

- The US signed an agreement with Cambodia, which is an LDC but not a WTO member, promising to increase its textile quotas under the ATC by $50 million, a miniscule amount relative to the US market but worth perhaps 18 000 jobs in Cambodia, on condition that Cambodia strictly enforced its labour laws, including the establishment of a minimum wage, the right to unionize and so on. Despite evidence of overall compliance and significant improvements, the US withheld the increase under pressure from textile unions (*Wall Street Journal*, 28 February 2000).
- The European Commission has adopted directives on waste electrical and electronic equipment aimed at reducing the hazardous waste caused by such equipment. The effect of these directives is likely to be very detrimental to developing-country producers and exports that have neither the capacity to develop new technology that excludes the pollutant in question nor access to alternative technologies patented

by developed-country producers (European Commission, 2000).

- The Commission directives on aflatoxin are likely to cost Sub-Saharan Africa more than $700 million in lost annual exports (see Chapter 6).
- The Quad countries are pressuring developing countries in the process of acceding to the WTO to become members of the Procurement Code at entry. Yet the code explicitly excludes from its provisions all economic assistance, which is provided primarily by the developed countries.[5]

In developing countries the problem of incoherence derives from a different source. In many cases trade policy reforms have been instituted by the government without 'ownership' by important stakeholders, inside and outside the government. Many reforms have been initiated, especially in Africa, under the pressure of 'conditionality' imposed by the Bretton Woods institutions. Frequently the negotiation of particular trade policies has occurred primarily between these institutions and Ministries of Planning or Finance, which are keen to gain access to external financing to meet urgent needs, and other ministries, including the Ministries of Trade and Foreign Affairs, are not part of the decision-making process.

It is well understood by now that if governments and stakeholders do not own the reforms the latter will neither succeed nor last. There is reason to believe that many trade reforms in Africa and elsewhere have not been implemented for this reason. In other cases representatives of developing countries in Geneva and New York, usually staff from Foreign Ministries, continue to use rhetoric based on traditional import substitution through protection rationale, even when their governments have fully espoused liberalizing trade reforms.

Questions of international coherence

The Bretton Woods institutions and GATT/WTO

The lack of coherence between the Bretton Woods institutions (BWI) and the GATT/WTO is far less significant than the incoherence between trade and development policies at the national level. The staff and management of the BWI are typically concerned with economic efficiency issues and hence tend to be strongly supportive of liberal trade policies, an objective that governments have also pursued within the GATT/WTO. Moreover governments are represented at these institutions primarily by Finance Ministries, which on the whole tend to have far more liberal views on trade policy than Trade Ministries in either developed or developing countries. In most cases the latter are strongly influenced by domestic producer interests, which frequently lobby for protection. Some problems arise, however, because the influence of the BWI is asymmetric: they have far more influence on trade policy in developing countries than in developed ones. And as the WTO agreements cover a variety of sectors and issues on which the BWI have an interest, such as the financial sector or environmental issues linked to sustainable development, greater cooperation among the institutions appears to be needed.

Until the 1980s the greatest interaction occurred between the IMF and GATT in the context of the IMF's participation in GATT's Balance of Payments Committee, but it seems that the IMF was able to exert little influence on the trade policies of GATT members as the GATT rules imposed few constraints on the policies of individual, especially developing countries.

During this early period there was far less interaction between the World Bank and GATT. The World Bank's activities were very strongly oriented towards project lending and little attention was paid to trade policy in that context. At the same time developing countries did not feel that their trade policies were particularly constrained by their participation in GATT (see Chapter 3).

In the early 1980s the situation changed dramatically. Both Bretton Woods institutions started to include trade-policy-related conditionality in their programmes of support, especially the World Bank in the case of its new Structural Adjustment Loans (SALs). This was because it was felt that outwardly oriented trade policies were essential to both long-term growth and medium-term adjustment to the emerging debt crisis. Indeed trade-related policy reforms were included in almost all World Bank SALs during this period. At the same time several developing countries were starting to consider more active involvement in GATT and in the exchange of reciprocal liberalizing concessions. Both developments were to give rise to problems with coherence.

The Uruguay Round

The link between trade and finance received explicit recognition at the launch of the UR. A negotiating group on the Functioning of the GATT System (FOGS) was established with the mandate to increase the contribution of GATT to the achievement of greater coherence in global policy making by strengthening its relationships with international organizations responsible for monetary and financial matters (Croome, 1995). There were two developments that brought the link to the forefront: some of the protection that existed in developed countries appeared to be due to persistent exchange rate misalignment; and it became obvious that the ability of the highly indebted developing countries to service their debts depended heavily on their export earnings, which in turn partly depended on the prevailing market access conditions in developed countries.

The FOGS group identified a number of areas of potential collaboration between GATT, the IMF and the World Bank in trade and finance. No concrete initiatives were implemented, however, in large part because the Bretton Woods institutions did not feel there was much to coordinate (Croome, 1995). Nonetheless cooperation with the BWI was identified as one of the WTO's explicit functions. Also, in the 'Decision on Measures Concerning the Possible Negative Effects of the Reform Program on the Least Developed and Net Food-Importing Countries', the IMF and the World Bank committed themselves to providing compensatory finance if they considered that the export subsidy reduction in the agreement on agriculture would cause problems. As noted in Chapter 4, no problem was found and this particular decision became and probably should continue to be, a dead letter.

One of the issues inconclusively examined by the FOGS group but which has remained important to the present, is whether and how developing countries that conduct autonomous trade liberalization can obtain credit for such liberalization in subsequent multilateral trade negotiations. The background to this is as follows. In the years leading up to the launch of the Uruguay Round in 1986, developing countries started to view the role that the World Bank and the IMF were playing in trade with some degree of suspicion. They were concerned that these institutions had far more leverage in promoting trade liberalization in developing countries, which were subject to conditional loans and credits, than in developed countries, whose trade restrictions appeared to be on the rise during this period. Also, some felt that their 'autonomous' liberalization (in the context of World Bank/IMF programmes) might reduce their negotiating leverage in the forthcoming trade negotiations.

It was to allay these concerns that the World Bank management first proposed that credit should be given in subsequent GATT negotiations for any autonomous liberalization undertaken in the context of World Bank/ IMF programmes (Krueger and Michalopoulos, 1985; Balassa and Michalopoulos 1986). The Bank was concerned that if some form of credit proposal was not put in place in advance of the negotiations, 'incentives may be created to postpone or not to undertake urgently needed policy reforms for adjustment in anticipation that trade concessions could be extracted from industrial countries at some future date' (Michalopoulos, 1985). The proposal was first made in a background document prepared by the Bank for a Development Committee meeting in April 1985. It was an idea that was from time to time internationally considered for the next 15 years, but which continues to face serious problems in terms of implementation.

During this period relations between the staff and management of the Bretton Woods institutions and GATT were becoming closer. As a symbol of their strengthened relationship, in 1984 Arthur Dunkel, then director general of GATT, was asked for the first time ever to address the World Bank/IMF Development Committee (a practice that continued in subsequent years),[6] and in the same year GATT staff made their first visit to the Bank.

The 'credit' idea was met with considerable suspicion by many developing countries in the run-up to the Uruguay Round because they perceived it as putting pressure on them to liberalize. During this period the Bank was insisting that all trade liberalization supported by its programmes should be made permanent through the binding of the reforms in GATT. During the Round discussions on the issue were conducted by the FOGS and Market Access groups. No action was taken in the context of trade in goods, but in GATS the principle received explicit recognition in Article XIX:3 which states that 'For each Round . . . negotiating guidelines shall establish modalities for the treatment of liberalization undertaken autonomously by Members since previous negotiations.' Yet no rule was set during the Uruguay Round negotiations and the issue has not been resolved in service negotiations, which started in 2000.

Despite their initially negative reaction, several developing countries warmed to the idea, which was articulated in a 'non-paper' submitted by Mexico and supported by 19 developing countries. The issue has also been taken up by the WTO Committee on Trade and Development and supported by the World Bank and IMF management in subsequent policy pronouncements, for example at UNCTAD X. However no enforceable rules have been developed in the context of either goods or services. One of the problems is that it is very difficult to devise a rule by which developing countries can be credited for autonomous reductions in *applied* rates when the GATT tariff negotiations deal with commitments on *bound* rates. The problem is especially difficult when tariffs are agreed to be cut on a 'formula' basis.

Indeed there have been reports that autonomous reductions in applied rates (but not unbound unilateral cuts) were taken into account in some developing country bilateral exchanges during the round (Finger *et al.*,

1999). It is difficult to gauge how much credit they actually received in the context of the overall tariff negotiations. It is conceivable that in such a negotiating mode a country might have been willing to 'pay' something, for example to reduce its own bound tariffs and thereby give credit for the benefits it had enjoyed in the past as a consequence of its partner's lower applied tariff rates. But the focus of the negotiations was the future, and the way to ensure the permanency of tariff rates at the time of the negotiations was through bindings; and the rules for this were the rules agreed on reciprocity, which themselves were not very tight.

When the Round started few developing countries had bound any rates. In the tariff negotiations the developed countries' main objective was to persuade the developing countries to bind their schedules rather than to liberalize as such. Indeed only in a few developing countries did the bindings result in a reduction in applied rates by the end of the Round. The mid-term review also agreed that participants would receive recognition for any liberalization measures adopted since the beginning of the Round (1 June 1986). As a consequence, in the case of agriculture a number of countries that had liberalized during the Round did not have to reduce their actual protection in many areas.

In the spring of 1999 the WTO Council considered a draft statement whereby WTO members would 'agree that the value of autonomous liberalization will be recognized as contributions to future multilateral trade negotiations ... subject to the government concerned agreeing to enter into contractual WTO commitments to guarantee the lasting character of the trade liberalization that is involved' (author's notes). While agreement on the statement was blocked by a few developing countries that feared it would encourage further liberalization commitments and bindings, it is possible that such a statement could be adopted as a principle in a new Round of negotiations. But even if that were to occur, it is unclear how the 'value' of autonomous liberalization would be recognized unless it involved future bindings.

Recently Mattoo and Olarreaga (1999) looked at the incentives that a credit rule creates for liberalization over time. They concluded that a credit rule is desirable if it is established at the end of a Round rather than at the beginning, as it will induce greater liberalization between Rounds. Such a rule was not established at the end of the Uruguay Round, and the authors suggest that it would undesirable to set up such a rule at the start of a new Round as it would tend to constrain liberalization during the Round.

While there are legitimate concerns about the incentives that setting a credit rule would have on future liberalization, Mattoo and Olarreaga's framework is not helpful in respect of designing practical measures to address the issue. Given that most of the tariff schedules for manufactures in developing countries are still either unbound or bound at much higher levels than the applied rates, probably the two most important developed-country objectives in future tariff negotiations should be to persuade developing countries to bind their remaining unbound tariff lines; and where they are already bound, to bring them as close as possible to the applied rates. As several developing countries have increased their applied rates on a number of occasions and others have reduced them since the end of the round, the probability that some of them will raise these rates again can hardly be viewed as zero. Hence the negotiations on binding tariff rates are not likely to start with the developing countries' currently applied rates, as Mattoo and Olarreaga seem to suggest, but much closer to the present ceiling bindings, where indeed there are bindings.[7]

At the same time, the fact that some developing countries have further reduced their applied rates implies that all other countries have enjoyed better access to their markets. The credit idea might be implemented by giving some recognition to past benefits though partial credit in any tariff-cutting formula, which would require developing countries to reduce their bound rates to below the currently applied ones in at least some items. This could be done as follows. Developing countries that have reduced their applied rates since the WTO agreements took effect on 1 January 1995 could be given the option of postponing such tariff cutting for a number of years, with product coverage being equal to the number of years (since 1 January 1995) that the applied tariff reductions have been in place. While such a rule may result in a somewhat smaller reduction of the applied rates during the Round, this may be small price to pay to bring down the bound rates and secure bindings on all the schedules.

Formulas are useful mechanisms for cutting tariff peaks but may be less so in services, where there is explicit provision for credit modalities. Here it is difficult enough to measure 'restrictiveness' and 'liberalization', so it would be even more difficult to design a credit mechanism. The fear is that any *ex post* credit for liberalization that is provided will result in no significant liberalization being achieved in the new Round over and above what countries have already done. It is for this reason that proposals on services have focused on increased commitments across the board for all modes of delivery, and that any agreed liberalizing formula should be based on the levels bound in the previous Round of negotiations.

The WTO period

Article III.5 of the WTO Agreement makes direct reference to the achievement of greater coherence in global policy making, and at the ministerial meeting in Marrakesh in April 1994 the senior management of the World Bank, IMF and WTO were instructed to review coherence issues and report to the WTO members on coherence in global policy making. After the establishment of the WTO a High Level Group on Coherence was set up, consisting of senior managers from the secretariats of the three institutions. At the same time the three organizations conducted extensive discussions that focused almost exclusively on procedural matters: which official WTO meetings should be attended by staff of the IMF and the World Bank, and *vice versa*; issues to do with the exchange of documents and databases; and possible collaboration in research and training, as well as staff exchanges.[8]

These lengthy discussions eventually led to the formal adoption of the agreements by the three institutions. Since then there has also been an increase in cooperative efforts in research, training and technical assistance, areas where the staff and management of the three institutions can collaborate most effectively (WTO, 1998f). These agreements are fundamentally procedural in nature, and some have questioned whether they are really worth the time the staff spent on negotiating them (Winters, 2000b).

Developing countries in particular were concerned that the very close coordination of the three institutions would result greater cross-conditionality being imposed on them. Nonetheless, over time the need has increased for strengthened collaboration in the provision of technical assistance, especially in connection with the Integrated Framework for the LDCs (see Chapter 5).

At the same time the staff of the three institutions have continued their informal consultations on policy issues at the level of individual developing countries. This was an area of concern to the WTO secretariat that proved to be unfounded, but it deserves consideration as it is characteristic of the differences between the culture and approaches of the WTO on the one hand and the Bretton Woods institutions on the other.

The issue is to do with concern that the Bretton Woods institutions would impose conditionality on individual countries, which would result in the latter violating legal commitments they had made under the WTO. A specific problem arose in the early 1990s when World Bank/IMF programme conditionality required Egypt to liberalize its trade by eliminating its extremely restrictive non-tariff barriers, involving licensing and import bans. In order to cushion the programme's impact on domestic producers, the Bretton Woods institutions proposed that the tariff level of a number of products be increased. Egypt had bound the tariffs on some of these products at low levels in earlier GATT Rounds, but the tariffs were meaningless as an instrument of protection because of the coexistence of very restrictive non-tariff measures. Nonetheless Egypt was legally obliged to offer compensation for any such increases, or to seek a waiver (author's files). It did the latter and the issue was closed. No similar problems have occurred since.

The controversy surrounding the case is indicative of the different approaches the institutions take on trade policy. The Bretton Woods institutions focus on the economic aspects while the WTO focuses on the legal aspects. In many cases the two approaches complement and reinforce each other. For example trade liberalization involving changes in applied tariffs can be strongly reinforced by legally binding tariffs at the WTO. WTO commitments can also act as a stimulus for economic and market-related reforms. At the same time legal agreements in the WTO may contain numerous provisions that make little sense from the economic or developmental point of view (see Chapter 3). Others may be far less or far more demanding of developing countries than is reasonable (see Chapter 5). One of the problems that arise when the WTO disciplines are very permissive is that the Bretton Woods institutions, when recommending reforms to particular developing countries, more and more frequently encounter the argument: 'Why should we go beyond what we are committed to do in the WTO?' At the same time many WTO commitments may have been unwittingly, but in good faith, made by developing countries that cannot possibly honour them. And in such cases it is appropriate to modify the legal commitments or take steps to help the developing countries to meet them.

Perhaps the greatest evidence of lack of international coherence in the WTO period is that the main global multilateral institutions supplying funding for development – the World Bank and the UNDP – reduced their assistance for trade-related capacity building at the very time the developing countries were asked to take on additional and costly trade-related commitments in the WTO (see Chapter 5). The Bretton Woods institutions and the WTO, under the direction of their members, were putting considerable effort into coordinating their procedures but not into raising the resources needed for trade-related capacity building. This has changed in recent years, especially since the Development Committee meeting of September 1999. But as noted earlier, problems remain – such as those related to 'mainstreaming' trade in World Bank operations. All this suggests the need for greater international coordination and collaboration on trade and development issues. But the main area in which additional coordination and collaboration has to take place is between the governments of the member countries.

The WTO secretariat, by virtue of the WTO being a member-driven organization, has far less leeway to suggest specific initiatives or policy proposals than the management of the World Bank and the IMF. The weakness of the WTO secretariat in this regard will become more and more pronounced if it is asked to play more of a role in anything remotely linked to trade policy. Characteristically the WTO secretariat takes no official position on any specific WTO policy issues and there is no official clearance procedure for secretariat documents or statements.[9] There is little chance that the WTO Members will press for changes to be made to the secretariat in order to make it more independent, so there is an even greater need for increased coordination among the governments themselves.

The management of the IMF and the World Bank do have the capacity and authority to take independent initiatives, but unless developed-country governments develop more coherent policies, any such initiatives are not likely to succeed. The recent experience with debt relief for the highly indebted poor countries is instructive in this respect.

Following the agreement reached in the IMF/World Bank meetings in autumn 1999 to increase the international debt relief efforts on behalf of these countries, and in advance of the Seattle ministerial meeting, the Managing Director of the IMF and the President of the World Bank proposed that the market access preferences provided to the LDCs should be extended to the highly indebted poor countries (HIPC). This proposal was an extension of an earlier proposal by the Director General of the WTO, supported by many countries, to extend duty- and quota-free treatment for all LDC exports.

The IMF and World Bank argued that as export growth in the HIPC countries was an important determinant of their ability to service their debts, this matter required extra attention and it would therefore make sense for these countries to be offered as much market access as the LDCs, for example through quota- and duty-free treatment. It turned out, of course, that the two lists coincided to a large extent, as 30 of the LDCs also appeared on the HIPC list of 40. The remaining 10 low-income countries – Bolivia, Honduras and Nicaragua in Latin America, Cameroon, Congo, Ghana, Côte d'Ivoire and Kenya in Africa and Vietnam in Asia – accounted for exports of $25 billion or 0.47 per cent of total world exports in 1999. Even combining the two lists together the countries involved accounted for less than 1 per cent of world exports.

Both the EU and the US signalled that they would not support the proposal – the EU by referring to its concern that such preferential treatment might have adverse implications for other low-income countries. EU's opposition appeared to derive in part from the political acceptability of the proposal to the Asian, Caribbean and Pacific countries (although five of the additional 10 low-income countries were ACP countries), which might wish to be included in any such extension of preferences; but most probably because the extension of duty- and quota-free treatment might not be acceptable to EU farmers, as the bulk of the exports of these countries were agricultural products, or raw materials upon which the EU applied no significant trade barriers.

The Bretton Woods institutions attempted to formalize this proposal as part of the joint declaration of the heads of the three institutions in advance of the Seattle ministerial meeting. However the WTO Director General balked and the proposal was dropped. Nonetheless it was revived by the World Bank and IMF at the UNCTAD ministerial meeting in early 2000, and there it stands.

As argued elsewhere in this book, there is little reason to believe that the problems faced by the LDCs are significantly different from those faced by other low-income countries. Therefore the measures taken by the international community should address both. In this case the international community and the Bretton Woods institutions have exhaustively analyzed the problems of the highly indebted poor countries. It now only remains for the trade ministers of the governments in question to be convinced of the usefulness of reducing their trade barriers to these countries. Continuing the trade restraints on the latter's exports means that consumers in developed countries are hurt twice: first by having to pay higher prices on imports from these countries and then by having to pay more in aid and debt relief to help them recover. Referring to the effect that such preferences would have on the exports of other low-income developing countries appears to be no more than a convenient excuse for doing nothing in an area where logic suggests that concerted international action is urgently needed.

Notes

1. One outcome of these efforts was the establishment of the STABEX fund, which until it was recently abolished permitted the ACP countries to obtain balance of payments assistance if they could demonstrate reduced earnings from commodity exports.
2. Some of the information in this chapter is drawn from personal files and recollections from the period 1975–95, when the author was involved with the coordination of trade and aid policy at USAID and the World Bank.
3. Trust funds financed by individual donors and administered by the World Bank tend to be tied, as are some contributions to IDA replenishment.
4. For a list of the agricultural products and developing countries that are adversely affected by EU export subsidies see EUROSTEP (1999).

5. Efforts to untie bilateral official development assistance have been pursued in the OECD for more than 25 years. The most recent effort, in 2000, focused on untying aid to the LDCs.

6. At a meeting with the author in December 2000, Dunkel recalled that his appearance before the Development Committee had been strongly opposed by the EU.

7. The underlying analytical framework of the study is also questionable: it rests on the assumption that a country produces a negative terms of trade externality by setting tariffs on its trading partners. It is hard to believe that more than a handful of developing countries are large enough to create such terms of trade losses for their trading partners.

8. The author was the first World Bank employee to be seconded to the WTO (in 1997–99) as part of this effort. The work experience in the WTO was extremely useful, but because of the administrative differences and bureaucratic obstacles that had to be overcome in the two institutions it took over 14 months to arrange.

9. This is in sharp contrast to the IMF, where strict procedures of clearance and accountability have been established, and the World Bank, where such procedures are being tightened. When I was asked to represent the WTO at an international meeting I was advised that secretariat staff spoke on a personal basis and could not speak on behalf of the secretariat as whole; and while it would be appropriate for me to seek the advice of a number of senior WTO staff and managers on the issues involved, it would be inappropriate to seek their clearance. I was told that there were no clearance procedures, because if they had existed the Members would wish to become involved and then nothing would be cleared as there was bound to be disagreement among the Members on the interpretation of the agreements. Such an environment does not encourage secretariat initiatives to forge agreement or promote collaborative action with other international institutions.

12
Conclusions and Recommendations

The main conclusion of this volume is that since the early 1980s the integration of the developing countries into the international trading system has been in many ways impressive, but also very uneven. A small number of countries, perhaps 15–20, have made giant strides, both in their institutional integration into the WTO system and in terms of their ratio of trade to GDP.

Most of the rest have struggled. By and large the ones that have struggled have been the poorest and the least developed. With few exceptions, for example China and India, the ones that have integrated most effectively have been the ones that started out with the highest incomes and most advanced institutional development. This increased integration is in part a result of the increased liberalization of trade regimes by both developed and developing countries during the Uruguay Round of multilateral trade negotiations, or for some developing countries, as a consequence of unilateral liberalization. It would have been impossible to achieve the large export growth rates of the 1990s if markets had not been becoming more open. Countries that have integrated more fully into the international economy have also tended to grow more rapidly.

The effect of these developments is greater polarization among developing countries. Those at the top of the income scale are achieving faster income and export growth than the developed countries, and as a consequence are converging to the level of development achieved by the latter. Others are being left behind. This uneven performance, amidst an environment of trade liberalization in both goods and services, has led many to argue that the latter is the cause of the former. And it has led to the conclusion that globalization is causing income levels to diverge and leading to the marginalization of the poor countries and people.

Chapter 2 showed that with few exceptions the fastest export growth has been achieved by the medium- and higher-income developing countries. They are the ones that are integrating the fastest in the sense that they have enjoyed the largest increases in their ratio of trade to GDP. Chapters 4 and 5 showed that low-income countries tend on the whole to have higher levels of protection and are characterized by serious institutional weaknesses, which have undermined their capacity to participate effectively both in international trade in general and in meeting their WTO obligations. Institutional constraints are especially pronounced in the LDCs, but are present in other low-income countries as well. These conclusions are reinforced by the analysis in Chapter 8 of the participation of developing countries in the WTO. Again a few countries, mostly higher- and middle-income ones, have been shown to be the most effective participants in the system by virtue of their representation in Geneva and their institutional capacity at home.

Which countries are these, and what are the characteristics of integration? First, integration should not be thought of as an admission ticket. It represents a continuum of institutional and policy accomplishments linked to performance, though it might be argued that WTO membership – a 'ticket' that Chapter 9 showed to be difficult to obtain – is an essential requirement.

Second, a variety of indicators can be used to define integration. The relationship of trade to GDP and its evolution over time has to be one of them. In Chapter 8 there was discussion of other institutional indicators that are designed to reflect the capacity of developing countries to take advantage of the opportunities of the WTO system, and it was concluded that rather few countries actually have the capacity to do so. These include the 'recent globalizers' – such as Argentina, Brazil, Costa Rica, India, Mexico and Thailand – and other economies with low protection that integrated into the system earlier, such as Chile, Hong Kong, Korea, Singapore and a number of others.

To what extent have the policies of the developed countries caused the uneven performance of the developing countries? Chapter 6 showed that developed countries have liberalized their trade regimes, but that their regimes are on the whole more closed to developing-country exports of goods and services than they are to the products and services of other developed countries. On average their tariffs are higher for products from developing countries; their remaining non-tariff barriers are concentrated in agriculture and textiles and clothing, which are products of primary interest to developing countries; and their use of trade remedies, especially antidumping actions, is skewed against developing countries.

But on the whole there is little evidence that this protection is particularly skewed against the low-income developing countries and the LDCs. Indeed the developed countries' use of protective measures against LDC products is much less than for developing countries as a whole. With the major exception of sugar, protection and export subsidies in agriculture focus on cereals and temperate-climate foodstuffs exported by the Cairns group – whose developing-country members are mostly middle-income countries – rather than the tropical foodstuffs exported by the LDCs and other low-income countries; although their export subsidies may undermine the achievement of efficient agricultural production in low-income countries as well. Developed-country antidumping actions have focused almost exclusively on developing countries other than the LDCs. It is only in the area of textiles that the existing quota arrangements tend to favour the more established, usually higher-income developing-country exporters and discriminate against lower-cost producers in low-income countries. But the main reason why developed-country policies towards the LDCs tend to be more liberal than those towards other developing countries is primarily that the production and export potential of LDCs is so small that it poses little threat to developed-country producers.

Thus the explanation of the uneven performance of developing countries must lie mainly in the institutional weaknesses and policy deficiencies of the developing countries themselves – although trade liberalization by developed countries would undoubtedly contribute to the welfare of all countries, including their own. But it is the more advanced and higher-income developing countries with stronger institutional and human capacities that have been able to take advantage of the opportunities offered by the more liberal international trade environment.

There is a never-ending debate on whether liberal trade policy is a cause or an effect of growth and sustainable development. While the bulk of evidence tends to support the proposition that liberal trade policies tend to be associated with long-term growth in income and output, there is extensive evidence that liberal trade policies alone are certainly not a sufficient condition for such growth. Thus the finding in Chapters 4 and 5 that low-income countries tend to have higher protection and weaker institutions should not lead to the naïve conclusion that if these countries liberalize their trade regimes they will automatically embark on a path of long-term growth. Indeed, in-depth country analyses of the issue have shown that for a liberal trade policy to be successful it has to be complemented by a variety of other policies at both the macro and the micro level, for example to improve the operation of factor and product markets.

On the other hand there is little evidence that sustainable growth can be stimulated by creating disincentives to export. A number of successful market integrators, for example Korea and most certainly India, have maintained protection, in some cases at rather substantial levels. But they have offset the disincentives created by protection by measures – for example tariff rebates, and in earlier days, export subsidies – that minimize the cost of protection on their exporters. For such a strategy to be effective, however, it is necessary to develop the institutional capacity to implement the required policies. There is evidence that countries in Africa that do not have the capacity to implement such policies have penalized their exporters, and held back their participation in international trade.

Thus we come back to the development of institutional capacity as the *sine qua non* both for developing-country integration into the international trading system and for grasping the opportunities and reaping the benefits that such a system can provide. Institutions are of course important for development in general. But here we are talking about trade-related institutional capacity, including the following:

- The capacity to design and implement trade policy and to represent the country's interests effectively in international fora such as the WTO.
- Trade-related human and physical infrastructure that affects the capacity to export.
- Supporting institutions to maintain quality standards and provide finance, insurance and marketing for exports.
- Appropriate safety nets to ensure that trade reforms that may benefit the country as a whole do not worsen the plight of the poor.

The experience of developing countries since the early 1980s shows that progress is possible. But without a concerted effort by the international community, progress in the twenty-first century will at best continue to be uneven, and at worst may be reversed. The very fact of continued polarization will give rise to further clamour for globalization to be arrested and for developing countries to be shielded from international trade. This could in turn lead to a reversal of the liberalization process, which may indeed result in a more even pattern of benefits but at the cost of a lower level of welfare for everybody.

A concerted effort will require action by the developing countries themselves, as well as the developed countries and the international institutions that support development. The focus of the effort should be not on all the developing countries, but primarily on those that need help to achieve more effective integration into the international economy. The main recommendations of this volume, presented in detail in the chapters above and summarized below, are limited to measures involving trade policies and trade-related assistance. A variety of other policies, for example on international finance, are also needed to promote a more equitable international economic order, but these have not been discussed.

Developing-country actions

Trade policies

Developing countries, especially the low-income and least developed ones, need to examine the suitability of their trade policies that affect both exports and imports of goods and services in the context of their overall development strategies. Where restrictive policies can be shown to be detrimental to long-term growth and poverty alleviation, a strategy for liberalization should be developed. An important part of developing such a strategy should be analyzing the possible effects of liberalization on the poor, and identifying other policies that need to be introduced in order to ensure that the effects of the liberalization are positive and lasting. Implementation of the strategy should take into account the possibility of binding liberalization commitments during a future WTO Round of multilateral negotiations, and of an exchange of commitments with developed countries to improve market access in products and services of interest to both sets of countries.

Opportunities for such mutually beneficial liberalization are available in the area of tariffs on manufactures as well as in agriculture and services. In agriculture, attention needs to focus on obtaining developed-country commitments to reduce export subsidies and on establishing rules that will permit continued developing-country support for the rural poor. In services, individual countries' liberalization efforts need to focus on sectors in which international supply factors offer the potential for a significant reduction of the cost of inputs, especially those which are necessary to export competitiveness; while developed-country commitments should be sought in modes of supply such as physical presence and in sectors such as maritime services, whose liberalization would make an important contribution to developing-country growth.

The TRIPS agreement has the potential to damage the interests of developing countries, especially the low-income countries and LDCs. Careful consideration needs to be given to modifying the agreement in a way that will increase the dissemination of knowledge and technology to low-income countries and LDCs; as well as to provisions that will allow them to benefit from the indigenous knowledge they possess.

Policy coordination within countries is needed to ensure consistency and coherence between the various policies that affect international trade, especially those which involve the wide-ranging commitments under the WTO. Coordination is also important among like-minded countries in the WTO. Regional groupings sometimes offer opportunities for such coordination; on other issues coordination needs to be pursued with developing countries in other regions and/or like-minded developed countries.

Trade-related institutions

The strengthening of trade-related institutional capacity should be given high priority in countries' development strategies as this is essential to effective integration into the international trading system. In this connection the establishment or strengthening of regional institutions may be of particular importance to smaller developing countries.

Assistance in strengthening trade-related capacity and institutions should be sought from international donors. In particular early action, in advance of any new WTO negotiations, is needed to implement an effective programme of technical assistance to the LDCs and other low-income countries. Developing countries should undertake no future commitments in the context of the WTO unless they have the institutional capacity to implement them, or unless they obtain legally enforceable promises that the assistance needed for their implementation will be forthcoming.

The existing transition periods for WTO commitments need to be carefully examined, and, where appropriate, action should be taken to seek their extension, in cooperation with other like-minded countries. Future WTO commitments must be carefully evaluated to ensure that they can be implemented on a timely basis.

WTO accession

Developing countries must become members of the WTO, if only in order to influence the way the trading system is shaped in respect of their interests. For a variety of reasons, the process of WTO accession has been and is likely to continue to be lengthy, complex and challenging for all countries, especially LDCs. Nevertheless there are a number of steps that the governments of acceding countries could take to facilitate and expedite accession:

- Establish a central coordination point to provide direction and manage the multiplicity of legislative and regulatory changes that are necessary for accession.
- Adopt relatively liberal trade policies, because such policies will both contribute to their effective integration into the international economy and facilitate WTO entry.
- Identify all aspects of the WTO agreements that will be affected by weaknesses in institutional infrastructure, seek technical assistance to help remedy the situation, and if necessary press for suitable delays in the implementation of the agreements as part of the accession process.

Strategy issues

Developing countries should be prepared to engage in a new Round of multilateral trade negotiations under the auspices of the WTO. As noted above, there should be three preconditions for the Round: agreement on a programme of technical assistance for capacity building in LDCs; reconsideration of the transition periods for implementation of the developing countries' institutional commitments under the Uruguay Round agreements; and liberalization of market access to LDCs, an important symbolic gesture. The negotiations in the new Round should involve a single undertaking that is limited to a small number of topics – these should be consistent with the developing countries' interests and their ability to implement future commitments.

While the interests of different groups of countries will differ, there are a number of important issues beyond the agreed topics of agriculture and services that developing countries as a group may wish to include in a new round. These are industrial tariffs and TRIPS. It may also be advantageous for environmental issues to be included, provided appropriate assurance can be obtained on the provision of institutional support to enable developing countries to meet their commitments. Other topics should be resisted because they are either counterproductive, premature or do not hold the promise of net benefits for large groups of developing countries.

The new Round should be a single undertaking in order to maximize the opportunities for trade-offs across issues and for political economy reasons, such as to permit liberalizing forces in both developed and developing countries to exert pressure on governments for a more liberal trading environment world-wide. But the Round should not contain too many issues, as doing so would strain the institutional and implementation capacity of many developing countries.

Developing countries should be prepared to exchange mutually liberalizing trade concessions, because that is the only way to maximize the benefits they can obtain from multilateral trade negotiations. Their focus in respect of special and differential treatment should be on the establishment of realistic transition periods and technical assistance to address institutional capacity constraints. The main exceptions to the above should be in agriculture. The most advanced developing countries, based on income level and share of world trade, should not be eligible for special and differential treatment. A look at the list of 15–20 countries that can be judged to have effectively integrated into the system (see Chapter 8) is a good starting point for discussions on which countries should be graduated, and hence be ineligible for special treatment.

Developed-country actions

The main thrust of future developed-country actions should be to increase coherence between their development and trade policies. As it is, developed countries devote significant resources to support development but then undermine the development efforts by implementing trade policies that damage the developing countries' interests as well as their own. In agriculture, developed-country consumers, and taxpayers, pay huge amounts to benefit a small group of domestic producers and support such elusive concepts as 'multifunctionality': they pay through higher prices for agricultural products consumed domestically; they pay through the budgetary support provided to agriculture; and they pay through the assistance they provide to developing countries to help the latter's agriculture. The agreement on textiles and clothing has resulted in developed-country consumers, usually the poorest segments of the population, paying higher prices for imports from developing countries. The main beneficiaries are developed and medium- to higher-income developing-country producers, which split the rents resulting from the quotas through which the system is administered.

The Uruguay Round made an important start in dealing with these issues. But over the next few years it will be vital to ensure that the textiles and clothing trade of developed countries is truly liberalized and that the huge distortions still characterizing their agricultural trade are progressively eliminated.

Making progress in these areas is of the highest priority for the global development agenda. It will require a very different approach from developed-country trade policy making: one in which development ministries and agencies are given a much greater role than has been the case in the past. It will also require a different approach in dealing with preferential arrangements. Special and differential treatment should be extended more on the basis of objective development criteria based on need, and less on the basis of rewarding political friends and punishing political enemies.

TRIPS raises some very special and thorny questions. IPRs are vital to long-term economic development based on private initiative and markets. But the TRIPS agreement has created problems in several areas, such as preventing access to cheap drugs to treat AIDS victims, arguably the most important issue in Sub-Saharan Africa; and preventing the protection of traditional knowledge.

The other side of the coherence issue, of course, has to do with strengthening the trade-related capacity of developing countries. This has many dimensions: the establishment of effective bilateral and multilateral assistance programmes, including the Integrated Framework for assistance to the LDCs; the linking of future developing-country commitments in the WTO to explicit developed-country assistance commitments; strengthening the technical cooperation role of the WTO and UNCTAD; and the linking of assistance initiatives, such as those extended to the HIPCs, to trade initiatives that affect poor countries.

Developed-country WTO members can also take steps to help expedite the accession process. Such steps are predicated on the assumption that it is in the interest of WTO members for the organization to achieve universal membership sooner rather than later, as they will benefit from the adherence of all countries to the rules and provisions of the WTO. In this connection the WTO members should be prepared to agree to suitable extensions of the time allowed to meet WTO obligations. If such extensions are not offered, either the negotiations will stall or acceding countries will end up accepting obligations they cannot implement. Developed countries should also continue to help non-WTO developing and transitional countries to strengthen their institutional capacity so that they will be better able to meet the requirements for WTO accession.

Priorities for international institutions

There are many international institutions whose programmes and policies affect developing countries' integration into the international trading system. The six institutions cooperating for the provision of assistance to the LDCs are very different. Some – such as the WTO and the ITC – focus exclusively on trade. Others – such as the World Bank and the UNDP – have a broad development focus within which trade-related activities play a small part. UNCTAD focuses on trade and development at the policy/ analysis level but has few programme resources of its own. The IMF is not a development institution as such, but its programmes and activities, of which trade is a small part, have increasingly focused on developing countries. And there are other international institutions – such as the regional development banks, the regional UN commissions, the South Center, the AITIC and the Advisory Center – that are also involved in various aspects of trade and development. What should be the future priorities for these institutions when helping developing countries to integrate more effectively into the world trading system?

The above analysis has focused on a few of these institutions, in particular the WTO, the World Bank and UNCTAD, because each of these institutions has a unique and vital role to play in the future integration of developing countries into the trading system.

The WTO's role is vital because it is the international institution within which the rules for the conduct of international trade are administered and where the agreements for trade liberalization are concluded. In broad terms, the main changes the WTO needs to make are to its internal budget priorities and the ways in which it conducts its business. Both of these need to reflect the fact that developing countries form the bulk of its membership. With regard to the budget, there is a need to increase very substantially the budgetary allocation for technical cooperation to assist low-income countries and LDCs to implement their WTO commitments, and to help them with the accession process. In addition the WTO needs to enhance the flow of information to developing-country members so that they will be better able to make decisions and protect their interests. A small step in this direction would be to ensure that documentation is available in all languages and on a timely basis, so as to ensure that non-anglophone developing countries are not disadvantaged. Finally, with regard to procedures it is important to develop ways to ensure transparency and participation by all members, as without it there can be no ownership of the organization and its policies by its members.

While playing a smaller role than in the 1960s and 1970s, as a political forum UNCTAD has an important role to play on two fronts: analyzing trade policy issues from a development perspective and using the analyses to support developing-country positions in multilateral trade negotiations; and providing technical assistance in a number of trade-related areas. To play such a role, the main constraint that needs to be addressed is its budget, and through it the quality and quantity of its staff. As in the case of the WTO, budgetary increases depend very much on action by the developed-country members, who hold the purse strings in both institutions.

The World Bank has a unique role to play because it is the only international institution that combines research and analytical capabilities in all aspects of trade policy issues, and has the capacity to provide very substantial technical and financial assistance to developing countries. It allowed both its research and analysis capability and its trade-related project and programme interventions to diminish very substantially in the 1990s, for a couple of reasons: it felt, erroneously, that its job of supporting trade policy reform had been accomplished; and it considered that trade-related capacity-building projects did not contribute to its main objective, which was to help developing countries alleviate poverty.

Its main priorities should be as follows. First, it should focus its analysis and research on issues of trade and poverty as well as on the aspects of developed-country policy coherence that have a bearing on developing-country trade and growth. Second, it should initiate a large number of trade-related capacity-building projects and programmes in the context of poverty-alleviation strategies and programmes elaborated by low-income countries. Finally, it should play an active role in coordinating trade-related assistance activities in low-income developing countries through the new Poverty Reduction Strategy Papers prepared by the individual countries. But only if the developing countries take the lead and develop their own strategies, as well as gain ownership of the assistance programmes that support these strategies, will there be any chance of these programmes succeeding.

While the role of the above three agencies is vital, the bilateral and other assistance agencies noted earlier should obviously continue or, if appropriate, increase their involvement in trade-related analysis and assistance to developing countries. Geneva-based institutions such as ITC, the AITIC and the Advisory Center can play a key role in strengthening the participation of developing countries in the WTO, and they deserve additional developed-country support. The progress made to date by many developing countries is reassuring. But the challenges currently confronting the low-income and least developed countries are daunting, and a coordinated effort by the international community and all its institutions is required if a more equitable international economic order is to be established.

Appendix 1: Country Groupings

As noted in Chapter 2, the major international organizations have no formal definition of 'developing country'. For statistical purposes the World Bank uses a per capita income grouping that does not distinguish between developed and developing countries, and this is used to some extent in this analysis. The WTO has no official breakdown of developed versus developing countries. For operational purposes the designation of 'developing country' is based on the principle of self-selection. The breakdown between developed and developing countries used in this analysis roughly follows the breakdown used by the WTO for statistical purposes – with a few changes, to be noted below.

In our analysis, developed countries include all members of the European Union, the four EFTA countries (Lichtenstein, Iceland, Norway and Switzerland), Australia, Canada, Japan, New Zealand and the US. This is pretty close to the WTO definition with the exception of South Africa, which the WTO classifies as developed but which we include in the developing-country group. There are no separate trade data for Lichtenstein, so our analysis only uses data on the trade in goods and services of the countries listed above, and excludes intra-EU trade.

Transition economies are the 15 economies that emerged from the former Soviet Union (FSU), plus the nine countries in Eastern Europe and the Balkans for which consistent data series are available (Albania, Bulgaria, Croatia, the Czech Republic, Hungary, Poland, Romania, the Slovak Republic and Slovenia), plus Mongolia, making a total of 25. Data on services are not available for the FSU for the whole period, thus the transition total for services excludes these countries.

All remaining countries and territories are designated as developing. For merchandise trade, the analysis uses data for 135 countries: 47 in Sub-Saharan Africa, 33 in Asia, 34 in Latin America and the Caribbean and 21 in the Middle East and Mediterranean. The latter region includes the five North African countries (Morocco, Algeria, Tunisia, Libya and Egypt) and stretches to the east to include Iraq and Iran (but not Afghanistan, which is in Asia). It also includes Israel, Turkey, Cyprus and Malta. Far less service data are available for developing countries. In this case our analysis uses information for 84 countries; 22 in Sub-Saharan Africa, 25 in Latin America and the Caribbean, 23 in Asia and 14 in the Middle East and Mediterranean.

OPEC consists of 11 members: Algeria, Libya, Nigeria, Indonesia, Iran, Iraq, Venezuela, Kuwait, Qatar, Saudi Arabia and the United Arab Emirates.

The income-level analysis uses the same definition for developed countries as above. Developing and transition economies are grouped into five categories based on the World Bank definition of groupings and per capita income for 1998, except that the LDCs are the 49 countries on the UN list, and are shown as a separate category. As Senegal was added to the LDC list after our analyis had been completed, the LDC totals are based on the other 48 countries. Senegal is included in the low-income countries. Low-income countries are those with a per capita income of less than $760 (except the least developed); lower-middle-income countries have a per capita income of $760–3030, upper-middle-income $3030–9360 and high income $9361 plus.

Data on merchandise trade are available for LDCs all except Eritrea, but information on services is available for far fewer countries – just 22. Similarly the low-income group includes 23 countries for merchandise trade but only 12 for services. The number of developing countries in the other groups are as follows: lower-middle income – 44 for merchandise trade and 29 for services; upper-middle-income – 31 and 22 respectively; and high income – 15 and 9 respectively.

Table A1.1 TPR country coverage

	GATT TPR	WTO TPR
Argentina	1992	1999
Bangladesh	1992	–
Benin	–	1998
Brazil	1993	1997
Bolivia	1993	–
Cameroon	1995	–
Chile	1991	1997
Colombia	1990	1997
Costa Rica	–	1995
Côte d'Ivoire	–	1995
Cyprus	–	1997
Dominican Republic	–	1996
Egypt	1993	–
El Salvador	–	1996
Fiji	–	1997
Ghana	1992	–
Hong Kong, China	1990	1994, 1999
India	1993	1998
Indonesia	1991	1994, 1999
Kenya	1994	–
Korea	1992	1996
Malaysia	1993	1998
Mauritius	–	1996
Mexico	1993	1998
Morocco	1990	1996
Nigeria	1991	1999
Pakistan	1995	–
Paraguay	–	1997
Peru	1994	–
Philippines	1993	–
Senegal	1994	–
Singapore	1992	1996
S. Africa/SACU	1993	1999
Sri Lanka	–	1995
Thailand	1991	1995
Tunisia	1994	–
Turkey	1994	1999
Uganda	–	1995
Uruguay	1992	1999
Venezuela	–	1996
Zambia	–	1996
Zimbabwe	1995	–

Note: The year refers to the date when the trade policy review was published, not the year when the review was undertaken. In the cases of Cameroon, Pakistan and Zimbabwe, the 1994 GATT reviews were published in 1995.
Sources: GATT, TPRs (1989–94); WTO, TPRs (1995–99).

Appendix 2: Method of Estimating Frequency Ratios

The TPR data enabled us to estimate frequencies in the application of non-tariff measures at the harmonized system (HS) two-digit level for 97 product categories. Thus the frequency ratios (f) calculated from the TPRs relate to the proportion of HS2 product categories out of the total affected by a particular measure. The weakness of this indicator is that it gives equal weight to the presence of a measure in a country that could affect only one or a few lines in an HS2 category, for example HS72 (iron and steel), while the presence of the same measure in another country might affect a large number of tariff lines, for example all steel products.

Formally, let N_{qm} be a non-tariff measure imposed by country m on a product or group of products q. The frequency ratio for that measure, $f_{nm} = \Sigma N_{qm} / \Sigma Q_m$ where Q_m is the total number of products, measured in total tariff lines or product groups. Thus for the calculation of f, using the HS2 product breakdown employed in most of the analysis, $Q_m = 97$. Where tariff line information was available, for example in the case of antidumping measures, for the calculation of f' a standard HS six-digit tariff line classification of approximately 5200 lines was used.

It may appear at first glance that f will always be larger than f'. This is not the case, however. The two different frequency ratios show different aspects of a country's trade regime: if a specific non-tariff measure involves a large number of tariff lines concentrated in one or two groups of products, f may be smaller than f'; the reverse will be the case if a particular measure applies to a few products in a large number of groups. A simple example from one of the countries – Thailand, for which tariff line and broader category measures are available for the same year – can be used to illustrate this point. In 1997 Thailand applied non-automatic licensing on a total of 25 product categories, involving 713 tariff lines. In this case $f = 26$ per cent while $f' = 14$ per cent. In the same year, Thailand's prohibitions were concentrated in six product categories involving 613 tariff lines. In this case $f = 6$ per cent and $f' = 12$ per cent.

An effort was made to complement the TPR analysis of non-tariff measures with data obtained from the UNCTAD TRAINS data base, which permits the calculation of frequency ratios (f') at the tariff line level. The TRAINS data are available for a fewer number of countries (22), and only in six cases was information available for the same country over a period of time. The f' ratios for similar non-tariff measures as those calculated from the TPRs but based on tariff line data from TRAINS are shown in Table A2.1. A comparison with Table 4.8 suggests that there is a pretty good correlation between the frequency ratios in countries that apply non-tariff measures on just a few products and those that apply them on a very large number of products, but there appears to be little correlation between the two frequency measures for countries in between.

On the other hand, when looking at the evolution of frequency ratios over time, the frequency ratios for Chile, Colombia and Thailand increased between the first period and the second, but using the TPR information they declined for the same countries. On closer investigation it appears that the reason for the increase was the introduction in all three countries of licensing and/or a prohibition on the importation of products that were either hazardous (radioactive materials and the like) and/or protected under environmental conventions (tropical wood and articles thereof); and there is no record in the TPRs of any changes to the commercial policy of the countries involved that would have affected these products. While an effort was made to exclude from consideration (using the TPRs) all products on which licensing and prohibitions were imposed for safety and environmental reasons, it was not possible to check all the TRAINS data in order to determine the extent to which they included restrictions for this purpose. As a consequence the TRAINS data cannot be readily compared with the data obtained from the TPRs, and were used only for general reference purposes and for the non-tariff measure estimates at the HS-2 level for India, as the information contained in the TPR for India was inadequate for that purpose.

Finally, it should be noted that the frequency ratios employed assume that the measure taken applied to all transactions involving the tariff line or product group and was not limited to transactions with one country or group of countries. This is not a major weakness in the set of measures being considered because, unlike most trade remedies (antidumping, countervailing duties), the measures included here were almost always applied to imports from all sources. There were a few exceptions. For example Korea applied tariff quotas on certain items only against imports from Japan, as did Cyprus against the EU. The measures applied by these countries were included in the calculated frequencies, as at the time they affected trade with a major partner. On the other hand several countries imposed total embargoes on imports from certain countries for political reasons, for example a number of Arab states against Israel. These embargoes were ignored in the calculations.

Table A2.1 Non-tariff measures in developing countries, 1989–97 (frequencies in per cent of total tariff lines for each measure)

	Non-automatic licensing		Prohibitions		Quotas		Foreign exchange restraints		Import monitoring		Administered pricing	
	1989–94	1995–97	1989–94	1995–97	1989–94	1995–97	1989–94	1995–97	1989–94	1995–97	1989–94	1995–97
Argentina	5.6	N/a	1.7	N/a	0.5	N/a	–	N/a	0.3	N/a	0.1	N/a
Bangladesh	3.7	N/a	7.6	N/a	–	N/a	–	N/a	–	N/a	–	N/a
Brazil	8.1	N/a	2.6	N/a	–	N/a	–	N/a	–	N/a	1.3	N/a
Cameroon	1.0	N/a	0.3	N/a	–	N/a	–	N/a	–	N/a	–	N/a
Chile	10.1	10.3	0.9	2.6	–	–	–	–	–	–	0.5	0.8
Colombia	3.0	8.4	–	0.9	0.0	–	–	–	–	–	–	5.4
Hong Kong, China	4.8	4.8	–	–	0.4	0.4	–	–	16.0	16.0	6.4	6.4
India	75.1	44.6	2.1	3.7	–	–	–	–	–	–	–	–
Indonesia	13.9	3.0	0.6	0.5	2.0	–	–	–	–	–	–	–
Malaysia	13.8	N/a	2.5	N/a	–	N/a	–	N/a	–	N/a	–	N/a
Mexico	11.5	N/a	4.3	N/a	0.5	N/a	–	N/a	–	N/a	–	N/a
Morocco	N/a	14.1	N/a	1.0	N/a	–	N/a	–	N/a	–	N/a	9.3
Philippines	33.0	N/a	2.7	N/a	1.9	N/a	23.0	N/a	–	N/a	–	N/a
South Africa	–	N/a	–	N/a	–	N/a	–	N/a	–	N/a	32.6	N/a
Sri Lanka	N/a	4.0	N/a	–	N/a	–	N/a	–	N/a	–	N/a	–
Thailand	19.3	14.2	6.5	12.2	–	–	–	–	–	2.8	–	–
Tunisia	5.6	N/a	–	N/a	–	N/a	–	N/a	–	N/a	5.9	N/a
Uruguay	16.1	N/a	1.6	N/a	–	N/a	–	N/a	–	N/a	–	N/a

Note: N/a = not available.
Source: UNCTAD.

References

Balassa, B. and C. Michalopoulos (1986) 'Liberalizing Trade Between Developed and Developing Countries', *Journal of World Trade Law'*, 20 (1).

Bhagwati, J. (1978) *Anatomy and Consequences of Exchange Control Regimes* (New York: National Bureau of Economic Research).

—— and T. N. Srinivasan (1996) 'Trade and the Environment: Does Environmental Diversity Detract from the Case from Free Trade?', in J. Bhagwati and R. Hudec (eds), *Fair Trade and Harmonization* (Cambridge, Mass: MIT Press).

—— and —— (1999) 'Outward Orientation and Development: Are Revisionists Right?', *Center Discussion Paper* no. 806 (New Haven, CT: Economic Growth Center, Yale University).

Binswanger, H. and E. Lutz (2000) 'Agricultural Trade Barriers, Trade Negotiations and the Interests of Developing Countries' (Bangkok: UNCTAD).

Blackhurst, R. (1997) 'The WTO and the Global Economy', *World Economy*, 20, 527–44.

—— (1998) 'The Capacity of the WTO to Fulfill its Mandate', in A. O. Krueger (ed.), *The WTO as an International Organization* (Chicago, Ill.: University of Chicago Press).

Braga, C. A. (1996) 'Trade-Related Intellectual Property Rights: The Uruguay Round Agreement and its Economic Implications', in W. Martin and L. A. Winters (eds), *The Uruguay Round and the Developing Countries* (Cambridge: Cambridge University Press).

——, C. Fink and C. P. Sepulveda (1999) 'Intellectual Property Rights and Development', *TechNet Working Paper* (Washington, DC: World Bank).

Chaytor, B. and M. Hindley (1997) *A Case Study of Sierra Leone's Participation in The World Trade Organization* (London: Cameron).

Correa, C. M. (1998) *Implementing the TRIPS Agreement* (Penang: Third World Network).

—— (1999) 'Review of the TRIPS Agreement', *Journal of World Intellectual Property* 2, 939–60.

Croft, A. (1997) 'EU Body Seeks New Russia, China Dumping Policy' (Brussels: Reuters, 16 December).

Croome, J. (1995) *Reshaping the World Trade System* (Geneva: WTO).

—— (1998) 'The Present Outlook for Trade Negotiations in the World Trade Organization', *Policy Research Working Paper*, no. 1992 (Washington, DC: World Bank).

Daly, M. and H. Kuwahara (1998) 'The Impact of the Uruguay Round on Tariff and Non-Tariff Barriers to Trade in the "Quad"', *The World Economy*, 21, 207–34.

Das, B. L. (1998a) 'Proposals for Improvement in the Agreement on TRIPS', *SEATINI Bulletin*, 1 (8).

—— (1998b) *The WTO Agreements: Deficiencies, Imbalances and Required Changes* (Penang: Third World Network).

Deardorff, A. V. (1990) 'Should Patent Protection Be Extended to All Developing Countries', *The World Economy*, 13, 497–508.

—— (1992) 'Welfare Effects of Global Patent Protection', *Economica*, 59, 35–51.

Dollar, D. (1992) 'Outward-Oriented Developing Countries Really Do Grow More Rapidly: Evidence from 95 LDCs, 1976–1985', *Economic Development and Cultural Change*, 40, 523–44.

—— and A. Kraay (2001) 'Trade, Growth and Poverty', paper presented at the World Bank-EU Conference on Trade and Poverty, Brussels, 6 March.

Dornbusch, R. (1992) 'The Case for Trade Liberalization in Developing Countries', *Journal of Economic Perspectives*, 6 (1).

Drabek, Z. and S. Laird (1998) 'The New Liberalism: Trade Policy Developments in Emerging Markets', *Journal of World Trade*, 5 (3).

Duran, E. and C. Michalopoulos (1999) 'Intellectual Property Rights and Developing Countries in the WTO Millennium Round', *Journal of World Intellectual Property*, 2 (6).

Edwards, S. (1993) 'Openness, Trade Liberalization and Growth in Developing Countries', *Journal of Economic Literature*, 31, 1358–93.

European Commission (2000) 'Proposal for Directives #2000/01/58; #2000/01/59 On Waste Electrical and Electronic Equipment, and on the Use of Hazardous Substances in Electric and Electronic Equipment' (Brussels: European Commission).

—— (2001) 'Everything But Arms' (Brussels: European Commission, 28 February).

EUROSTEP (1999) 'Eurostep Dossier on CAP and Coherence' (Brussels/The Hague: EUROSTEP, April).

Evans, J. (1968) 'The General Agreement on Tariffs and Trade', *International Organization*, XXII, 72–98.

Evenett, S. and B. Hoekman (1999) 'Government Procurement: Do Border Barriers Matter?', Center for Economic Policy Research (CEPR) Workshop, London, 19–20 February.

FAO/AITIC (1998) 'The Relationship between the FAO International Undertaking on Plant Genetic Resources, the Convention on Biological Diversity and TRIPS', Uruguay Round Agreements – Implications for Agriculture, Forestry and Fisheries in the Less-Advantaged Countries (Geneva: AITIC).

Finger, J. M. (1993) *Anti-dumping: How It Works and Who Gets Hurt* (Ann Arbor: Michigan University Press).

—— and M. Ingco (1996) *The Uruguay Round: Statistics on Tariff Concessions Given and Received* (Washington, DC: World Bank).

——, W. Reincke and A. Castro (1999) 'Market Access Bargaining in the Uruguay Round: Rigid or Relaxed Reciprocity', Policy Research Working Paper no. 2258 (Washington, DC: World Bank).

—— and L. A. Winters (1998) 'What Can the WTO Do for Developing Countries', in A. O. Krueger (ed.), *The WTO as an International Organization* (Chicago, Ill.: University of Chicago Press).

—— and L. Schuknecht (1999) 'Market Access Advances and Retreats Since the Uruguay Round', Policy Research Working Paper no. 2232 (Washington, DC: World Bank).

—— and P. Schuler (2000) 'The Implementation of Uruguay Round Commitments: The Development Challenge', Policy Research Working Paper no. 2215 (Washington, DC: World Bank).

Fisch, G. and B. Speyer (1995) 'TRIPS as an Adjustment Mechanism in North–South Trade, *Intereconomics*, March/April, 65–9.

Francois, J. and I. Wooton (1999) 'Trade in International Transport Services: the Role of Competition', mimeo, Erasmus University, Rotterdam, August.

Frankel, J. and D. Romer (1999) 'Does Trade Cause Growth?', *American Economic Review*, 89 (3).

Gabunia, G. (1998) 'Reasonable Protectionism', *Expert* (Russia), 33 (September).

GATT (1948) *Preamble to the Establishment of GATT.*

—— (1954) *Basic Instruments and Documents (BISD)* 3rd supplement.

—— (1955) *Report of the Review Working Party on Quantitative Restrictions*, L/332/Rev.

—— (1958) *Trends in International Trade* (Geneva: GATT).

—— (1964) *BISD*, 12th supplement.

—— (1972) *BISD*, 18th supplement.

—— (1979) *The Tokyo Round of Multilateral Trade Negotiations*, Report of the Director General (Geneva: GATT).

—— (1980) *BISD*, 26th supplement.

—— (1982) *Directory* (Geneva: GATT).

—— (1987) *Directory* (Geneva: GATT).

—— (1989–94) *Trade Policy Review* for 29 developing countries, various years, (Geneva: GATT – for details see Appendix A).

—— (1994) 'Measures to Deal with Members in Category IV of the Administrative Arrangements on Arrears', PC/7, L/7578, December.

—— (1995) 'A Description of the Provisions Relating to Developing Countries in The Uruguay Round Agreements, Legal Instruments and Ministerial Decisions', COMTD/510.

Harrison, G., T. F. Rutherford and D. G. Tarr (1996) 'Quantifying the Uruguay Round', in W. Martin and L. A. Winters (eds), *The Uruguay Round and the Developing Countries* (Washington, DC: World Bank).

Herfkens, E. (2000) 'Free Trade: Far from an Everyday Reality', in *From Havana to Seattle and Beyond: The Quest for Free Trade and Free Markets* (The Hague: SDU Publishers).

Hertel, T. and W. Martin (1999) 'Developing Countries Interests in Liberalizing Manufactures Trade', CEPR Workshop, London, 19–20 February.

Hoekman, B. (1996) 'Assessing the General Agreement on Trade in Services', in W. Martin and L. A. Winters (eds), *The Uruguay Round and the Developing Countries* (Washington, DC: World Bank).

—— and P. Holmes (1999) 'Competition Policy, Developing Countries and The WTO', Policy Research Working Paper no. 2211 (Washington, DC: World Bank).

—— and K. Saggi (1999) 'Multilateral Disciplines for Investment-Related Policies?', paper presented at the Conference on Global Regionalism, Instituto Affari Internazionali, Rome, 8–9 February.

Hudec, R. E. (1987) *Developing Countries in the GATT Legal System* (Hampshire: Gower).

Inside US Trade (1998) 28 August.

International Grains Council, Food Aid Committee (1999) *Food Aid Convention*, London, 24 March.

International Herald Tribune (2001) 'Drug-makers Drop AIDS Suit Against South Africa', 20 April.

International Task Force on Commodity Risk Management (ITF) (1999) 'A Proposal for a Market Based Approach' (Washington, DC: World Bank).

Jay, K. and C. Michalopoulos (1989) 'Donor Policies, Donor Interests and Aid Effectiveness', in A. O. Krueger, C. Michalopoulos and V. Ruttan, *Aid and Development* (Baltimore, MD: Johns Hopkins University Press).

Karsenty, G. and S. Laird (1987) 'The Generalized System of Preferences: A Quantitative Assessment of the Direct Trade Effects and of Policy Options', Discussion Paper no. 18 (Geneva: UNCTAD).

Keesing, D. B. (1998) *Improving Trade Policy Reviews in the World Trade Organization* (Washington, DC: Institute for International Economics).

Kemper, R. (1980) 'The Tokyo Round: Results and Implications for Developing Countries', Staff Working Paper no. 372 (Washington, DC: World Bank).

Kessie, E. (2000) 'Enforceability of the Legal Provisions Relating to Special and Differential Treatment under the WTO Agreements', paper presented at the WTO Seminar on Special and Differential Treatment of Developing Countries, Geneva, 7 March.

Krueger, A. O. (1974) 'The Political Economy of the Rent Seeking Society', *American Economic Review*, 64 (3).

—— (1978) *Liberalization Attempts and Consequences* (New York: National Bureau of Economic Research).

—— (1995) *Trade Policies and Developing Countries* (Washington, DC: Brookings Institution).

—— (1999) 'The Developing Countries and the Next Round of Multilateral Trade Negotiations', *The World Economy*, 22 (7).

—— and C. Michalopoulos (1985) 'Developing-country Trade Policies and the International Economic System', in E. Preeg (ed.), *Hard Bargaining Ahead: US Trade Policy and Developing Countries* (Washington, DC: Overseas Development Council).

——, M. Schiff and A. Valdes (1988) 'Agricultural Incentives in Developing Countries: Measuring the Effects of Sectoral and Economy-wide Policies', *World Bank Economic Review*, 2 (7).

Kwa, A. and W. Bello (1998) 'Guide to the Agreement in Agriculture', mimeo Chulalong University, Thailand.

Laird, S. (1999) 'Multilateral Approaches to Market Access Negotiations', in M. R. Mendoza, P. Low and B. Kotschwar (eds), *Trade Rules in the Making* (Washington, DC: Brookings Institution).

Lerner, A. (1936) 'The Symmetry between Import and Export Taxes', *Economica*, 3, 306–13.

Leutwiler, F. *et al.* (1985) *Trade Policies for a Better Future: Proposals for Action*, (Geneva: GATT).

Lindbland, J. (1997) 'The Impact of the Uruguay Round on Tariff Escalation in Agricultural Products', ESCP no. 3 (Rome: FAO).

Little, I., T. Scitovsky and M. Scott (1970) *Industry and Trade in Some Developing Countries* (London: Oxford University Press).

Low, P. (1995) 'Pre-shipment Inspection Services', *Discussion Paper* no. 278 (Washington, DC: World Bank).

—— and A. Subramanian (1996) 'Beyond TRIMS: A case for Multilateral Action on Investment Rules and Competition Policy', in W. Martin and L. A. Winters (eds), *The Uruguay Round and the Developing Countries* (Cambridge: Cambridge University Press).

Martin, W. and L. A. Winters (1996) 'The Uruguay Round: A Milestone for the Developing Countries', in W. Martin and L. A. Winters (eds), *The Uruguay Round and the Developing Countries* (Cambridge: Cambridge University Press).

Maskus, K. (2000) *Intellectual Property Rights in the Global Economy* (Washington, DC: Institute for International Economics).

Mattoo, A. (1998) 'Financial Services and the WTO', Policy Research Working Paper no. 2184 (Washington, DC: World Bank).
—— (1999) 'Developing Countries in the New Round of GATT Negotiations. From a Defensive to a Proactive Role', mimeo (Washington, DC: World Bank).
—— and Marcelo Olarreaga (1999) 'Should Credit be Given for Autonomous Liberalization in Multilateral Trade Negotiations', Policy Research Working Paper no. 2374 (Washington, DC: World Bank).
Matusz, S. J. and D. G. Tarr (1999) 'Adjusting to Trade Policy Reform', Policy Research Working Paper no. 2142 (Washington, DC: World Bank).
Michalopoulos, C. (1985) 'Non-Tariff Measures', *Trade and Development*, 6 (Washington, DC: Development Committee, World Bank).
—— (1998) 'The Participation of Developing Countries in the WTO', Policy Research Working Paper no. 1906 (Washington, DC: World Bank).
—— (1999a) 'Developing Countries in the WTO', *The World Economy*, 22 (1).
—— (1999b) 'Trade Policy and Market Access Issues for Developing Countries', Policy Research Working Paper, no. 2214 (Washington, DC: World Bank).
—— (1999c) 'Developing Country Strategies for the Millennium Round', *Journal of World Trade*, 33 (5).
—— (2000a) 'Special and Differential Treatment for Developing Countries in the GATT and the WTO', Policy Research Working Paper no. 2388 (Washington, DC: World Bank).
—— (2000b) 'The Integration of China into the World Trading System: Implications of WTO Accession', paper presented at the International Forum on China's Reform, Haiku, Hanan, 25–7 March.
—— and L. A. Winters (1997) 'Summary and Overview', in P. D. Ehrenhaft, B. V. Hindley, C. Michalopoulos and L. A. Winters, *Policies on Imports from Economies in Transition*, Studies of Economies in Transformation no. 22 (Washington, DC: World Bank).
Miranda, J., R. A. Torres and M. Ruiz (1998) 'The International Use of Antidumping: 1987–1997', *Journal of World Trade*, 32 (5).
Nogués, J. J. (1993) 'Social Costs and Benefits of Introducing Patent Protection for Pharmaceutical Drugs in Developing Countries', *The Developing Economies*, 31 (1).
—— (1998) 'The Linkages of The World Bank with the GATT/WTO', in A. O. Krueger (ed.), *The WTO as an International Organization* (Chicago, Ill.: University of Chicago Press).
——, A. Olechowski and L. A. Winters (1986) 'The Extent of Non-Tariff Barriers to Industrial Countries' Imports', *The World Bank Economic Review*, 1 (1).
OECD (1997) *Indicators of Tariff and Non-Tariff Barriers* (Paris: OECD).
—— (1998, 2000) *Outlook* (Paris: OECD).
—— (1999) 'Trade Measures in Multilateral Environmental Agreements: Synthesis Report of Three Case Studies', COM/END/TD(98) 127 FINAL (Paris: OECD).
Onguglo, B. P. (1999) 'Developing Countries and Trade Preferences', in M. R. Mendoza, P. Low and B. Kotschwar (eds), *Trade Rules in The Making* (Washington, DC: Brookings Institution).
Otsuki, T., M. Sewadeh and J. S. Wilson (2000) 'What Price Precaution? European Harmonization of Aflatoxin Regulations and African Food Exports', mimeo (Washington, DC: World Bank).
Oyejide, A. T. (1990) 'Africa and the Uruguay Round', *The World Economy* 13 (3).

Palmeter, D. N. (1998) 'The WTO Antidumping Agreement and the Economies in Transition', in T. Cottier and P. C. Mavroidis (eds), *State Trading in the Twenty First Century* (Ann Arbor: University of Michigan Press).

Panagariya, A. (2000) 'Preferential Trade Liberalization: The Traditional Theory and New Developments', *Journal of Economic Literature*, 38 (2).

Papageorgiou, D., M. Michaely and A. Choksi (1991) *Liberalizing Foreign Trade, Lessons of Experience in the Developing World*, vol. 7 (Washington, DC: World Bank).

Prebisch, R. (1950) *The Economic Development of Latin America and its Principal Problems* (Santiago: UN ECLA).

Rodriguez, F. and D. Rodrik (1999) 'Trade Policy and Economic Growth: A Sceptic's Guide to the Cross National Evidence', mimeo (University of Maryland, College Park).

Rodrik, D. (1992) 'The Limits of Trade Policy Reform in Developing Countries', *The Journal of Economic Perspectives*, 6 (1).

Sachs, J. D. (1999) 'Helping the World's Poorest', *The Economist*, 14 August.

—— and A. Warner (1995) 'Economic Reform and the Process of Global Integration', Brookings Papers on Economic Activity (Washington, DC: Brookings Institution).

Sapsford, D. and V. N. Balasubramanyam (1999) 'Trend and Volatility in the Net Barter Terms of Trade', *Journal of International Development*, 11 (6).

Shahin, M. (1997) *Trade and the Environment in the WTO: A Review of its Initial Work and Future Prospects* (Penang: Third World Network).

Singer, H. (1950) 'The Distribution of Gains between Investing and Borrowing Countries', *American Economic Review, Papers and Proceedings*, 11, 473–85.

Smeets, M. and C. Fournier (1998) *Trade and Tariffs in Leather and Leather Products* (Geneva: WTO).

South Center (1997) *The TRIPS Agreement: A Guide for the South* (Geneva: South Center).

Srinivasan, T. N. (1998) *Developing Countries and the Multilateral Trading System* (Oxford: Westview Press).

Stiglitz, J. E. (1999) 'Two Principles for the Next Round, Or How to Bring Developing Countries in from the Cold', Statement at WTO Seminar, 21 September.

Subramaniam, A. (1995) 'Trade-Related Intellectual Property Rights and Asian Developing Countries: An Analytical View', mimeo (Asian Development Bank) Manila.

Tansey, G. (1999) *Trade, Intellectual Property, Food and Bio-diversity* (London: Quaker Peace and Service).

Third World Network (1998) *Options for Implementing the TRIPS Agreement in Developing Countries* (Penang: Third World Network).

United Nations (1997) *Directory of Geneva Agencies* (Geneva: United Nations).

UNCTAD (1968) *The Kennedy Round. Estimated Effects on Trade Barriers* (Geneva: UNCTAD).

—— (1980) *Assessment of the Results of the Multilateral Trade Negotiations* (Geneva: UNCTAD).

—— (1997a) 'Post-Uruguay Round Tariff Environment for Developing Country Exports', UNCTAD/WTO Joint Study, TD/B/COM.1/14 (Geneva: UNCTAD, October).

—— (1997b) *The Uruguay Round and Its Follow-up: Building a Positive Development Agenda* (Geneva: United Nations).

—— (1998) *The Least Developed Countries 1998 Report* (Geneva: United Nations).

—— /WTO (1996) *Strengthening the Participation of Developing Countries in World Trade and the Multilateral Trading System*, TD/375 (Geneva: UNCTAD).

—— / —— (1997) *Market Access Developments since the Uruguay Round: Implications, Opportunities and Challenges, in Particular for Developing Countries, and Least Developed Countries, in the Context of Globalization and Liberalization* (Geneva: UNCTAD).

US Congress (1999) House Committee on Government Reform, Subcommittee on Criminal Justice, Drug Policy and Human Resources, testimony by J. Papovich, Assistant US Trade Representative, 22 July.

Whalley, J. (1987) *Dealing with the North: Developing Countries and the Global Trading System*, CSIER Research Monograph (London, Ontario: University of Western Ontario).

—— (1999) 'Special and Differential Treatment in the Millennium Round', *World Economy*, 22 (3).

Whichard, O. G. (1999) 'Measurement, Classification and Reporting of Services Activities: An International Perspective', mimeo (US Department of Agriculture), Washington, DC.

Winters, L. A. (2000a) 'Trade and Poverty: Is There a Connection?', in *Trade, Income Disparity and Poverty*, Special Studies (Geneva: WTO).

—— (2000b) 'Coherence with no "here": WTO co-operation with the World Bank and the IMF', paper presented at the CEPR/ECARES/World Bank Conference, Brussels, 14–15 July.

World Bank (1995) 'The Trade Co-operation Program with the Former Soviet Union', Project Completion Report, Operations Evaluation Department (Washington, DC: World Bank).

—— (1998) *World Development Report: Knowledge for Development* (Washington, DC: World Bank).

—— (1999) 'World Bank Support for Developing Countries on International Trade Issues', Development Committee, September (Washington, DC: World Bank).

—— (2000a) *World Development Indicators* (Washington, DC: World Bank).

—— (2000b) 'The Impact of Oil Prices on Developing Economies', PREM Economic Policy and DEC Prospects Group (Washington, DC: World Bank).

—— (2000c) *Trade Blocs* (Washington, DC: World Bank).

—— (2000d) *Global Economic Prospects* (Washington, DC: World Bank).

WTO (1995) *The Results of the Uruguay Round of Multilateral Trade Negotiations: The Legal Texts* (Geneva: WTO).

—— (1997a) 'Report of the Panel on India – Patent Protection for Pharmaceutical and Agricultural Chemical Products', WT/DS50/R, September.

—— (1997b) 'Market Access for Least Developed Countries', High Level Meeting on Integrated Initiatives for Least Developed Countries' Trade Development, WT/LDC/HL/14, November.

—— (1997c) 'Report on the Implementation of the Agreement on Textiles and Clothing', Textiles Monitoring Body, G/L/179, July.

—— (1997, 2000) *Directory* (Geneva: WTO).

—— (1997–99) 'Trade-Related Technical Assistance Needs Assessments', Committee on Trade and Development, WT/COMTD/IF/No. 1–42, various dates.

—— (1998a) 'Cairns Group Ministerial Meeting, Communique', WT/L/263, April.

—— (1998b) 'Declaration on Global Electronic Commerce', WT/MIN/(98)/DEC/2, May.

—— (1998c) 'Market Access for Exports of Goods and Services from the LDCs: Barriers and Constraints', WT/COMT/LDC/W/11/REV.1, December.

—— (1998d) 'Second Biennial Review of the Implementation and Operation of the Agreement on Import Licensing Procedures', Committee on Import Licensing, G/LIC/6, November.

—— (1998e) 'India – Patent Protection for Pharmaceutical and Agricultural Chemical Products', Report of the Panel, WT/DS79/R, August.

—— (1998f) 'Coherence', GC/13, October.

—— (1999a) 'Developing Countries and the Multilateral Trading System: Past and Present', Development Division, background document prepared for the High Level Symposium on Trade and Development, Geneva, 17–18 March.

—— (1999b) 'Special and Differential Treatment and the Spaces for Policies in the WTO', communication from Venezuela, WT/GC/W/279, July.

—— (1999c) 'EC Approach to Trade Related Aspects of Intellectual Property in the New Round', General Council WT/GC/W/193, June.

—— (1999d) 'Semi-Annual Reports under Article 16.4 of the Agreement', Committee on Anti-Dumping Practices, G/ADP/N/41 and N/47 Add.1. April.

—— (1999e) 'Report of the Working Party on Pre-shipment Inspection', G/L/300, March.

—— (1999f) 'Communication from Venezuela', General Council, WT/GC/W/282, August.

—— (1999g) 'Communication from Kenya on Behalf of the African Group', General Council, WT/GC/W/302, August.

—— (1999h) 'Work Programme on Electronic Commerce', S/C/8, March.

—— (1999i) 'Third Progress Report on the Follow-up to the High Level Meeting', Subcommittee on Least-Developed Countries, WT/COMTD/LDC/W/13, February.

—— (1999j) 'Technical Note on the Accession Process', WT/ACC/7, March.

—— (1999k) 'Communication from CEFTA and Latvia', General Council, WT/GC/W/275, July.

—— (1991l) SPS Review G/SPS/12, 11 March.

—— (2000a) 'Integrated Framework for Trade-Related Assistance to LDCs: The Process to Date, Concerns and Suggested Improvements', WT/COMTD/LDC/W/18.

—— (2000b) 'Implementation of Special and Differential Treatment Provisions in WTO Agreements and Decisions', WT/COMTD/W/77.

—— (2000c) 'Disputes Status Report', July.

—— (2000d) 'Developing Country Agricultural Negotiations Submission', G/AG/NG/G/13, June.

—— (2000e) 'US Agricultural Negotiations Submission', G/AG/NG/G/15, June.

—— (2000f) *Directory* (Geneva: WTO).

—— Integrated Data Base.

—— Rules Division, Antidumping Measures Data Base.

—— *Trade Policy Review* (1995–99) for 31 individual developing countries, various dates (Geneva, WTO). For details see Appendix A; also *Trade Policy Review* for the EC (1997), Canada (1998), US (1996), Japan (1998).

Index